FIRE IN BEIRUT

Also by Dan Bavly:
   The Subterranean Economy
   With David Kimche, *The Sandstorm* (published in paperback as *The Six Day War*)

Also by Eliahu Salpeter:
   With Yuval Elizur, *Who Rules Israel?*

FIRE IN BEIRUT

Israel's War in Lebanon with the PLO

Dan Bavly
and Eliahu Salpeter

STEIN AND DAY/*Publishers*/New York

First published in 1984.
Copyright © 1984 by Dan Bavly and Eliahu Salpeter
All rights reserved, Stein and Day, Incorporated
Designed by Louis A. Ditizio
Printed in the United States of America
STEIN AND DAY/*Publishers*
Scarborough House
Briarcliff Manor, N.Y. 10510

Library of Congress Cataloging in Publication

Bavly, Dan.
　Fire in Beirut.

　Includes index.
　1. Lebanon—History—Israeli intervention, 1982–
2. Munaẓẓamat al-Taḥrīr al-Filasṭinīyah.　I. Salpeter,
Eliahu.　II. Title.
DS87.53.B38　1983　　　　956.92′044　　　　83-42636
ISBN 0-8128-2924-7

Contents

Maps

Preface

After a long life I have come to the conclusion that when all the establishment is united it is always wrong.

—Harold Macmillan.

THE announcement by Prime Minister Menachem Begin at the end of August 1983 that he intended to resign coincided, in effect, with the realization that Israel had failed to bring about a new Lebanon. It was not yet the last and final chapter of the war, since Israeli and Syrian troops still occupied more than two-thirds of that tragic country and the civil war had flared again in its full cruelty, this time between the Christians and the Syrian-supported Druse. There was no indication as to how long Israeli soldiers would be positioned in their new, shortened lines in southern Lebanon, to prevent it from becoming PLO country again.

The Israeli government's political targets and ambitions that followed the 1982 move into Lebanon had not been fully achieved, and Begin's resignation marked an implicit but clear admission of failure.

In the days following the Israeli invasion of Lebanon and the start of the war, many Israelis, even those who instinctively supported it, questioned the reasons for the northern campaign. Later, as the Israel Defense Forces spent the fall and winter stuck in the muddy maze of Lebanon and opposition to the policy of the government became more vocal, an increasing vagueness became apparent about the actual facts. As we corresponded and spoke with Europeans and Americans who have for many years been interested in the Middle East, it became obvious to us, from the views they offered, that much of what had happened had not been brought to their attention. What and who were the powers in the area? Why and how were they operating? These were among the many questions that were always asked but rarely answered. In an attempt to clarify some of the interaction among Israel, the PLO, and Lebanon, which reached its climax in the summer of 1982, we set out to write this book.

We found data and material in the Israeli daily newspapers and especially in the articles published by Ze'ev Schiff in *Ha'aretz.* We also drew upon such British and American weeklies as *The Economist, Time, Newsweek,* and *Business Week.* We met with many people involved in or close to the events happening in the region: Israelis, Lebanese, Palestinians, Americans. The majority prefer not to have their names acknowledged. We honor their expressed wishes and, without divulging their identities, thank all those who were of so much help.

We do, however, mention by name Yuval Elizur, whose assistance, encouragement, and enthusiasm was and is appreciated. With his wife, Judy, Yuval offered important corrections to the sensitive chapter on the power of the media.

We also thank Miranda Kaniuk, whose support, keen observations, and fine comments helped put into more accurate focus some of the points we tried to make.

To Penina Barkai, who for months typed and retyped our manuscripts, successfully maintaining order and helping us edit each other, a special thanks.

D.B. AND E.S.
October 1983

1
The War Bound to Happen

BARRING total self-restraint on the part of the Palestine Liberation Organization—which was impossible if the PLO wanted to maintain its credentials—the war in Lebanon had become inevitable one year before it actually started. In the spring of 1982, the war "was just waiting to happen," as one leading diplomat closely involved in the events remarked.

Two factors were pushing the parties toward armed conflict. One was the PLO buildup in southern Lebanon, which was seen by a number of people in the Israeli cabinet as an increasingly serious military threat. The other was the wish of the Israeli government to eliminate the destructive influence emanating from the PLO headquarters in Beirut, Lebanon's capital, against the effort to build a pro-Israel Palestinian political factor in the West Bank.

As early as October and November 1981, in his talks with American diplomats, Israel's defense minister, Ariel Sharon, was open on this score. In the following months, responsible Americans became convinced that it was only a matter of time before sufficient provocation would occur for Israel to start to mop up the PLO forces governing the "state within a state" in southern Lebanon.

From the late summer of 1981 onward, several incidents involving the PLO threatened to become the immediate cause of the Israeli operation; but various events, including very strong American messages, prevented the commencement of the invasion. It was clear, however, that each new development was bringing Israel closer to the decision to launch the attack.

The last straw was the shooting of Shlomo Argov, the Israeli ambassador to London, on June 3, 1982. There was some evidence that the attack was carried out by the Abu Nidal terrorist group, which had a history of Syrian and Iraqi influence, and not by the mainstream PLO. The next day, Israel retaliated with an air attack on PLO arms depots in the Beirut sports stadium. Had Yasser Arafat, chairman of the PLO Executive, been in complete control of his organization and not responded to the Israeli bombing, the war might have been postponed once again. There are indications that the PLO leader's first order was indeed to avoid direct response to the Israeli air attack but that George Habash, head of the Popular Front for the Liberation of Palestine, a PLO component, apparently refused to accept the restraining order. Under pressure, Arafat revised his position and gave his approval for what he probably saw as a limited artillery attack on settlements in northern Israel. If he expected that Israel, too, would be content with a limited reaction, he grossly miscalculated.

This time, things were different. The Israeli tanks were ordered to move.

The Americans, who on previous occasions had helped prevent the outbreak of hostilities, failed in early June 1982. Why? Had the election of Ronald Reagan as president and the appointment of ex-NATO commander in chief and ex-general Alexander Haig as secretary of state changed the American position? Some diplomats suspect that the nature of the Reagan administration might well have been conducive to creating the atmosphere that led to the Israeli invasion. There was a different turn of mind in the new administration on how to deal with friends and allies: stress common views publicly, it said, and discuss differences in private. There was a publicly shared view between the president and the secretary of state and the Israeli leaders concerning the nature and villainy of the PLO. These points of common outlook combined to create a pattern of American-Israeli relations quite different from those of the previous administration, adding to the inevitability of the war.

The Americans never actually encouraged Defense Minister Sharon to start the war. Indeed, Secretary Haig warned him that the consequences of an attack were unpredictable, as far as the Syrian reaction was concerned. The cost, he said, might ultimately be much higher than it was worth to destroy the PLO apparatus in southern Lebanon. There were other warnings, such as when Sharon, on one occasion in the fall of 1981, indicated to Ambassador Philip Habib in some detail what Israel planned and could do in southern Lebanon, and the ambassador "became quite apoplectic."

But in the general atmosphere, the Israeli leaders apparently misread the conflicting signals from Washington. Prime Minister Begin and Defense Minister Sharon evidently believed that whatever was said by American administration spokesmen, they would not be too disturbed by an attack on the PLO and the Syrians in southern Lebanon.

The war in Lebanon was, in more senses than one, unique in the history of modern Israel. Wars often bring into sharp focus the strengths, weaknesses, and dilemmas of nations. The Lebanese war, like the five others that have marked Israel's thirty-five years of independence, demonstrated the qualitative superiority of its manpower and its impatience stemming from the closeness of the battlefields to home and from the nature of an army of reservists. On the operative level, the war in Lebanon was the first in which the major achievements were of a technological nature. But the real uniqueness of the Lebanon war was in its political aspects.

The 1948 War of Independence started with an invasion by five Arab armies on the very day the new state was born. In the 1956 Suez War, Israel joined Britain and France in sending its troops against Egypt—but only after Egyptian-controlled Palestine commandos, attacking from the Egyptian-held Gaza Strip and from Jordan, had for months made life unbearable for the settlements on the Israeli side of the border. Again in the Six Day War of 1967, while it was Israel that fired the first shot, the *casus belli* was the Egyptian initiative in closing the Straits of Eilat to Israeli shipping, expelling the United Nations peace-keeping forces from the Sinai, and moving most of its own army, contrary to the demilitarization agreements, into the Sinai and toward the Israeli border. The

1969–1970 War of Attrition across the Suez Canal was also initiated by the Egyptians. The Yom Kippur War of 1973 started with a coordinated surprise attack by Egypt and Syria on the holiest day of the Jewish calendar. With its political objectives, the Lebanon war was the first one initiated by Israel and not by its enemies.

The timing appeared to be excellent. The Arab world was divided more than it had been for a long time, minimizing the danger that Israel would have to fight on several fronts simultaneously. Iraq was stuck in its protracted war with Iran. Jordan was at logger-heads with Syria, which had become the odd man out of the Arab camp by siding with Teheran against Baghdad. Egypt, the most formidable potential enemy, had just recovered the last portion of the Sinai under the recent peace treaty with Israel and was still in the initial stages of rejoining the Arab fold. In Lebanon itself, the Kataeb (Phalangist militias), the most powerful local force, was acting as an informal ally and protégé of Israel.

The initially proclaimed aim of the Israeli invasion was strictly defensive: to clear out the terrorists from a 25-mile zone north of Israel and to push the PLO beyond the range of its heavy guns that had been shelling Israeli settlements in the Galilee. Soon, however, the Israeli public discovered that the operation actually had three political aims: first, to destroy the PLO infrastructure in southern Lebanon; second, to bring about the departure of all foreign forces, PLO as well as Syrian, from Lebanese soil; and third, to help the reestablishment of an independent Lebanon, whose government was expected to sign a peace treaty with Israel. Beirut, Jerusalem, and Cairo were to join in a "Triangle of Peace" in the Middle East.

These three aims may serve as one kind of yardstick for evaluating the extent to which Israel's Lebanese initiative failed or succeeded.

But there was a fourth, perhaps even more important aim motivating the Israeli government that provides the main criterion by which to judge the political consequences of the Lebanese war. In the spring of 1982 the Palestinian autonomy negotiations had reached a complete deadlock, and Israel was expecting increased American pressure for concessions and flexibility on its part, which would induce the Arabs to join the talks. Yet it was the stated belief of the Israeli government that PLO threats were preventing the emergence of more moderate West Bank leaders, who would be prepared to enter into autonomy negotiations on the basis of Israel's limited offer. Once the PLO was crushed in Beirut, its powerful hold on the West Bank would be broken and, with it, resistance to autonomy on the terms set by Israel's prime minister, Menachem Begin.

The Begin government thus had a special incentive to strike out and destroy the "state within a state" in southern Lebanon.

From the outset to its inconclusive conclusion, the war reflected the dominance of domestic considerations over events directly influencing the country's foreign policy and international relationships. It started in Lebanon—to serve the government's political aims on the West Bank. And the soldiers stayed on—to prove that it was no mistake to have sent them into Lebanon in the first place.

It was, therefore, in the eyes of a great many Israelis, a doubly contentious war. Many Israelis disputed the wisdom or morality of going to war for anything but national survival in the immediate sense. Most of those who shared this view were also opposed to the narrow concept of West Bank autonomy, which they judged to be unfair, impracticable, or ultimately not viable.

The war in Lebanon thus became the first Israeli war in which there was no national consensus about the war's aims, or its inevitability, or even its necessity.

Margaret Thatcher, the British prime minister, once quoted a Commonwealth colleague as having said that "consensus is the word you use when you cannot get an agreement." Certainly, Arab opposition to the very existence of Israel, from the day it was founded in 1948, was one of consensus rather than of unity. The late Egyptian president Gamal Abdel Nasser explained patiently, time and again, that the Arab leader who signed a peace treaty with Israel would undoubtedly be killed. Without seriously attempting to make peace, the charismatic Egyptian president died prematurely but peacefully, in his bed. His successor, Anwar Sadat, took up the challenge for peace in the fall of 1977, traveled to Jerusalem, and permitted the beginning of the peace process between Egypt and Israel. Within four years he was murdered by Moslem zealot extremists. A year later, young Bashir Gemayel, the Lebanese president-elect, suffered a similar fate. Said Hamami before him and

Dr. Issam Sartawi after him, two of the more moderate PLO leaders, both of whom had indicated that they believed in some sort of accommodation with the Israelis, were similarly assassinated. The message implicit in the killing of Dr. Sartawi, in the early spring of 1983, was crystal clear to two more prominent Arab leaders, Jordan's King Hussein and PLO chairman Yasser Arafat, both of whom were under considerable pressure from their Western connections to join the Camp David process. Should you seriously parley with the Israelis, they were being told in effect, you may well be the next casualty. Realistic believers in self-survival rather than idealists, both men understood the warning and stepped back to safer ground. But there are and will be others who dare. It is an extraordinary fact that in spite of assassinations being more common in the Arab world than in most parts of Judeo-Christian society, courageous Arabs who are proud nationalists but also moderates do from time to time stand up to be counted.

Amin Gemayel, who inherited the presidency of Lebanon from his assassinated brother, is more of a survivor, rather than a courageous risk-taker. This contributed much to the difficulties of the protracted Israeli-Lebanese-American negotiations in the spring of 1983, and to the weaknesses showed by his government in the following months. Yet even Amin Gemayel realized that some move must be made toward normalization—that there can be no simple retreat to the PLO-Syrian anarchy of 1976–1982. It compelled him to seek a compromise between his old fears and the new openings created by the Israeli invasion. This, perhaps, is one of the indications that hope and sanity are also becoming a political requirement in the Middle East, and may, in the not too distant future, overcome the tradition of terror, assassinations, and fratricide.

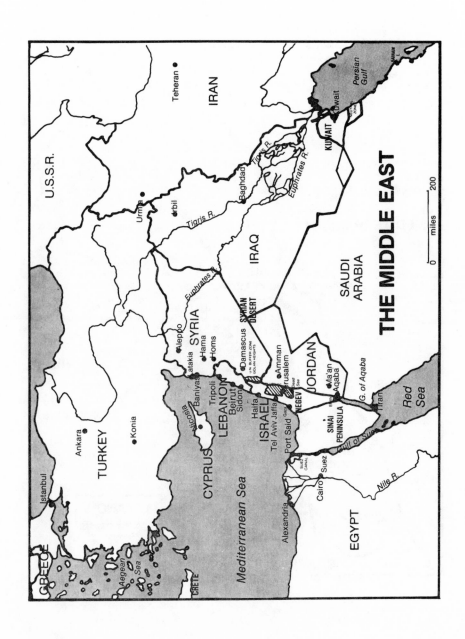

THE MIDDLE EAST

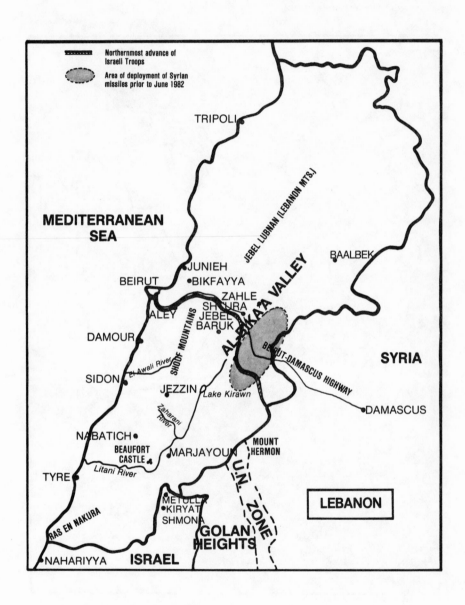

Northernmost advance of
Israeli Troops

Area of deployment of Syrian
missiles prior to June 1982

TRIPOLI

MEDITERRANEAN
SEA

JEBEL LUBNAN (LEBANON MTS.)

BAALBEK

JUNIEH

BEIRUT •BIKFAYYA

ZAHLE
SHTURA
JEBEL
BARUK

ALEY

AL-BIKA'A VALLEY

SHOUF MOUNTAINS

DAMOUR

BEIRUT-DAMASCUS HIGHWAY

SYRIA

El-Awali River

SIDON

JEZZIN   Lake Kirawn

DAMASCUS

Zaharani
River

NABATICH •

BEAUFORT
CASTLE

MARJAYOUN

MOUNT
HERMON

Litani River

TYRE

U.N. ZONE

METULLA
•KIRYAT
SHMONA

LEBANON

RAS EN NAKURA

GOLAN
HEIGHTS

• NAHARIYYA   ISRAEL

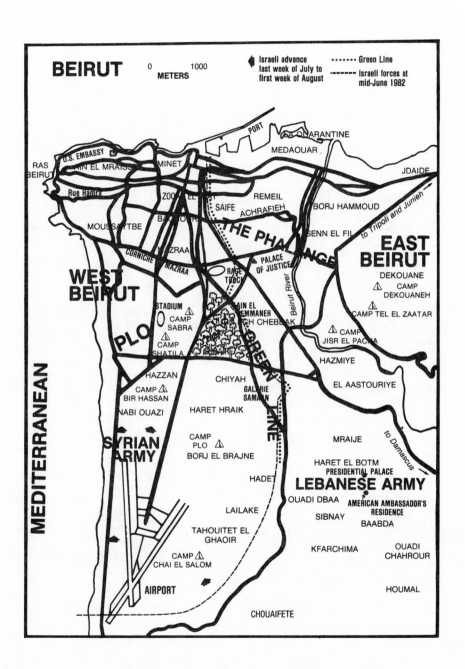

The PLO

THE Lebanon war was, first and foremost, a war against the Palestine Liberation Organization and its influence on the West Bank, an influence which Israel wanted to erase. The PLO rocket attacks on settlements in northern Israel were the direct cause of the war, and the substantial caches or armaments found in PLO depots in southern Lebanon were taken as proof that the government had been right to set out to demolish the PLO infrastructure.

The PLO is usually seen as the Palestinian response to the Israeli occupation, organized by Yasser Arafat. It is not. The PLO came into being long before the 1967 Six Day War, in which Israeli forces, in a preemptive response to threatening moves by Syria, Jordan, and Egypt, occupied the Golan Heights, the West Bank, the Gaza Strip and the Sinai Peninsula. Officially, the PLO resumed terror operations on January 1, 1965, when the Fatah, which later became its main fighting arm, carried out its first attack. The PLO had been established while Israel was still within its 1949 frontiers, and it was the territory of pre-1967 Israel that the organization wanted to "liberate" from the Jews.

Ideologically, the PLO was the successor to the Arab Higher Committee, active a generation earlier in British-ruled Palestine. Both the PLO and the Higher Committee wanted all of Palestine, with no room for a Jewish state. As the noted historian Bernard Lewis has said, "The Committee directed the destinies of the Arab population in Palestine . . . and finally led them to disaster. Their most consistent and characteristic feature was their maximalism— their unwillingness to compromise at any point."[1]

This attitude did not change after the Six Day War, which brought fundamental organizational and personal changes to the PLO, nor after the Yom Kippur War, which led to Israeli-Egyptian negotiations and to a peace agreement between these two countries.

This was still the PLO stand when the PLO Central Committee, representing its component bodies, met in Damascus in the last week of November 1982, for the first time after the PLO's defeat in Lebanon. They reiterated their public position that Israel must be replaced by a secular, nondenominational, democratic state of an entirely different composition. When the full Palestine National Council met in Algiers in February 1983, PLO moderates tried to create an opening toward the United States by some sort of implicit recognition of Israel's existence. The hard-liners, however, would have none of it and Arafat took the more negative approach.

The fact that the council repeated its old credo after the events in Lebanon showed that the PLO could not give up the idea of an Arab state replacing Israel. It should have come as no surprise: whatever political successes or frustrations they encountered over the years, in no way have any of the PLO leaders ever considered dropping, cancelling, or changing the articles of the PLO Covenant that call for the annihilation by armed struggle of the State of Israel. Thus Articles 9, 19, 20, and 21 state that:

> Armed struggle is the only way to liberate Palestine (Article 9).
>
> The partition of Palestine in 1947 and the establishment of the State of Israel are entirely illegal, regardless of the passage of time (Article 19).
>
> The Balfour Declaration, the Mandate for Palestine and everything that has been based upon them are deemed null and void . . . nor do Jews constitute a single nation with an identity of its own; they are citizens of the states to which they belong (Article 20).
>
> The Arab Palestinian people, expressing themselves by the armed Palestinian Revolution, reject all solutions which are substitutes for the total liberation of Palestine (Article 21).[2]

18

The PLO probably would not have been able to find so many well-wishers were it not for the newfound Western respect for Arab financial power. The world economic crisis of the 1970s added the mighty clout of petrodollars to the growing international opposition and criticism of Israel and its policies. The PLO thus became the beneficiary of the self-righteous and often hypocritical pro-Arab attitudes of a dispirited West.

Many years ago, the PLO recognized the roots of the pro-Israel attitude of Western public opinion and, with great persistence, managed to erode them badly. PLO proclamations, resolutions, and public appearances aimed at Arab audiences were virtually always phrased in radical, rejectionist, and extremist terms. In English, however, they presented a moderate, somewhat romantic image. PLO representatives in the West are encouraged to adopt a reasonable, conciliatory stance. They admit that there are certain "uncompromising elements" in the organization and seem to beg for support for their own, liberal faction—to strengthen the bloc of sanity and reduce the danger of extremist action. Western media often quote these "moderate" PLO spokesmen to support their argument that the Fatah has, for several years, ceased to demand the outright liquidation of Israel and that it is more inclined, instead, to rely on the United Nations Charter and the recommendations of the General Assembly. The media often point at the criticism leveled at Yasser Arafat by his more radical comrades, George Habash, Ahmed Jibril, and Naif Hawatmeh, as proof of his moderation.

In Arabic, to Arabs, however, PLO leaders continued to call for the destruction of Israel:

> There will be no existence for either the Palestinian people or for Israel unless one of them disappears. The Arabs must deal with the Palestinian problem from the vantage point that there will be no peaceful coexistence with Israel. The PLO has no right to discuss recognition of the enemy Zionist state. The final goal of the PLO is to restore to the Palestinian people sovereignty over its lands, and there to establish the independent state.[3]

And:

The liquidation of Israel is one of the means we adopt to achieve unity and freedom in the Arab world. We know that liberation is a long-term goal, but I . . . [can say with confidence] that, at the end of this year, a democratic Palestinian state will be established.[4]

What the moderates present to the world is a step-by-step plan which will bring them recognition by the United States, oblige Israel to accept the PLO at the political negotiating table, and result in a PLO state in the West Bank and Gaza. They do not deny that the final goal of this process still remains the control of all the territory now held by Israel.

But this plan presents a problem. If the PLO demands for a Palestinian state were met, they would have to recognize and to accept all the obligations of statehood: permanent borders, international treaties, membership in the United Nations, and the like. They would no longer have legitimacy for their struggle to control all the land, including the pre-1967 territories, now held by Israel. The solution to this dilemma offered by the PLO moderates was a resolution, adopted at the twelfth Palestinian Council, calling for the establishment not of a Palestinian state (*duala*) but only of an authority (*sulta*). An "authority" would give them all the benefits of statehood without any of the obligations, responsibilities, or restrictions.

The so-called moderates, such as Walid al-Khalidi, explicitly stated that the Palestinian state which would arise in the West Bank and Gaza would continue to demand the return of the Palestinian refugees to Israel, would establish an army with heavy weaponry including artillery pieces, tanks, and planes, and would follow the Palestine National Covenant (which calls for the elimination of Israel).[5]

The standard PLO explanation is that there is no reason to change the Covenant because it is but a "dream, a ritual, an old document from the early days of the PLO, long outdated." The Israelis respond with the question: If it is so unimportant, why the refusal to change the Covenant, to delete the disturbing paragraphs?

Although the PLO has been a failure militarily and has brought much suffering on the Palestinian refugees themselves, it has become a political and public relations success, not only in the Arab world but also in the West. It evokes basic, compelling associations, such as the search for a "homeland" and the inalienable right of a people to "self-determination." Israel involuntarily strengthens PLO claims to sympathy by its apparent total refusal to recognize the national rights of the Palestinians or to meet with PLO representatives.

In Israeli eyes, PLO moderation can begin only after it has nullified the Covenant and replaced it with another that recognizes Israel's inalienable right to exist (and not just the evident fact that it does exist, as stated by "moderates" as the ultimate proof of their moderation).

Indigenous terror organizations in Europe or Latin America choose as their victims individuals with symbolic importance, such as Prime Minister Aldo Moro or U.S. General William Dozier in Italy or industrialist Hans Shleier in West Germany. The PLO have, so far, preferred safe, unprotected civilian targets: a busload of children, a school, or a busy marketplace. Therefore it irritates Israelis to hear them called "guerrillas" or "freedom fighters." They point out that, outside Lebanon, the PLO carefully refrains from attacking military installations or armed military personnel. Their exploits are acts of terror. Guerrilla operations have military objectives or, at the very least, are directed against national or public symbols. But the PLO, almost without exception, attacks unarmed, anonymous civilians.

Until Israel's invasion of Lebanon, "the armed struggle against Israel" involved only such terror attacks, aimed almost exclusively against civilian targets. In their operations they seemed to prefer to veer toward the spectacular, to publicize the PLO and its exploits. The first of these big operations was the explosion of a booby-trapped car in the Mahane Yehuda market in a new part of Jerusalem, on November 22, 1968. Twelve Jewish civilians were killed and fifty-three wounded.

Later, there was a bazooka ambush on May 20, 1970, of a school bus carrying children from Avivim, a *moshav* (agricultural cooperative) village on the Lebanese border. Nine children and three teachers were killed; nineteen children were wounded.

On April 11, 1974, there was a massacre in Kiryat Shmona, in which sixteen civilians, eight of them children, were killed, along with two soldiers. This was followed on May 15 by terrorist seizure of a school in Ma'alot; seventeen children were killed.

Probably the best-remembered attack was the March 11, 1978, massacre near a Tel Aviv hotel country club. It cost the lives of thirty-four passengers, including children, of a hijacked tour bus. This outrage led, five days later, to "Operation Litani," the first Israeli occupation of southern Lebanon.

There were many other terrorist attempts inside Israel. Most failed or caused far fewer casualties. Since the late 1960s and the 1970s, the PLO also engaged in repeated terrorist attacks abroad. The most common were attempts to hijack airplanes of El Al and other international carriers. Several were successful. From time to time, there were attacks on embassies or ambassadors, mostly of Israel and the United States. These culminated in the attempt, on June 3, 1982, on the life of Shlomo Argov, Israel's ambassador in London. The attack, which left him completely paralyzed for life, was the signal for the start of "Operation Peace for Galilee" that became the war in Lebanon.

The terror accomplishments of the PLO were of little significance compared to the political publicity it had achieved in the fifteen years preceding the war in Lebanon. No other underground terrorist liberation movement has caught the fancy of the international public as has the PLO and its chairman, Yasser Arafat. He is an unquestioned media star, the only representative without a country to have addressed the General Assembly of the United Nations. No other speaker has been permitted, as he was in November 1974, to walk up to the podium of that gathering armed with a pistol. His extraordinary capacity to make political capital out of military disaster saved him and his organization after it was decimated and expelled from Jordan in the "Black September" of 1970 and again after the severe beating at the hands of the Syrians in Lebanon in 1976.

As Arafat realized once again during the Israeli invasion of Lebanon, the PLO has no military allies on whom it can count in any emergency. But the organization did accumulate enormous political support. Since 1974 there have been few international gatherings to which the Arab delegates have not insisted on inviting a PLO representative. Whether it was a United Nations symposium on health and preventive medicine, a UNESCO meeting or a convention of the International Monetary Fund, the Saudis, Libyans, Yemenis, and/or Somalis were sure to demand the invitation of a PLO delegate. Very often, they got their way.

He was a welcome conciliator when the Third World "77" assembled in New Delhi early in 1983. Despite the beating he took when expelled from Beirut in 1982 and the Syrian-sponsored rebellion within the PLO ranks that severely tested, and probably weakened, his position among his forces the following summer, he remained an unquestioned favorite when the United Nations convened an international conference on the question of Palestine in Geneva at the end of August 1983.

One of the more shocking discoveries made by the Israelis during the Lebanon war was evidence of the close working ties between the PLO and the UN institutions. At the large Technical and Teacher Training Institute run by the United Nations Relief and Works Agency at Siblin, some 5 miles northeast of Sidon, the dormitories were full of PLO uniforms and propaganda posters—clear indications that the institution had been used as a terrorist training center. Classrooms served as ammunition stores, with crates full of rockets as well as training manuals. The plaque outside the institute building declared that the structure had been put up in 1963, with Swedish funds, and that "it is dedicated to the training of young Palestinian refugees in the fields of education and industry."

There were also cases in which some of the close to 10,000 staff and troops of the United Nations International Emergency Forces (UNIFIL), established soon after the Litani operation to police southern Lebanon, actually had close contacts with the PLO and supplied them with arms, intelligence information, and other support. Documents found when Israeli forces entered southern Lebanon revealed that the involvement of UNIFIL with the terrorists was deeper than had previously been believed and even included military training programs.

Unlike other struggling nationalist movements, the PLO did not have to operate underground, in poverty or want. Until the Lebanon war, rather than being persecuted, they were often the persecutors.

Though they excelled in presenting the image of the underdog, they collected hundreds of millions of dollars; the organization's functionaries enjoyed luxurious facilities. An affluent group to begin with, the PLO has been spoiled by the ample funds provided by wealthy Arab countries and by the supply of more arms than they could use, mostly from the Soviet Union via Libya and Syria. The *New York Post* recently reported, "With an income of $300 million a year from its own investments, a further $400 million in subsidies from Saudi Arabia's rulers and an unlimited supply of Soviet weapons, the PLO can well afford to boast that it is now 'the richest liberation organization in the world.'"[6] In fact, it has become a source of pride to PLO leaders that they are able to help other guerrilla and terror organizations.

The PLO attained its paramount standing and connections in the sphere of terrorism because it was the best-equipped organization in the world for planning and perpetrating acts of terror. Lebanon provided a safe territorial base; from there the PLO could organize its actions in broad daylight, without any concern for surprise police operations such as faced by the Red Brigades in Italy or the Baader-Meinhof group in Germany.

Until the 1982 war, there was hardly a terror movement in the world, rightist or leftist, that had not, in the preceding decade, enjoyed some PLO support—not only in weapons but also in training.

An examination of the international terrorist acts perpetrated over the past fifteen years reveals the major part played by various PLO groups in their planning and execution. Most of the acts of terrorism—explosions, hijackings, taking of hostages, murder—are connected in one way or another with the PLO and with facilities provided by the Arab states: training, finance, intelligence aid, documentation, weapons and ammunition, and escape routes.

Men from other countries were sent to train in PLO camps, and made use of their weapons—which the PLO could easily transfer from one country to another through the diplomatic services of Arab states.

Such help was especially prevalent in Latin America. In Nicaragua, for example, an extensive PLO training and aid mission was virtually integrated into the local Sandinista army framework, with PLO instructors training the Nicaraguans in the operation of Soviet weapons. That fact has been published in the *White House Digest* and has been reiterated by President Reagan in a July 20, 1983 briefing. Sandinista press spokesman Jorge Mandi has also confirmed that many Sandinista units have trained at PLO camps in Jordan and that "Nicaraguan and Palestinian blood was spilled together in Amman and in other places during the Black September battles."[7]

Early in January 1982, addressing the General Federation of Palestinian Writers and Journalists in Beirut, Yasser Arafat acknowledged that PLO fighters were serving in Nicaragua, El Salvador, and Angola. His aides later added that relations with revolutionary movements in Latin America had been established for more than a decade, and included various forms of military support.

PLO ties with the El Salvador rebels are especially interesting. The Communist leader of the latter is Shafik Handal, whose father emigrated from Bethlehem.[8] Some observers believe that the El Salvador Communists are working together with Cuban dictator Fidel Castro's operatives in several trouble spots of the world, on behalf of the Soviet Union.

Financed by the oil-rich Arab countries, mainly Saudi Arabia and Kuwait, the PLO in 1981 transferred $12 million worth of arms to the Sandinista Government in Nicaragua. Other governments in the developing world received similarly liberal supplies of weapons.

During 1980 and the first half of 1981, the PLO and its affiliates brought some 2,250 international terrorists from twenty-nine countries to participate in training courses of one to four months' duration at PLO camps in the Middle East. They came from four continents:

Latin America—some 500 terrorists from Argentina, Brazil, Chile, Uruguay, Mexico, and El Salvador

Europe—some 950 terrorists from Turkey, Spain, West Germany, Italy, and Ireland

Asia—some 450 terrorists from Pakistan, Bangladesh, Iran, Armenia, the Philippines, Japan, and Sri Lanka

Africa—Some 350 terrorists from South Africa, Zimbabwe, Niger, Somalia, Ghana, Nigeria, Tunisia, Egypt, Togo, and Mali

The principal PLO training camps which hosted these courses were Hamouriya, near Damascus in Syria; Damour, Baalbek, Shatilla, Bourge ash-Shimali, and Nahr al-Bared, in Lebanon; and Halamek, in South Yemen.

Among the more prominent terrorist organizations represented in these courses have been:

Movimiento Peronista Montonero (MPM, Argentina-Uruguay)
Operaia Autonomia (Italy)
Brigada Rosa (Red Brigades, Italy)
SWAPO (Namibia, Southwest Africa)
Zimbabwe African National Union
Euzcadi Ta Askatauna (ETA, Basque, Spain)
Moro National Liberation Front (MNLF, Philippines)
Secret Army for the Liberation of Armenia (Turkey)
Movimiento Izquierda Revolucionaria (Movement of the Revolutionary Left, MIR, Chile)
Baader-Meinhof Red Army Faction (West Germany)
Tupamaros (Uruguay)
Japanese Red Army (Japan)
Dutch Red-Aid (The Netherlands)
Irish Republican Army (Northern Ireland)
Turkish People's Liberation Front (TPLF, Turkey)
Front for the National Liberation of Corsica (FLNC, France)

Concurrently, the PLO expanded its overseas training activities among the international terrorist organizations. During 1980 some fifty PLO instructors were active in Latin America, Africa, and Asia.

Control of Beirut and southern Lebanon was essential for these activities. The disappearance of effective governmental authority in the Lebanese state had given the PLO uncontrolled access to seaports, to a major international airport, to international banking and communications facilities; it provided territory for arms and ammunition depots, for training camps and command posts. Some of these also could have been (and were) obtained elsewhere. But for the more important functions, Beirut was essential: arms could be imported—and exported—without control or law enforcement, and telephone and telex contact could be maintained with terrorist cells and terrorist organizations in the West and in the East—all within a four- to twelve-hour air distance from Beirut. Beirut, in short, was the ideal place for the terrorist capital of the world.

In the international political arena, since the early 1970s the PLO has usually been assured of a majority vote for every issue raised. In private, however, many people in the Third World and in the Arab countries viewed the PLO's affluence and public standing with mixed feelings, if not jealousy. The reaction of a top Somali minister, at a conference held in London, was typical. Over coffee with his British counterpart, he complained that he himself was helpless to deal with the plight of well over a million Somali refugees driven out of the Ogaden district by the Ethiopians. Infuriated by the total apathy of the big powers and the European community, he exclaimed bitterly, "The PLO, they are the worst con men in the world." It is true that there are many other issues in the Arab world, besides the Palestinians, which should be taking up the attention of the West, but which are in fact hardly noted. These range from the terrible Somali refugee problem to the Iraq-Iran war to the massacre by the Syrian government of Moslem fundamentalists and the destruction of a great part of the town of Hama. Yet it is the PLO confrontation with Israel that is invariably news.

The brightest among the PLO members were trained and indoctrinated in one of some forty different military academies in the Soviet Union, Pakistan, Hungary, and other East European or Asian countries. Often, during the fifteen years leading up to the invasion of southern Lebanon, the PLO was also aided by Western terrorist organizations, whose members gathered intelligence about Israel and acted as go-betweens, messengers, and postal drop-offs. In many operations, from the Japanese Red Army massacre at Lod Airport in 1971 to the hijacking of an Air France plane to Entebbe in June 1976 by a team that included German terrorists, the PLO enjoyed direct foreign aid and participation.

The image of the PLO was enhanced not only by its allies and sympathizers but also by the unwillingness of Israel's leaders to recognize the rights of the Palestinians. Golda Meir, when prime minister, once proclaimed publicly, to the delight of the PLO, that there was "no such thing as a Palestinian nation." Indeed, the decision not to parley with the PLO as long as it adheres to their Covenant goes back to the Meir era. Early in 1975, when General (Res.) Aharon Yariv, then a member of the Israeli cabinet, and Victor Shemtov, the left-wing minister of health, proposed that the government adopt a policy of talking to any Arab body that would recognize Israel's inalienable right to exist and acknowledge UN Security Council resolutions 242 and 338, the majority of the Labor party coalition would have none of it. By the time Menachem Begin assumed the premiership, any Israeli who suggested a meeting with a PLO leader was suspect of being just this side of treasonous. From the day the Likud government took office, the PLO was the Enemy, and treated accordingly.

Important forces in the West, concerned with the spread of multinational terrorism, at first agreed that terror could not in any way be condoned, and sympathized with the Israeli approach to the PLO. But, with time, they began to have second thoughts. In the 1970s, for reasons having to do with human rights in some cases and with purely mercenary concerns in others, there was increasing criticism of Israel's apparent intransigence concerning everything related to the Palestinians in general and to those under Israeli administration on the West Bank and in the Gaza Strip in particular. Many people, even some in Israel, began to feel that ostracizing the PLO was counterproductive. They argued that through some kind of dialogue, moderation could be achieved; that failure of such talks, in itself, could cause no real damage. Why indeed, they argued, should indirect talks—and they contended that such had taken place—be better than direct contact? When humanitarian problems arose, the Americans had talked with the PLO, as had the Israelis. Late in 1978, Defense Minister Ezer Weizman indirectly approached the PLO and negotiated the return of a single Israeli prisoner captured soon after the Litani campaign. The Americans asked the PLO to employ their good offices with the Khomeini regime, in the fall of 1979, to try to release the captive U.S. embassy staff in Teheran. Even in 1982, the PLO would not have agreed to withdraw from Beirut without negotiations; in those talks the

Americans and the Lebanese were actually intermediaries between the Israelis and the PLO. Also, a considerable number of West Bank and Gaza Strip leaders and notables are followers of the Fatah or pay lip service to it. In their travels to the Arab world, these notables meet with senior members of the PLO to compare notes and coordinate steps. Through them, Israel has, from time to time, been in limited contact with the PLO.

Politically, the PLO consists of several groupings, each maintaining its own paramilitary arm. The largest and most active is the Fatah, founded by Yasser Arafat in 1959 and operational since 1965, when Arafat became head of the eleven-man Central Committee of the PLO. He is also chairman of the PLO's Executive Committee, and his organizational control of the PLO has since been complete, at least until the June 1983 Syrian-sponsored revolt. In the 1960s the PLO, and especially the Fatah, were greatly influenced by the successes of the Algerian National Liberation Front (FLN) a generation earlier, which had led to the independence of that country. The Algerians were eager teachers and were happy with their Palestinian students. It was in that country that the first training camps were set up and to which the first plane hijacked by the PLO was diverted. In the late 1970s, as the leaders of Algeria grew in respectability, their involvement in the Middle East decreased. Today, they still espouse the ideals of the PLO but do little more than that. The PLO has relations with as many countries as does Israel, and receives money, arms, logistic support, and training camp facilities from all Arab and most Communist states. At its peak, early in 1982, it had more than 20,000 active members. One of its main aims has long been to obtain international recognition as "the sole representative of the Palestine People."

Fatah's main method of gaining attention was to attack civilian targets. It was responsible for a series of terrorist acts, from the murder of eleven Israeli athletes at the Munich Olympic Games to the assassination of U.S. ambassador Cleo A. Noel, Jr. and several other diplomats in Khartoum and the triple airplane hijack to Jordan. In order to advance its efforts for political recognition, the Fatah announced that it had ceased to engage in direct terror operations after the Yom Kippur War. It signified its willingness to join certain political processes in the Middle East and thus helped the West to accept it as a moderate. It was ready to join negotiations on the future of the West Bank and the Gaza Strip, with a view to establishing a Palestinian state in these regions, as the first step toward replacing Israel. Significantly, the Fatah never indicated that, even if the first step were achieved, it would consider recognizing Israel, let alone sign a peace treaty.

The Palestinian Liberation Army (PLA) was established in the mid-1960s as a "regular" military arm of the PLO. But its rapid expansion took place in 1981 and early in 1982. It included the Hittin Brigade of nearly 2,000 Palestinians, most of whom resided in Syria and were, for all practical purposes, under Syrian command. The Qadasiya Brigade had a similar background and command but was somewhat smaller. Both were based in Beirut, as part of the Arab Deterrent Force.* Under direct PLO command was the Ayn Jalut Brigade, as well as a smaller separate unit, a battalion. The Kerameh, Kastel, Yarmuk, and Egendine brigades, distinct from the PLA, were also part of the PLO.

The military tables of organization of the various brigades were similar to those in other Arab armies. But in combat with the Israeli forces it became clear that their training had been more limited. In mobile battle they did not give a creditable account of themselves, but when the fighting reached the built-up areas of Tyre, Sidon, and the nearby Ein Al Hilwe refugee camp and, later, Beirut, the motivation of the individual fighter appeared at its strongest and slowed down the pace of Israeli advance. Indeed, some of their defense efforts were impressive.

Back in 1969, after the Syrians realized that Yasser Arafat and the Fatah were too independent for their convenience, they organized the Al-Saika forces to enable them to intervene directly in the workings of the PLO. Headed by Zuheir Muhsein until he was murdered on the French Riviera in 1979, Al-Saika is still under Syrian aegis but has been on the decline in recent years. Most of its members are, in fact, of Syrian rather than Palestinian origin. Indeed, a substantial number of terrorists in all the PLO organizations, including the Fatah, are non-Palestinian.

---

*See Chapter 3 for greater detail.

The Al-Saika doctrine takes its lead from that of the ruling Syrian Ba'ath party. It is totally "rejectionist," opposing any peaceful accommodation, even interim, in solving the Palestinian problem. It strongly disapproves of the Egyptians, who signed a peace treaty with Israel, and is critical and suspicious of the Jordanians. In the past, Al-Saika carried out a few token attacks in Western Europe, but their terror activities have all but ceased in recent years. Since the death of Muhsein, the Syrians have concentrated on encouraging the paramilitary arm of the Saika to become part of the Palestinian Liberation Army.

The politically most indoctrinated faction of the PLO is the Popular Front for the Liberation of Palestine (PFLP). It came into being in 1967 following the merger of three quite small organizations, each with a modest terrorist record. Headed by George Habash, who was trained as a doctor, the PFLP were pioneers in air hijacking. Possibly their most notorious exploit was the hijacking of an Air France plane to Entebbe in Idi Amin's Uganda in June 1976, leading to the dramatic rescue of the passengers by Israeli commandos on July 4.

The principal supporters of the PFLP are Iraq and South Yemen (to which PFLP men moved when they were forced to leave Beirut in August 1982), but they also enjoy support from Algeria and Libya. The PFLP claims to be Marxist-Leninist and forms part of the Rejectionist Front, which as a matter of principle opposes any negotiation on Palestine or the participation of the PLO in such negotiations. For several years after the PLO Executive Committee meeting of September 1974, the PFLP refused to be part of the PLO because the umbrella organization had adopted a relatively less radical position.

The PFLP maintains close contacts with radical underground organizations throughout the world, from the Italian Red Brigades to the Japanese Red Army, from what remains of the German Baader-Meinhof group to the outside fringe of the Irish Republican Army (IRA) and the extremist groups of Latin America. These relations include training members of the other underground groups at PFLP bases, helping them acquire arms, and receiving volunteers from among their ranks to carry out operations against Israel and Israeli targets abroad.

In 1969, following a split with George Habash, Naif Hawatmeh established the Popular Democratic Front for the Liberation of Palestine. This organization is ideologically close to both the Soviet Union and Red China but, concentrated logistically in Beirut and Lebanon until August 1982, it was linked to Fatah.

Another group that broke away from George Habash, in 1969, was called the Popular Front—General Command. It was headed by Ahmad Jibril, a retired Syrian army captain. Largely dependent on Syrian support, Jibril and his followers were active in the fratricidal fighting in the Palestinian camps in Beirut in the mid-1970s, joining other leftists against the Lebanese forces.

There is also the rather mysterious Abu Nidal faction, of which relatively little is known. Sabri el Bana, better known as Abu Nidal, began to serve the PLO cause in 1969 as the Fatah representative in Iraq. He resigned in June 1974, following the twelfth Palestinian National Council meeting which resolved to use political means along with its regular terrorist tactics. Abu Nidal discarded the restraints of the PLO and launched his own terrorist operations. He took over control of all Fatah institutions in Iraq and began to organize an independent terrorist group. Although he left the PLO in 1974, Abu Nidal's independent operations actually began in September 1973, when he organized an attack on the Saudi Arabian embassy in Paris. He is held responsible for the deaths, among others, of Said Hamami, PLO representative in London, and Az Al-Din Kalak, PLO representative in Paris. Attacks on the Syrian embassies in Rome and Pakistan, in the fall of 1976, are also attributed to his group. The three men eventually convicted in a British court of attempting to assassinate Israel's ambassador, Shlomo Argov, testified that Abu Nidal was responsible for the operation.

There are, in addition, smaller and less active splinter groups. In recent years, most of them were located in the camps in southern Lebanon and around Beirut.

Some of the groups besides the PFLP regard themselves as Marxist. All are secular and include both Moslems and Christians. George Habash is a Christian. Yet the growth of Moslem fundamentalism did not bypass the PLO. It is penetrating its ranks gradually. The leaders are worried about this threat from within, and it has already led to several internal disputes. PLO leader Shafik el Hut was quoted in Toronto on October 27, 1982, as saying that Moslem fundamentalism was "putting a strain" on the PLO.

In the seventeen years leading up to the war in Lebanon (excluding the period of the Yom Kippur War), the PLO killed 674 civilians in Israel and the administered territories and wounded nearly 3,700. Abroad, in close to 300 acts of terror, the PLO killed 326 people, sometimes in collaboration with organizations whose roots are outside the Middle East, and wounded 768 (see table). The non-Arab country of their preference, in which they operated most freely, was West Germany, followed by France, the United Kingdom, and Italy. More than twenty attacks were perpetrated in each of these four countries.

Persons Killed or Wounded by the PLO, 1965–1982

	Wounded	*Killed*
1. Israelis and tourists in Israel and the Administered Territories	3,694	674
2. Israelis abroad	59	45
3. Total Israelis (1 + 2)	3,753	719
4. Jews abroad	42	15
5. Gentiles abroad	667	266
6. Foreigners abroad (4 + 5)	709	281
7. Total casualties abroad (2 + 6)	768	326
8. Palestinians in Israel and the Administered Territories	1,977	392
9. Israelis and Palestinians (1 + 8)	5,671	1,066
10. Total casualties in Israel and abroad (7 + 9)	6,439	1,392

The total would have been higher, were it not for the very expensive but effective efforts of the police forces of Israel and the respective European countries. In comparison, for instance, with the British achievement against the IRA, the police of Israel and Europe have done an impressive job of keeping down the number of successful acts of PLO terror.

In the late 1970s and early 1980s there was a shift in the focus of PLO activities. More and more attacks emanated directly from southern Lebanon, against Israeli targets across the border. Utilizing the long range of their Katyusha rockets and Soviet-made artillery, they began the sporadic shelling of towns and settlements in northern Galilee.

The PLO may have felt a kind of triumph in chasing Israelis out of their homes and making them seek refuge in other parts of the country. But their attacks led, in June 1982, to the inevitable Israeli reaction: "Operation Peace for Galilee" and the war in Lebanon.

3

The Lebanon—
A House Divided

I N the morning of April 13, 1975, a car full of unidentified Palestinians opened fire on a group of Christians who were coming out of a church after a wedding in Ein Rumanah, a small town in the hills above Beirut. In the group were members of the Gemayel family, bosses of the Kataeb, the Phalangists. The Moslem attackers killed three of the worshipers. Later the same day, not far from the site of the first atrocity, the Phalangists ambushed a bus full of Palestinians on their way to the Tel el-Za'atar refugee camp* in East Beirut, killing twenty-seven.

On that day, effective government, however modest, ceased to exist in Lebanon and anarchy began to rule.

It seems to be human nature to accept the massacre of peoples other than one's own. The West has not kept alive the memory of the Turkish slaughter of the Armenians in 1915; it showed no remorse when, soon after World War II, the British shipped more than 2 million White Russians, German allies who had been made prisoners of war, back to their home country to meet their deaths at the hands of the Soviets. Nor was the public in Europe a century ago particularly shocked by the wholesale killings of Lebanese Christians by the Druse Moslems in 1859–1860.

---

*Later completely destroyed in the fighting of the summer of 1976.

Much of the hatred of recent years between Lebanese Moslems and Christians goes back to events in the middle of the nineteenth century, when the Lebanon was part of the decaying Ottoman Empire. Some eighteen years of discord, riots, and intermittent bloodshed among the Turkish rulers, the Druse clans of the Al-Shouf mountains, and their more numerous but weaker Christian neighbors preceded the bloodbath.

The massacre began in the summer of 1859, when Druse from the Al-Shouf attacked Christians living in the nearby Gharb and Matten districts. They were soon joined by Sunni and Shiite peasants, and together they set out to burn and raze some sixty Christian villages in the mountains and down to the coast. They went on to occupy Zahle and committed many murders and other atrocities. In Deir el Kamar,* more than 2,000 Christians were slaughtered in one day. By June 1860 there were no Christians left south of the Damascus Road. When they heard of the massacre of the Christians in Lebanon, the Damascus Moslems staged their own, killing several thousand more Christians. It was only when they attempted to push on to the Christian center in the north and reached Bikfayya (today the home of the Gemayel family), that the Moslem advance was stopped and the attackers were forced to withdraw.

In 1860 and 1861 the European Great Powers held three conferences in Paris and a fourth in Constantinople,† in the aftermath of which the semi-independent, autonomous entity of Lebanon was established, comprising the then predominantly Christian parts of the country. A representative government, unique in the Middle East, came into being in a mountainous area which the Turkish troops generally refrained from entering.

Under the mandate of the League of Nations after World War I, the French became responsible for that part of the Levant. They made what later turned out to be a fatal mistake: in 1920 they added to the Christian area predominantly Moslem territories, creating a Greater Lebanon, which gradually became a democratic republic—

---

*Today, the home of former president Camille Shamoun. In the summer of 1983, when the Druse were attempting again to expel the Christians from the Al-Shouf, the population of this town was once more threatened with mass murder.

†On August 3, 1860, February 19, 1861, March 15, 1861, and June 9, 1861.

but a divided nation. On November 16, 1943, Lebanon was granted independence.

Just as the three-century-old battles between Catholics and Protestants are as vivid to the Irish as if they occurred yesterday, so the Lebanese clans have lived with their feuds and hatred for well over a hundred years, from revenge and carnage to counterrevenge and more bloodletting.

Compared to a 78 percent Christian population in the original "small Lebanon," the expansion reduced their proportion to 53 percent in 1932, when the last official census was held. It is certain that since then the percentage of Christians has gone down and that of Moslems has risen. The total population now may be close to 3 million.

Economic and social statistics can be baffling and, more often than not, unreliable. The figures relating to land area are less controversial. With a total of some 4,000 square miles, Lebanon is approximately four-fifths the size of Connecticut. It is about 125 miles long and its width varies between 20 and 35 miles.

In the first three decades of its independence, as the hashish poppies bloomed in the Al-Bika'a valley, Lebanon's laissez-faire economy thrived. Beirut became an international financial center, the hills above offered a cool retreat for businessmen and Saudi sheikhs, and the country provided a haven for opposition leaders of all persuasions from other Arab lands.

Syria, however, never fully recognized the independence of Lebanon, considering it part of "Greater Syria." Syrian involvement has long been an integral part of Lebanese politics and intercommunity clashes.

When serious outbreaks of Moslem and Christian rioting occurred in May and July 1958, and there was a danger of the conflict spreading, President Camille Shamoun asked President Dwight Eisenhower to send in the U.S. marines. The troops landed and hostilities ended as abruptly as they had begun. The American soldiers spent several weeks in Beirut, basking on the sunny beaches, and then departed. Economic growth resumed and, at the same time, Beirut became the political and ideological show window of the Arab world. Almost every country had its exiles, its bank accounts, and at least one newspaper in its pay in the city.

At the beginning of the 1970s, clouds appeared. The Palestine
Liberation Organization, established in 1965, had tried to take control of Jordan but was mercilessly beaten down by King Hussein's
army. Suffering heavy casualties, after a spectacular triple airline
hijacking, the terrorist army was forced to flee from Jordan in the
"Black September" of 1970. Aware that the PLO had tried to create
a state within a state in the land the Palestinians had called a refuge,
no other Arab government was now willing to accept them. There
was only one Arab country in the region that was too weak and
disunited to resist the unwanted guests: Lebanon. Yasser Arafat
and his colleagues moved in and established their new bases in
southern Lebanon and in a number of teeming Palestinian camps*
along the Mediterranean and near Beirut.

In the early 1970s, there were nearly 200,000 Palestinian refugees
in Lebanon. Although still socially separate, most were gradually
absorbed into the Lebanese economy. There were precedents for a
refugee community settling in the country and thriving: the Armenians to this day maintain their special status and regard themselves,
however affluent, as being in exile in Beirut.

But the PLO soon disrupted life in Lebanon. First, they took over
management of the Palestinian camps and gradually assumed
quasi-governmental authority. They handed out jobs and permits,
ran schools and hospitals, dispensed their own brand of justice, and,
most important, compelled the youth to join their ranks and
undergo paramilitary training.

The Lebanese government probably could not and certainly did
not seriously attempt to stop the PLO from taking over and expanding in parts of the country.

The secret of the PLO's easy success was the sectarian strife,

---

*The Palestinians had become refugees in the spring and summer of 1948,
when the then Grand Mufti of Jerusalem, Haj Amin El Husseini, an admirer of
Hitler who had spent the years of World War II in Nazi Germany, called upon the
Arabs living in the Coastal Plain, from south of Jaffa to Haifa and Acre, and their
cousins in the Galilee, to leave their homes, temporarily he said. He promised
them that the Palestinian fighters would soon win a victory and, supported by
the neighboring Arab states, would overwhelm, destroy, and conquer the budding Jewish State. Most of the Palestinian refugees never returned; gradually,
the temporary refugee camps became permanent establishments.

which deprived the Lebanese government of effective power and authority. From the beginning of independence, it was clear that the idea of a multiethnic state would work only if it was backed at least by the four main religious groups: the Maronite Christians, the Sunni Moslems, the Shiite Moslems, and the Druse. It was a fragile situation, with many tacit, unwritten agreements. The different groups lived together by the principle of a National Covenant, established with the coming of the republic and known in Lebanon as "confessionalism." In it, both Christians and Moslems agreed to prevent foreign domination; to avoid alliances with other countries, including those in the Arab world; and to seek to maintain the country's cultural ties with the West. Yet, as people with an international outlook, they could not ignore the developments among their neighbors, and these changes gradually upset the delicate balance of the Lebanese Republic. Still, for several decades and certainly on the face of things, the system worked. It was accepted that the president of the republic should always be a Maronite, the prime minister a Sunni Moslem, the chairman of the parliament a Shiite Moslem, and the minister of defense often (but not always) a Druse. The chief of staff of the armed forces was usually a Maronite.

As time went by, it became clear that this understanding did not really forge a single nation. Old enmities just would not die and new demographic realities developed.

For one thing, there are many Christian denominations. For every ten Maronites, there are probably three Greek Orthodox, two Greek Catholics, and two Armenian-Georgian Christians. Among the Moslems, the poorer Shiites probably outnumber the richer, better-educated Sunnis. The number of Druse is comparable to that of the Greek Orthodox, but not much more. No one could give a definite figure of the number of Palestinian refugees; before June 1982, some Lebanese sources estimated that there were as many as 600,000 while other officials doubted whether there could be more than 250,000.

The birthrate of the Christians was for decades lower than of the Moslems and their emigration rates were higher—both because of a higher level of education and because of wider family ties abroad, especially in Catholic Latin America and in North America. The change in the Christian-to-Moslem ratio was dramatically accelerated with the influx of Palestinian refugees in 1948, since the great majority of them were also Moslems. The Christians of Lebanon, therefore, felt threatened. This fear increased with the PLO take-over of southern Lebanon after Black September because it was accompanied by a second wave of Palestinian refugees, the "illegals." The growing Maronite militancy—and the wish to expel the Palestinians—was, to a large extent, a reflection of Moslem ascendancy.

But the change wrought by the PLO takeover was not only demographic, it was also social. In Lebanon, as in many Moslem countries, the Shiites were generally the lowest on the socioeconomic ladder. The Palestinian Arabs who moved to Lebanon found an affinity with the Shiite community, which became their link for merging with the local economy.

When the PLO established its state within a state in southern Lebanon, the new power structure also reinforced and elevated the status of the Shiites vis-à-vis the Sunni and Christian landowners and industrial employers. Thus, the first link was forged in the PLO's Lebanese alliance, later joined by the majority of the Druse, traditionally hostile to the Christians, as the second link.

The Druse are a minority wherever they live—in Syria, Lebanon, and Israel. They are proud and jealous of their rights and traditionally ally themselves with the apparent strongest power in the country they live in. In Syria, they collaborate with President Hafez al-Assad, and play a large part in his army and in his political party, the Ba'ath. In Israel, they serve in the Israel Defense Forces and are represented in the Knesset. In Lebanon, their position was usually in total opposition to what Israel stands for.

But this overall division had and still has subdivisions as well as cross-currents. Shiite rural interests do not necessarily run parallel to urban Palestine refugee interests and loyalties. Shiite proletariat often confronts Sunni bourgeoisie in the Moslem sector of Lebanese society. Similarly, on the Christian side, the dominant Maronite group must contend with Greek Orthodox and other smaller denominations, and even within the Maronite community loyalties can be divided along family lines. Class definitions can be as meaningless as the terms "right" and "left" in a country where a Walid Junblatt, one of the few remaining feudal chieftains, is described as a "leftist

40

leader" while Christian peasants are identified as "Phalangists," who are sometimes also described as social democrats or fascists.

This divisiveness had a major impact on the years of civil war that preceded the Israeli invasion. On each side of the main Moslem-Christian divide there were several military and paramilitary organizations, forming alliances (occasionally even across the divide) and breaking them as yesterday's ally becomes tomorrow's enemy, sniping from the next roof, ambushing from behind the next bend of the mountain road.

When wars come to a halt and exchange of fire subsides, a tourist visiting Beirut today after years of warfare, upheaval, and destruction, is impressed by the pace of construction, with buildings going up in most parts of the city. One notes its Western look, its handsome young men and pretty young women. One may think of Naples but Beirut looks far more prosperous, far more affluent. The architecture is sometimes dull but more often imaginative. The mixture of Oriental and supermodern Western styles is striking and attractive. There are few beggars; even the poorly dressed look healthy; the young are certainly fit.

For most of the day, the roads and wide boulevards suffer from chaotic traffic problems as slick Rolls-Royces, Porsches, and other luxury cars tangle with dilapidated, unroadworthy jalopies. Yet generally, the drivers are fatalistically patient.

There are many uniformed men in the streets, and some uniformed women. Looking rather bored, some direct the traffic; others just stand around.

Similar to the situation earlier, since 1975 most Lebanese have derived income from any number of sources, as well they might in this state of laissez-faire. In addition to official donations from America and Saudi Arabia, these sources of revenue have included at least seventeen different foreign intelligence services and forty-odd militias. Until the summer of 1982, the largest single provider was probably the PLO, looking after 10 percent of the Lebanese population. Besides its terrorist activities, the PLO operated some hundred schools, eight hospitals, a broadcasting service, and a newspaper, as well as a garbage collection service and other instruments of government.

From the day warring started in 1975 until the seige of 1982, it was business as usual for the more than eighty banks* with many branches listed in the Beirut financial directory. Despite a lack of police, financial activity expanded and total amounts deposited with the commercial banks more than quadrupled between early 1975 and late 1982. As hard a currency as could be found in the Middle East, while most European currencies dropped in value the Lebanese pound increased in value by 40 percent compared to the U.S. dollar in the second half of 1982.

Lebanon holds an almost unique reserve position, with about 80 percent of its currency backed by gold and with foreign debt as low as $320 million. Its success in managing its finances is attributed to the fact that it has a small government budget and laissez-faire policies that kept the banks alive. With its practice of strict secrecy and protection, throughout the wars of the mid-1970s to this day, Lebanon has encouraged Saudis and Kuwaitis as well as the PLO and other armed militants to channel their transactions through Lebanese banks.

The Maronites and the Shiites have considerably stronger nationalistic pride than the Sunnis, who often see themselves as pan-Arabists first and Lebanese second. The Maronites regard themselves as descendants of the Phoenicians of ancient times, inventors of the alphabet and allies of the Tribes of Israel. They maintain that:

> The country of Lebanon has risen up out of the territories which in ancient times, belonged to the Phoenicians. The Phoenicians, being separated from the inland areas by two chains of mountains, turned, naturally enough, towards the Mediterranean, that is to say towards the West with which they exchanged both goods and ideas. Similarly, in modern times, the Lebanese have always been attracted by the sea and by commerce. Thus the same circumstances have produced the same results.[1]

Indeed, the wealthier Lebanese consider themselves part of Western society. Many Beirut families and their landed brothers

---

*There were 104 banks that had permits to operate but some, not necessarily for reasons of political security, chose not to.

and cousins in the mountain towns and villages speak French at home, and the older generation is often more comfortable reading and writing that language than Arabic. They pride themselves on being civilized, cultured, worldly, and well traveled, compared to their Moslem neighbors.

It takes some time, even for the discerning, to discover that, behind this façade there exists an inner man, belonging to the feudal Middle Ages. Well before the outbreak of hostilities, Lebanese civilians were reputed to be among the most heavily armed in the world. No self-respecting citizen moved in Beirut without a gun. Leaders such as Camille Shamoun, Oriental-style "godfathers," attended even private meetings surrounded by well-armed bodyguards. One gets the first glimpse of the rougher side of Beirut when, on a peaceful day, one watches a jeepful of armed toughs precede the limousine driving up to one of the swank restaurants. The escort is there to protect a leader of one of the clans who now steps out of the car: a Shamoun, a Gemayel, or a Karameh. Suddenly, one realizes how much violence is still the way of life here, as it has been for centuries. There is a mixture of Renaissance cunning and earlier-day Scottish clannishness running in the blood of the people. Family vendettas are carried on for generations. Feuds are fought not only among adherents of the different religions but among tribes and families; both Moslems and Christians indulge. Thus, a journalist could truthfully report, in the late 1970s, that he had counted as many as seventeen different paramilitary groups operating in the tiny country. Some of the quarrels are more than a century old. Even at the peak of Lebanese economic growth the feuds were carried on, albeit with less public notice.

When fighting erupted on April 13, 1975, the first round, which lasted for about a week and spread northward from Beirut to Tripoli, involved virtually all the factions. They all evidently felt they had passed the point of no return and that legal government was no longer capable of maintaining law and order. The Lebanese knew that the warring would be a long and costly free-for-all.

A cease-fire stopped the fighting, but it resumed in mid-May. This time it took longer to reach a cease-fire. Gradually, the breaks between hostilities grew shorter, the battles more intense.

One of the problems facing the combatants was how to get new

43

supplies of arms and ammunition. They soon realized that in the past, anticipating the outbreak of hostilities, they had often miscalculated how fast they would use up their supplies. In the spring of 1975, the so-called leftist units, as well as the Druse in the al-Shouf mountains under Kemal Junblatt, the Moslems in Tripoli led by Rashid Karameh, and the PLO in Beirut all had substantial caches of material that they had accumulated gradually over the previous five years. They were assured of replenishment from many sources in the Arab world. There was a continuous supply from Damascus, which the Lebanese army knew about but did not dare stop. Shipments from Libya, too, arrived periodically at the PLO base in Sidon, toward the south.

The Christians, on the other hand, found themselves with fewer assured resources. They soon approached potential suppliers in the West, but since no Western government showed any interest in supporting them, they began to canvas the main private weapons dealers. Having sound business instincts, the European arms merchants assessed that they could afford to raise their prices, making Lebanese fratricide costly as well as bloody.

It was in the late spring of 1975 that one of Camille Shamoun's allies, who spent a considerable part of his time in Europe, called on an Israeli contact in Western Europe and suggested an arms deal—on a purely commercial basis. He proposed that the Israeli, who, he knew, had excellent relations with several arms merchants, agree to become the business intermediary supplying arms to the followers of Shamoun.

The Israeli agreed and soon the supply of weapons, mostly light arms, to the Shamoun forces commenced. Payment was made promptly.

The exchange of fire in Lebanon continued throughout the summer. At first the incidents caused relatively few casualties and the combatants made little effort to occupy new positions. But as shooting became more intense, the influence of the Lebanese regular army, as the military arm of the state, diminished. The soldiers gradually withdrew to their barracks or moved to guard crucial government positions, such as the presidential mansion and the Defense Ministry building.

By autumn 1975, the fighting had imposed a new lifestyle on the residents of Beirut. Most Christian and some of the Moslem combatants, being part-time militiamen, were also employed in civilian occupations. They would don uniforms for several days a week, overalls or business suits for the rest. On payday, at the end of every month, there was an almost complete cease-fire as everybody went to collect his wages. Similarly, shooting usually came to a standstill on days of important sports events or during a favorite television show (since 1980, it has been "Dallas").

In the first two years of the war, an estimated 70,000 men, women, and children were killed or wounded; yet, all this time no matter how fierce the fighting, how heavy the casualties, abundant fresh food supplies were always available at the markets and shops on both sides of the battle line. Similarly, the electricity, gas, and water supplies, running across the lines, were never cut off.

In the summer of 1975, when the fighting intensified, demand for arms increased both in quantity and in firepower. The Shamounists became more and more dependent on their Israeli source. The Gemayel family's Phalange units did not, as yet, have any weapons supply contact with the Israelis but began to establish it toward the end of the year. It was then that the Israelis began to consider more seriously the political implications of the war in Lebanon, and they presented their clients with a number of requests. One grew out of Israel's concern that there be a better exchange of information; another was that Camille Shamoun himself meet with a senior Israeli leader. Negotiations in Europe over these two points lasted for some time. Finally, the Israeli terms were accepted and, at the turn of the year, ex-president Shamoun of Lebanon met with then prime minister Yitzhak Rabin on board an Israeli missile boat as it cruised up and down the coast off the bay of Junieh.

It is reported that the sea was far from calm, the ship's engines were very noisy, and quite a few on board were seasick. Yet both sides felt it had been a good meeting. Rabin agreed to a series of steps to strengthen ties with the Christian forces. These included an accelerated supply of antitank artillery and other weapons as well as communications equipment. He also agreed in principle that Christian troops were to receive military training in Israel; these courses for various groups of Lebanese personnel continued well into the 1982 war.* Camille Shamoun, at the time in his seventies, upgraded the responsibility for contacts with the Israelis, putting his elder son, Danny Shamoun, in charge. Danny was also responsible for the military arm of the organization.

Soon afterward, on January 8, 1976, following a statement by the Syrian foreign minister in which he threatened an invasion of Lebanon, Israeli Defense Minister Shimon Peres issued the first public warning that Syrian intervention in the Lebanon would force Israel to consider steps it might take in response. In Washington, the State Department stressed its opposition to any intervention in the internal affairs of Lebanon, either by Syria or by Israel. The pattern of the diplomatic side of the fighting began to emerge.

At the beginning of 1976, the fighting moved into a new phase. The Moslem factions and the PLO established more powerful bases in West Beirut and along the coastal highway southward. The Christians were concentrated in East Beirut and in their fiefdoms to the east and northeast. But both sides occupied pockets of territory, some quite large, close to major bases of their opponents. Both felt strong enough to attempt to seize territory heretofore in the hands of the other side.

In mid-January the fighting spread and a force of some 8,000 Syrian-trained PLO men moved into the Al-Bika'a Valley from Syria. Within a few days they had encircled Zahle, a major Christian town on the main Beirut-Damascus highway, at the western approaches to the Al-Bika'a. Other Moslem militiamen attacked Damour, a predominantly Christian town some 15 miles south of Beirut, on the coastal highway to Sidon. Taking the town, they carried out one of the largest massacres of recent years: some 6,000 Christian men, women, and children who did not manage to escape were butchered. The survivors abandoned Damour. On the hilltop outside the town, overlooking the scene of the devastation, about 100 Damouris gathered in the Church of St. Elias White Cross.

---

*When the new Likud government assumed office in Jerusalem in the early summer of 1977, they were delighted at the relationship with the Lebanese bequeathed by their predecessors and looked forward to strengthening the ties with their potential new friends to the north. Begin's administration soon invited them to visit Israel; the government liked what it saw, and promised the Lebanese continued support.

By a miracle, Phalange militiamen arrived in time to take them to safety. The church itself was not so lucky; the Palestinians first looted it and then burned it down. An unfinished cathedral building next to the church became the headquarters of a pro-Iraqi PLO faction. At the head of the cathedral nave, where the altar had been, the terrorists erected a target for firing practice.

At the same time, the Christians were attacking and laying siege to small Moslem areas near the business center of East Beirut. At the end of January this round of fighting subsided. It resumed in mid-March with even more ferocity.

While fighting went on in the field the political leaders of the country, almost all in their sixties or seventies, were negotiating and dealing, forming tenuous alliances only to break them, declaring eternal enmity only to embrace the next day. President Suleiman Franjieh, whose six-year term in office was to end by September 1976, is generally considered the chief villain of the piece. In his quest for compromise with the radical Arab governments, the PLO, and the Lebanese Moslems, he was responsible for the collapse of the government. Kemal Junblatt, the wily Druse leader of the Progressive Socialist party, civilized and charismatic, was one of the main destablizers. He was often in collusion with Rashid Karameh, the Sunni leader of Tripoli. Junblatt demanded that the political structure of Lebanon be "modernized," by which he meant the transfer of the power constitutionally vested in the Christians to the Moslems, who were by now believed to be in the majority. Pierre Gemayel and Camille Shamoun insisted on the upholding of the present constitution and on the maintenance of the status quo. The PLO leaders, headed by Yasser Arafat, supported their fellow Moslems. Virtually everybody was worried about the possibility that the Syrians would move their army into Lebanon.

By the spring of 1976 the fighting encompassed the four largest cities, Beirut, Tripoli, Sidon, and Zahle, as well as virtually all of the countryside and the south nearly as far as the Israeli border. April 13 saw the first anniversary of the outbreak of hostilities. During this first year, some 17,000 had been left dead, some 35,000 wounded, and there was no end in sight. It was also clear that overt Syrian interest in Lebanon was increasing. Until that time the outside world, Arabs included, had considered the mounting fratricide an internal Lebanese affair. But a gradual reassessment was taking place: the aid of external peace-keeping forces was considered more necessary, and many people were coming to believe that the Syrian army could help stem the bloodletting.

Meanwhile, at the end of April and early in May, Elias Sarkis, encouraged by all those elements who favored the status quo (that is, the Christians and the Shiite Moslems) conducted a zealous campaign for the Lebanese presidency. Although he was not to assume office until September, parliament convened on May 8 and, with 66 votes out of the 69 members present, Sarkis was elected; but this had no affect on the fighting.

After reconnaissance visits by token Syrian forces early in May, the first large contingent of Syrian troops—some 2,000 men and sixty tanks—crossed the Lebanese border on May 31. Officially, they were entering Lebanese territory to reduce the military pressures on the Christian supporters of the status quo. Within a week, there were nearly 8,000 Syrian troops in Lebanon. By mid-June, the Syrians were the largest of the more than twelve fighting forces in the country. On June 21, the Arab League retroactively approved the invasion that had taken place three weeks earlier. The 10,000-troop Syrian force and a token Libyan contingent were together renamed the inter-Arab Peace-keeping Force, or the Arab Deterrent Force, and President Hafez al-Assad stated, on July 20, 1976, that "the Syrian Army entered Lebanon to protect the Palestinian resistance and the Arabic nature of Lebanon." Yet the fighting continued uninterrupted, with the same degree of cruelty and at the same level of ferocity. In no way can it honestly be said that the Syrian forces made a contribution to peace.

On June 16, as the Syrian army was moving toward the capital, a PLO terrorist murdered the American ambassador to Lebanon, Francis E. Meloy, Jr., and his economic councillor, Robert O. Waring.* Meanwhile, the Christian forces, composed mainly of Sha-

---

*Ambassador Meloy was the second American ambassador killed by the PLO. Three years earlier, Ambassador Cleo A. Noel Jr., and his deputy chief of mission, George C. Moore, were among several diplomats killed at a reception held by the Saudi ambassador, when PLO fighters seized the embassy compound in Khartoum, Sudan.

moun's faithful, now under increased pressure, completed their plans to launch an attack on the Palestine refugee camp of Tel el-Za'atar. Tel el-Za'atar, with some 25,000 residents, was situated on the main approach to Beirut from the east and, with its concentration of PLO troops and weapons, continuously threatened Christian communications with their hinterland. The Christian attack on the fortified refugee camp commenced on June 4. Meanwhile, by the end of the month, the smaller camp of Gisher el-Basha had been occupied by the Christian forces.

By August 12, the siege of Tel el-Za'atar was all over. Although no official figures were issued, the PLO announced that 4,000 men, women, and children had been killed in the camp, from the commencement of the siege until its final occupation.

The fighting continued in Beirut and around the countryside. The Syrians occupied key points to enable them to reach the three major cities on the coast but were careful not to penetrate areas that were held by the Christians or within the Christians' sphere of influence.

In the autumn, several Lebanese leaders made calls to contain the PLO, to whom they referred as "the Palestinians." In a farewell broadcast on Radio Beirut on September 19, 1976, on leaving the presidency, Suleiman Franjieh made the following points:

> Lebanon was suffering from a war launched against it by the Palestinians and their supporters, Arabs and others.
>
> The Palestinians had deceived many naive Moslems and convinced them that the Lebanese army was composed of Christians only, thereby winning those Moslems over to the Palestinian side.
>
> The Palestinians demanded changes in Lebanon's form of government and constitution.
>
> The Palestinians were not content with subjugating only the Moslems of Lebanon; they imposed their own puppet leaders to rule all of Lebanon from behind the scenes.
>
> When their plot failed, the Palestinians changed their strategy and tried to establish a state of their own in southern Lebanon.
>
> Taking advantage of this situation, communist governments tried to bring Lebanon into their orbit, to make it their stepping-stone to the Arab world and the Middle East.

The Palestinians incited communal strife, made impossible demands, and endorsed the efforts of the Lebanese leftists to change
the system of government and constitution.

The Palestinians brought about an escalation of murder, pillage,
kidnapping, and looting, leading to the outbreak of civil war
which, in effect, is a war between Lebanon and the Palestinians.

The lesson to be learned from the Lebanese tragedy is that the
Palestinians in Lebanon should be treated just as they are in the
other Arab countries, which restrict their freedom of movement.

A month later, on October 14, Edouard Ghorra, Lebanese delegate
to the United Nations, declared to the General Assembly that:

Lebanon's tragedy should be a warning, indeed a stern one, that the
security, nay the survival of member states cannot be viewed with
indifference. . . .

The Palestinians increased the influx of arms into Lebanon. They
transformed most of the refugee camps—if not all—into military
bastions. . . . Common criminals fleeing Lebanese justice found
shelter and protection in these camps.

In fact, these camps became centers for the training of mercenar-
ies sent and financed by other Arab states. . . . Palestinians belonging to various organizations kidnapped Lebanese and foreigners,
holding them prisoner, questioning them, torturing them, and
sometimes even killing them.

On October 17, 1976, King Khalid hosted a conference in Riyahh,
Saudi Arabia. Presidents Assad of Syria and Sadat of Egypt
attended, as well as the emir of Kuwait, Lebanese president Elias
Sarkis, and Yasser Arafat. The main decision adopted was a resolution to bring about a cease-fire in Lebanon, based on a return to the
status quo ante. The PLO would be committed to adhere to the
Cairo Agreement of 1969, which recognized a limited autonomy for
the PLO in the Palestinian camps and in southern Lebanon, and to
the strengthening of the Arab Deterrent Force. Although far from
satisfactory for the Lebanese, the Riyadh conference proved to be
the first, after many Arab summit meetings, to diminish the
fratricide.

By autumn, the areas under the control of each of the various forces had been recognized and militiamen patrolled the boundaries between them as well as the ports. The fighting lessened somewhat, although it was clear that the basic problems remained unsolved and that it was only a question of time before the Lebanese volcano erupted again.

Even before the Riyadh conference, as early as mid-December 1975, the various Christian forces had recognized that the then current cease-fire (the sixteenth in eight months), and subsequent cease-fires, would almost inevitably be broken. So they put together a joint command,* including:

> The Social Democratic Kataeb party (the Phalange).
> The Tanzim, headed by George Adwan. This is the most radical of the Christian factions and distrusts the ideas of any equitable coexistence with the Moslems.
> The Guardians of the Cedars, the radical Lebanese nationalist wing headed by Etiyane Sakar. It emphasizes the concept of a separate and unique Lebanese identity, distinct from the rest of the Arab world, and seeks latter-day inspiration from the glories of the Phoenician past.
> Nonaffiliated combatants.

While their elders bickered, a younger generation of Lebanese was gradually asserting itself. Each of the leaders had at least one son in his twenties or thirties. Some were busy being playboys, but others were involved in the fighting or in the political struggle. A few even found time to do all three.

There was Toni Franjieh, son of the outgoing president. In the elections of 1970, when forty-nine members of parliament voted for his father and forty-nine for Elias Sarkis, it was parliamentary deputy Toni who walked up to the dais, drew his pistol, and asked the Speaker how he intended to use his tie-breaking vote. "For your father, of course," was the answer Toni got.[2]

---

*It was not until August 1976 that a United Lebanese Front was officially created under Sheikh Bashir Gemayel with his father Pierre as president of the Council of Leadership.

There were Danny and his brother Dori Shamoun. In 1975, Danny was considered the most politically attractive and promising Young Christian of his generation.

And there were Amin Gemayel and his younger brother Bashir, also rising stars of the Christian community.

Among the Druse, there was Walid Junblatt, a weak, sensitive, untried young man, still living in the shadow of his father.

All, aching for power, were arrogant and jealous of their siblings, often imitating or resembling their fathers and their strengths and weaknesses. Camille Shamoun and Pierre Gemayel had often been allies for the sake of convenience and necessity, but there was little personal love lost between the more aristocratic Shamoun "Pasha," scion of an old family, and the more bourgeois Sheikh Pierre, ruthless challenger to the lay leadership of the Maronite and other Christian communities.

Danny Shamoun had many of his father's characteristics, and similarly Bashir Gemayel reminded many observers of his father in his youth. Danny was nearly ten years older than Bashir and in 1975 he had a far larger backing. He was considered to be politically less adventurous and more astute. He conducted himself well in the Battle of Tel el-Za'atar, although it gradually became clear that, among the various militia volunteers, those under his command were the least motivated and disciplined. Even before the massacre in the camp, there were some who called Danny's men riffraff.

Bashir was the younger Gemayel. In the mid-1960s, as a teenager, he was already spending his time with the Kataeb militia. Later, he took part in all their training and gradually rose in rank, position, and prestige. By the end of the first year of the fighting, in the spring of 1976, he was the unquestioned leader of the Kataeb military arm. They went on to become the most disciplined, serious, and professional of all the militias operating in Lebanon.

The younger Lebanese Christians, especially those involved with the armed forces, looked on with warmth and affection as Bashir gradually rose to leadership. The people preferred him to the more conservative older brother, Amin. In public, Amin grudgingly accepted the predominance of Bashir. But there was, to the end, considerable jealousy between the two. Both brothers loathed the Syrians and were interested in the new opening to Israel. Amin, however, was the more thoughtful and temperate of the two, taking fewer risks. This made him popular with the older generation, who characteristically preached compromise and moderation. Though less daring, Amin should not be underestimated. His courage is unquestionable. In the crucial years of the late 1970s he was a forceful commander of the militias confronting the Syrians in the Matten mountain range.

The Kataeb, and its leaders the Gemayels, were not only ambitious but also understood, respected, and exercised power. It was clear to them that, in the absence of any operative government, they should increase not only the territories under their control but also the economic resources available for the welfare of their followers. Accordingly, they pushed the Moslems out of approximately half of the jobs they had traditionally held in the Beirut Port Authority and replaced them with Christian longshoremen and laborers. They moved north into the mountains, toward Tripoli, into territories previously claimed by the Franjieh family, and asserted control of a large quarry, until then part of the interests of their on-again, off-again Christian ally. This inroad into the domain of the northern clan was resisted and two Kataeb guards were killed one night. Toni Franjieh's troops were believed to have been the attackers.

In revenge, Bashir ordered that Toni be eliminated. But his friends say that he was shocked when he learned how efficient his men had been: Toni was killed on June 13, 1978, together with his wife, their baby, and eighteen others.

As early as the summer of 1976, when the Israeli ties with the Lebanese Christians were being strengthened, some delicate questions had already arisen concerning the relations between the Shamouns and the Gemayels. Periodically, an Israeli missile boat or a smaller Dabour-class gunboat would arrive at the bay of Junieh, towing a barge full of arms. The arms would be handed over and the empty barge would be towed back to its home port.

The arms deliveries proved to be a more complicated problem than the Israelis anticipated; they had to share out the shipments, including the appropriate working manuals, evenly between the Kataeb and the Shamounites. Each item and each publication had to be supplied in duplicate.

53

The Israelis training the young Lebanese were impressed by the dedication of these idealistic young men and women, who deeply believed in their mission. To some veteran Israelis, they were reminiscent of the Canaanite movement, fashionable among Palestine Jewish youth in the days before the establishment of the state. Its members had regarded themselves as a new breed of Hebrews, with roots going back to the pagan tribes of Bible times. When they met with these latter-day Phoenicians, they found much in common. Others were charmed by the delightful, francophile, well-educated style of the young Lebanese. The young women were both proud and charming, some even strikingly beautiful. Solange was one of them—a young woman training as a radio operator. Later, she was to become the bride—and the widow—of Bashir.

Until the end of July the Israelis hardly ever landed in Lebanon. But then short visits began. One of the first to step onto Lebanese soil was Brigadier General (then Colonel) Binyamin ("Fuad") Ben Eliezer. He commanded the Israeli troops across the border from southern Lebanon and he also acted as adviser to the military command of the Lebanese Front. It was he who, in late July, observed the penultimate stages of the siege of Tel el-Za'atar.*

Enlarged programs were developed for training soldiers of the Lebanese Front in Israel. Some of their leaders visited Israel as well. Camille Shamoun visited Jerusalem and his son Danny crossed the border often, as did Bashir and Amin Gemayel. Each usually arrived without the other. Wherever they went, they were lauded and feted. As with his own men, Bashir gradually became the favorite of the Israelis. They were impressed by his natural courage, leadership, and creativity, and they believed that he would be the most dependable of their Lebanese connections.

The Christian Lebanese forces were not the only ones under continued pressure. On March 16, 1977, on the way to his country mansion at Muchtara in the Al-Shouf Mountains, Kamal Junblatt, the Druse chieftain and the most powerful presence among the

---

*This episode became a minor political issue six years later when, after another massacre, at another Palestinian camp, Israel's defense minister, Ariel Sharon, was fighting for his political life. Sharon incorrectly insinuated that Israeli officers were present during the final capture of Tel-el-Za'atar and the killings there.

leaders of all the Moslem factions, was ambushed and assassinated. It was never conclusively determined who had ordered his murder, but the consensus in Beirut was that the Syrians were behind it; because of his independent stand, they regarded him as too danger- ous to survive.

Another meeting of Arab leaders followed, again paying lip serv- ice to the need for a cease-fire. Meeting in Shtura, a small town west of Zahle on the Beirut-Damascus road, where the Syrians had established their Lebanese command post, the Syrians, the PLO, and the Lebanese government issued a joint proclamation reiterat- ing the need to carry out all previous decisions. In exchange for helping bring the country back to normal, the PLO would be given a substantial degree of autonomy within the Palestinian camps. They promised to obey the laws of the land outside the camps but, as frequently happened, got what they wanted without keeping their side of the bargain. The story of Beirut is probably the best illustra- tion of this.

By the end of 1976, the city had been divided into two parts: East Beirut, controlled by the Lebanese Forces, and West Beirut, occu- pied by the Syrian army and the PLO. West Beirut included the business center, the foreign embassies, the American University, the big international hotels, the attractive Corniche, and, on the outskirts, four Palestinian camps. It also encompassed the Interna- tional Airport. Not only did the Lebanese Forces avoid this whole area, but even the official Lebanese army dared not enter it until the PLO was expelled in the summer of 1982.

Counting the cost to Lebanon, it was apparent that the country had taken a severe beating. By 1977, not only had some 70,000 persons been killed and possibly double that number wounded, but Lebanon seemed even further away from resuming self-rule. Four- fifths of its territory was occupied and administered by foreigners: the south by the PLO, and most of the center and north by three Syrian divisions which, at full muster, totaled 40,000 men. The Christian Lebanese forces controlled East Beirut and the moun- tains to the northeast, but found it no mean task, and at times dangerous, to operate within their tiny enclave.

Bashir Gemayel, who assumed military command of the Leban- ese Forces in 1976, had a considerable gift for organization. As a result, East Beirut soon had its own municipal services operating and a fairly effective police force. In West Beirut, the situation was different. Garbage piled up in the streets, thefts and bank robberies were common, and rape and murder the order of the day. The law courts ceased operating in 1975, as there were no law-enforcement authorities and nobody to whom to appeal. In Sidon, Tyre, and other towns controlled by the PLO, there was similar anarchy.

Suddenly there was an escalation of fighting in the south. At the end of February 1978, in a series of thrusts, the PLO took up positions in the hills overlooking Israel and cut off communications among various towns and villages under the control of Saad Haddad. A year and a half earlier, in the late summer of 1976, following the contacts with the Israelis, Major Haddad of the Lebanese army had been ordered by his president and commander in chief to cross, via Haifa and Metullah, in Israel, into southern Lebanon, cut off from Beirut by PLO-held areas. There, he was to assume command of the local military and paramilitary units. He was to try to prevent the PLO from disrupting life and to do his best to maintain law and order. This was the beginning of Haddad's ties with Israel.

Haddad, to some an adventurer, to others a hero and a true Lebanese patriot, is a personable soldier with a record of courage. Initially, both he and the Israelis had grave doubts about working together, but Israeli officials came to admire him and the cooperation became strong. After the 1978 Litani campaign, Haddad's connection with the Israel Defense Forces also took on a political character, which intensified with the "Peace for Galilee" operation of 1982. At first he was regarded with distrust and disdain by Western officials, but his sensible, moderate political stance gradually won over many of them.

Early in March 1978 a small gang of PLO men landed on the Israeli coast, opposite Maagan Michael, about 40 miles north of Tel Aviv. They surprised a young American, Gail Rubin, who was photographing birds in a nature reserve, murdered her, and went on to hijack a bus carrying passengers to Tel Aviv. Some 2 miles north of the city, they were stopped by Israeli forces; in the ensuing shootout, thirty-four Israeli civilians were killed, including women and children.

56

On March 16, Israeli troops entered southern Lebanon and moved up to the Litani River, in what came to be known as the Litani campaign. They did not occupy the town of Tyre, which remained a PLO center. But they succeeded in destroying or flushing out all PLO positions in other parts of southern Lebanon. By the end of April, in accordance with Security Council Resolution No. 425 the Israelis had transferred responsibility for the territory they had occupied to the United Nations Forces in Lebanon (UNIFIL). Within two months, some 800 PLO terrorists were back in their bases, under the tolerant eye of the international peace-keepers.

These developments were of secondary importance for the Lebanese Front leaders. They were more interested in what was going on in Lebanon proper, immediately under their noses. They snubbed Major Haddad, regarding him as a country bumpkin who was lacking in refinement. They resented him—perhaps because, paradoxically, he was the only officer with a record of having fought both against and with the Israelis.

At the end of June 1978, the day the Lebanese Christians had long feared finally arrived. The Syrian army turned against them. Taking advantage of the shock in the Christian community following the murder of Toni Franjieh, the Syrians attacked. They relied on heavy artillery bombardment rather than any movement of forces, but even so, caused many civilian casualties and much destruction. Earlier, for five days starting April 8, the Syrians had had a bloody shootout with Lebanese forces in Ein Rumanah, east of Beirut. Now, the artillery pounding went on almost continuously from June 28 until September 23 and was far more serious than anything that had gone before. The heavy bombardment of East Beirut continued while the Syrians overran strongholds of the Lebanese Forces in Bsharri and Batrun, in the north.

There was another conference, on October 17, 1978, this time in the splendid, century-old presidential palace, situated in the pretty town of Beit Eldin, in the Al-Shouf Mountains. The meeting was attended by the foreign ministers of the countries participating in the Arab Deterrent Force. Resolutions adopted in earlier summit meetings were reiterated, this time in somewhat different phraseology, and the shooting lessened for a while.

During the summer fighting, the Lebanese Christian leaders

57

became worried and asked for more help from the Israelis. Prime Minister Begin met with them in Jerusalem. He promised that if the Syrians were to attack by air, Israel would intervene. Beyond that, all he offered was warm and encouraging words.

By the end of 1978, most Christians were ready to accept Bashir Gemayel's growing power and agreed on the need for a unified Lebanese force. There was, however, one group which objected to domination by Sheikh Bashir: the Liberal militias under the command of Danny Shamoun, who resented the power of his young adversary. Finally, in the summer of 1980, as an act of compromise and as a last resort, Shamoun proposed transferring authority over his militia outposts in Ein Rumanah to the Lebanese army. Bashir would have none of it. Rather than enter a cumbersome alliance, it was his design to establish a clear, unified Christian command. In a well-planned, sudden sweep on July 7, 1980, the Kataeb militias occupied the power bases of the Shamoun family. The beaten Danny Shamoun thought it safer to go into voluntary and, as it turned out, temporary exile in Paris.* His father, Camille, and his followers, however, now unquestioningly accepted the leadership of Bashir, which was an important political as well as military victory.

Bashir Gemayel began a slow, careful consolidation and expansion of Kataeb power. A major aim was to reinforce lines of communications with Zahle, the prosperous Christian town in the Al-Bika'a valley. For several years the Syrians had regarded the Al-Bika'a as part of their first line of defense to the west of Damascus, and a major part of their troops in Lebanon were stationed there. The fact that Zahle was out of bounds was a constant thorn in their side. Their consolation was that they controlled the roads out of the city, linking Zahle with both Beirut and Damascus. Late in 1980 the Lebanese Forces began laying a new road leading up to their positions near Jebel Senin in the mountains some 7 miles away.

In December the Syrians indicated to Sheikh Bashir their dissatisfaction with his plans, by light fire on Zahle. When the road work continued, the Syrians opened a full offensive on Zahle on

---

*He remained there until after the murder of Bashir Gemayel and the election of Bashir's brother Amin as president, two years later.

April 2, 1981. It was a brutal attack in which the Syrians pounded the city heavily, virtually laying siege to it and inflicting heavy casualties. But the Christian forces held out valiantly and the Syrians decided to step up the fighting by another increment. They brought commandos in, by helicopter, to occupy Christian positions on Jebel Senin. Once again the Lebanese Forces appealed to the Israelis for help. They obliged and Israeli planes shot down two Syrian helicopters carrying troops. This was the first time the Israelis used their air force to intervene in the Syrian-Lebanese fighting and it marked a new high in Israeli-Syrian tensions.

The Syrians reacted by moving a substantial number of Soviet-made SAM-6 missile batteries into the Al-Bika'a valley. The escalation spiral that was to culminate one year later in the Israeli invasion of Lebanon had begun.

4

A Change of Mixed Blessings

I T was eleven P.M. on May 17, 1977, when Haim Yevin, Israel's star TV news broadcaster, in a shocked voice announced the computer forecast of the national election results: the Labor party would probably have thirty-one or thirty-two members in the incoming ninth Knesset, the new Democratic Movement for Change (DMC) possibly sixteen, and the Likud, a coalition of conservative parties, as many as forty-three. When the final result confirmed the forecast, to most Israelis, including the majority who had voted for Likud, it was unbelievable. For many, the news was frightening; for others, a dream come true. The impossible seemed about to happen. The solid, stable Labor party, the rock of endurance which had ruled long before the establishment of the state, through the 1973 Yom Kippur War and beyond, had now toppled. Most Israelis had expected Labor to take a beating and lose up to half a dozen Knesset seats. The newly established DMC had hoped to pick up these and more, and to hold the balance between the two big blocs. As it turned out, the DMC achievement, impressive though it was, fell short of its aims. More than 200,000 Israelis, including most of the upper-grade civil servants, academics, and military men who had voted for the DMC had, by doing so, unwittingly weakened Labor to such an extent that it could not prevent Menachem Begin, head of the Herut party and leader of the Likud coalition, from forming a Likud-led coalition government.

As it turned out, the new government did not have a vital need for the votes of the moderate DMC; when, months later, the new party was co-opted by an already functioning cabinet, their lack of influence was predictable. Begin, the new prime minister, had, since his arrival in Palestine in 1941 during the darkest hours of World War II, always lived as the leader of a minority. Often hated by the establishment, tolerated at best, at the age of sixty-four he was regarded as a perennial loser and his followers, with few exceptions, were seen as uninspired sycophants. He himself at first was not quite clear about the meaning of his victory. At the Herut party headquarters,* Begin made a subdued though sentimental victory speech. By the end of the week, he had a heart attack more serious than the one he suffered in the election campaign, and convalescence kept him out of politics for several weeks.

When he appeared before the Knesset, on June 21, to ask for a vote of confidence, Begin seemed still overwhelmed by his victory. In an attempt to pacify the new Opposition, his government included Moshe Dayan as foreign secretary and former Air Force chief Ezer Weizman as minister of defense. Controversial, opportunist Ariel Sharon was appointed to what was believed to be a back-seat ministry: agriculture. Begin extended an open invitation to the DMC to join the government and four months later they did so. Professor Yigael Yadin, as Deputy Prime Minister, joined the familiar faces of Dayan and Weizman. All three were well-known, generally respected personalities. The transfer of power was being implemented much more peacefully than might have been anticipated. It was an important day for Israeli democracy. Its institutions stood up successfully and the changes went through smoothly.

Seen with hindsight, the demise of the Labor government is not all that surprising. Sclerosis had already begun to set in in the early 1960s. Infighting—ostensibly over the so-called Lavon Affair following a bungled cloak-and-dagger operation in Egypt—caused the the secession of the independent Israeli workers' list, known as Rafi,

---

*Named Metzudat Zeev after Zeev (Vladimir) Jabotinsky (1880–1940), founder of the Zionist Revisionist party that was the forerunner of Herut.

from the Labor party. In the general elections in the fall of 1965, Rafi, headed by David Ben Gurion, Israel's first prime minister, was one of the options offered to the Israeli voter but its success was limited. Of its own accord it entered the political wilderness of the Opposition, until just before the Six Day War, when the prime minister invited Rafi to return to the fold of the Labor party and they seized the opportunity. When Golda Meir assumed the premiership upon the death of Levi Eshkol, early in 1969, her leadership and authority were for a while accepted by the entire party, indeed the whole country. In-party bickering for a time almost disappeared.

The Yom Kippur War had a traumatic effect on the whole of Israel. It came in the midst of an election campaign and the vote had to be postponed for two months, until the end of 1973. The questions posed after the war were many: Why was the leadership so surprised by the Egyptian and Syrian strikes? Where were Israel's intelligence services? Why were so few troops in the front-line positions? These were asked with bitterness and much personal recrimination. Moshe Dayan, who was regarded as the architect of the striking victory in the Six Day War and the hero of 1967, became the scapegoat of 1973 and was blamed by many for the shock and surprise that caused so many casualties in the Yom Kippur War.

Elections took place on December 31, 1973. Although the Labor party suffered a beating and was left with fifty-one seats in the seventh Knesset compared with fifty-seven in the previous one, Golda Meir had no difficulty in setting up a new coalition. It appeared as if the Israeli public were willing to give the party one more chance—even though they still wished to understand who was to blame for the lack of preparedness.

The Agranat Commission, appointed by Golda Meir to investigate responsibility for the events leading up to the Yom Kippur War, conducted its work *in camera* and its completed findings were never fully published. Basically, however, the commission addressed itself only to the shortfalls of the military, by omission clearing the political leadership of any responsibility. The chief of staff, Lt. Gen. David Elazar, was forced into early retirement, as were the chief of intelligence and several other officers. Mrs. Meir, having read the report, nevertheless felt weighed down by her share of the responsibility and she retired voluntarily. By a small majority the Labor party chose Yitzhak Rabin over Shimon Peres as their leader and candidate for the premiership. In June 1974, again by a small Knesset majority, he won the office, which he held for three years.

These were not happy years for Israel, for the Labor party, or for Rabin. The trauma of the war had injected a new pessimism into the people. Inflation, running at more than 30 percent annually, the lack of new investments, political squabbling among the government ministers, as well as the slow, flat, crickety voice and manner of their prime minister, all contributed to the public sense of malaise.

It became clear that Rabin and Shimon Peres, the minister of defense, were devoting the largest part of their energies to fighting with each other. It is still arguable who was more responsible for this infighting, but there is little doubt that it badly damaged the party.

Although, on the face of it, Rabin and Peres share many things in common, closer study reveals the differences between them. Rabin, considered a hero of the Six Day War, a retired chief of staff of the IDF, and ultimately the first Israeli-born prime minister, was educated at the Kadoorie Agricultural School in the Lower Galilee; he was also a senior officer in the Palmach defense force before the establishment of the state. He is widely admired for his brilliant analytical mind but has many enemies who recall that he cannot take much stress and suffered a breakdown on the eve of the Six Day War and on one or two previous occasions. In public office he was suspicious—some thought close to paranoic. He displayed many prejudices and pronounced opinions and showed little patience or willingness to listen. To some, Rabin's least forgivable sin is that he lacks social graces and seems unable to make small talk.*

The climax of the Labor party's leadership crisis came at the end of March and early April of 1977. The Washington correspondent of *Ha'aretz,* Israel's leading independent newspaper, Dan Margalit, discovered that, upon Rabin's return five years earlier from his assignment as Israeli ambassador to the United States, his wife

---

*Israelis who accompanied Yitzhak Rabin to a dinner party held in his honor by Jimmy Carter at the White House in March 1977 were shocked by Rabin's monosyllabic answers to Carter's efforts at conversation. To ease the mood before his private talk with the prime minister, the president reportedly showed him around the private quarters of the White House and asked him whether he would like to meet Amy doing her homework. Rabin replied with a curt "No."

Leah had, contrary to Israel's foreign currency regulations, kept her American bank account open. In the ensuing furor, Rabin resigned as the party's candidate for prime minister in the then upcoming elections.

Soon after the 1977 elections Rabin wrote an autobiography, highlighting his then recent tenure as prime minister. In it, he accused Peres, his defense minister, of vile behavior and of deviously and continuously trying to undermine him.

Peres, two years older, is far more sociable. He was born in Eastern Europe but arrived in Israel as a boy, became a leader in the youth movement of the Labor party and, as a young man, joined a Haganah contingent active in arms procurement abroad. Though he never served in the army, he rose in the Defense Ministry hierarchy to become its director general under David Ben-Gurion, Israel's first prime minister. Later, Peres was deputy minister of defense until he resigned in 1964 to help Ben-Gurion establish Rafi. Loyal to both Ben-Gurion and Moshe Dayan, he was for years overshadowed by the latter and was an uninspired member of the two Meir cabinets. Peres has some intellectual leanings and good friends in the arts and sciences. Even to supporters, he seems far too comfortable among his foreign peers in the international labor movement but somewhat detached from what should be his domestic grass roots. He repeatedly appears strained and fatigued in his appeals to the electorate, trying too hard to please everybody. His TV appearances are often disastrous. The camera does him grave injustice. On the screen his shifting eyes give an impression of a lack of credibility which drives his admirers to despair.

The politically astute Likud may be grateful to Rabin for his ineptness, which helped get them elected. For years they have regarded Rabin as their favorite political opponent and have used his utterances as one of their main offensive gambits against the Labor party in general and Peres in particular.

All but the most loyal Labor supporters had, by that time, become disenchanted with the government's ministers.* The sense of a lack

---

*Within the previous six months, Asher Yadlin, Rabin's candidate for governor of the Bank of Israel, had been sentenced to a five-year jail term on charges of corruption and embezzlement, and Minister of Housing Abraham Ofer had committed suicide on learning that the police investigation of corruption allegations was to be continued.

of leadership was accompanied by a general feeling that things were slipping and shaky; the system just was not working well any more. Prices kept rising, economists worried about the growth in foreign debt, and gross national product almost stagnated. Ominous for the Labor party in the coming elections was the fact that the workers felt that their standard of living was declining. There was also a widespread suspicion that Rabin and Peres did not have the guts to stand up to increased American pressure for Israeli concessions to the Arabs.

Labor leadership was amazingly ignorant of the change in public sentiment. Throughout the spring campaign, they kept repeating slogans with humorless pomposity, confident that they would be reelected. They seemed unaware of the impact of Likud's populist messages or the intellectually attractive appeal of the untried innocents of the DMC, headed by Professor Yadin and Dr. Amnon Rubinstein. Even after they were turned out of office, and throughout the six years of Begin's tenure, they seemed not to understand or accept what had happened or why.

The Likud administration took over, elated and hesitant, as if not quite believing that government was really theirs. Most of the new ministers impressed their senior civil servants by their first steps. They appeared to grasp the matters at hand and were careful not to upset previous decisions. In the months that followed, optimists could hope that although the actors had changed, the scenario was still the same. Some felt that it was, from Menachem Begin down, a caretaker government seeking legitimization. They saw it as no accident that Begin's two senior ministers were Moshe Dayan, Ben-Gurion's number one protégé, and Ezer Weizman, nephew of Israel's first president, Chaim Weizmann. In those days many shared the view but few had the audacity of Avraham Kidron, ambassador to the Court of St. James's, who was quoted by *The Guardian* newspaper as having declared that Mr. Begin's administration may be considered a "temporary apparition." (Although Kidron later claimed he had been quoted out of context, he was soon dispatched to faraway Canberra, Australia.)

During the first Likud term of office it was unnoticed just how much weaker the Labor party had become. As long as they had been

in office, they had encouraged many of their brightest young followers to join the government as senior civil servants. The enormous
contribution of these "backroom boys" to the strength of the party
was taken for granted. But, with the ascent of the former Opposition, these employees were encouraged to stay at their posts. In
these changed circumstances, they could be of little help to their
party. Their wings were clipped by their new bosses, who made up
for what they lacked in administrative experience by a better inside
knowledge of politics.

Learning how to manipulate the newly acquired power was often
difficult and laborious, and public opinion began gradually to turn
away from them and their new allies of the DMC. But the Likud
government was digging in and the leaders had no intention of being
passing phenomena. Toward the end of the ninth Knesset, at
the close of 1980, they finally understood that what was hurting
them most were the economic policies of their first two ministers of
finance. Simcha Ehrlich, nominal head of the Liberal party and
number two to Begin, had ordered almost complete liberalization of
currency controls but also fathered three-digit inflation. His successor, Yigael Horowitz, a successful businessman with an abrasive
personality, understood the source of Israel's economic difficulties
and, warning that it might hurt the public, seriously tried to
improve the foreign trade and currency situation. When it became
clear that Horowitz was responsible for the increasing unpopularity
of the government, he lost Begin's support and resigned at the end of
1980. The premier appointed Yoram Aridor, the by then almost
perennial deputy minister and general stand-in, as the new minister
of finance.

Unlike other factions that make up the Likud alliance, an important element within the rightist Herut party is passionately populist. The two most senior ministers to adopt and preach these beliefs
were Deputy Prime Minister David Levy and Yoram Aridor. Begin
showed little evident personal interest in economics and its attend-
ant problems, yet in principle—though rarely publicly—he supported the Levy and Aridor positions.

Ever since it was reestablished in 1948, Israel has had a negative
balance of trade and a substantial foreign debt. Its social-democrat-
dominated governments were committed not only to building a high

level of social welfare and a powerful army as an effective deterrent to Arab aggression—very expensive investments in themselves—but also to the absorption of massive immigration from socially and economically underdeveloped countries in Eastern Europe, Southwest Asia, and North Africa, providing the newcomers with housing, jobs, schooling, and other services. In addition, until 1977 the economic leaders of Israel also strived to reduce the country's foreign debt by increasing the gross national product and exports as well as by restraining consumption by means of indirect taxation. The then government ministers understood that Israel should strive to attain a positive balance of payments and that economic independence was essential, not least to prevent political pressure from abroad.

A close second in economic priority was the realization that inflation—13 percent in 1972 and 56 percent in 1974, in the aftermath of the Yom Kippur War—had to be fought. But in 1976 it was still 38 percent. Foreign currency controls were widely applied and the government promulgated various export incentive schemes. Most economists, while unhappy about the pace of progress, concurred in principle with the general direction they pursued.

The victory of Begin and his Likud coalition changed matters completely. Economic controls were almost totally abolished. But Israel did not become the Switzerland of the Middle East; instead, its economic indices took a serious turn for the worse.

Over the years Israeli administrations have devised a system of indexing, or pegging, that is far-reaching and intricate. Some sectors have to calculate costs, trade, and profits in dollars, so that relating the dollar to inflation has become like a "differential in mathematics, which measures constant reality with ever-increasing numbers of shekels."[1] Indeed, in 1981 and 1982 dollar prices barely moved.

As the government entered 1981, with elections only six months ahead, Finance Minister Aridor began, with energy, indeed panache, to practice what he had for years been preaching. By cutting the taxes levied on them, within days he reduced the prices of medium-range to expensive consumer goods, mainly electric home appliances, television sets, refrigerators and air conditioners, as well as small and medium-sized cars. The public, thinking that the bonanza would not last forever, went on a buying spree and, happy with their new possessions, felt more optimistic than they had for a long time.

The Labor leaders never attempted to convince the electorate how dismal they believed the record of the Likud administration to be nor the real cost to the nation of the constant increase in the standard of living: foreign debt was reaching horrendous proportions, inflation had settled in the three-digit range, and the cabinet members and their ministries often demonstrated a surprising degree of ineptness. Yet, during the election campaign Labor never clearly indicated to Israeli voters that their party was capable of offering better reasoned, more effective social and economic policies.

The fact that it was during Begin's premiership that the first peace treaty with an Arab nation had been signed was not a major campaign issue. There were other important reasons why the Likud did so well in the elections of 1981. Certainly, the number of the party's hard-core supporters had grown in the preceding four years. They were the working class, composed mostly of families who had immigrated to Israel from Arab countries in the decade after the establishment of the state. These voters had never had it so good. Encouraged by Begin's dramatic rhetoric, they pinned their hopes on him and voted accordingly. It was probably the charisma of Begin together with Aridor's populist steps that contributed most to the final results.

Running against Begin was a nervous Labor party headed by the disunited leaders it had elected. They were clutching at the straws held out during the preceding three years by the pollsters. Instead of policy they offered election gimmicks; they promised patronage jobs which there was reason to doubt they could provide. By the end of the spring, public support was rapidly moving back to the Likud.

Although the Labor party recovered most of what it had lost in 1977, the Likud more than regained popular support in 1981. When the polls for the tenth Knesset election closed, both parties had won the same number of seats. But with the support of the minority parties, it became clear that the Likud would remain in power. This rightward swing continued after the elections.

This trend began to change in the autumn of 1982; public opinion polls began to indicate diminishing support for Likud and a corre-

69

sponding improvement of Labor's position. The Government's inability to translate the military achievements of the war in Lebanon into tangible political benefits, as well as the widespread dissatisfaction with Israel's continued military presence there, began to detract from Mr. Begin's popularity. But the fast-deteriorating economic situation probably contributed much more to the change in popular mood. Still, despite turbulent events such as the evacuation of Sinai, the war in Lebanon, the massacres in the Sabra and Shatilla camps, and the findings of the Inquiry Commission, and even after it was announced in September 1983 that Itzhak Shamir would be the next prime minister, each subsequent opinion poll showed that if elections were then held, the Likud would return with a larger number of seats and Labor would lose some of the seats it held.

From 1977 on, there was one exception to the generally low standard of ministerial efficiency: Ariel Sharon, minister of agriculture. While most veteran farmers complained that they had never been so neglected by their ministry, Ariel Sharon seemingly directed all his energy to settling Jewish residents in the Gaza Strip and, even more intensively, in Judea and Samaria (the "West Bank"). As the West repeatedly heard of "one more" and "another couple" of new settlements on the West Bank, Sharon, ignoring the chorus of Laborite criticism at home and abroad, was busy completing his settlement program. Sharon's personality seems larger than life. With a gluttonous appetite and enormous energy, he is impatient with the niceties of democracy and eager for results. A strong believer in the use of power and a shrewd manipulator, Sharon apparently assumed, during his tenure in the Ministry of Agriculture, that the Labor party would return to office in 1981. He was therefore in a hurry to leave behind him a network of settlements that any force, from within the country or without, would find it hard to dismantle. Encouraged by the prime minister, he sought to create such a strong living bond between the West Bank and the Jews as to constitute *de facto* annexation. Although his achievements there, like the peace with Egypt, were not a major issue of the election campaign, they could well prove to be of no less historic significance. When, after the 1981 elections, he gave up the agriculture portfolio for that of defense, he left behind him a significant monument: 103 settlements, most of them established during his tenure, with plans for some 60 more to be established in the 1980s. By the summer of 1983 the number of settlements on the West Bank and in the Gaza Strip has grown to 126. Over the past 15 years another 28 had been established on the Golan Heights.

Compared to the indigenous Arab Palestinian population of some 700,000, the actual number of Jewish residents on the West Bank— probably less than 30,000—was insignificant. But the number would grow. There were many attractions, in the form of building subsidies and other financial incentives, drawing Israelis to settle there. No longer did it seem fantastic to think that, by the end of the decade, 100,000 Jews would actually travel the well-paved roads, commuting from their bedroom towns and villages on the West Bank to work inside the Green Line, the pre-1967 border. Paying little concern to the political or legal measures that may bring about annexation and which, their opponents say, involve questions of human and civil rights, the majority of Israelis now regard the West Bank as part of Israel.

On June 7, 1981, just three weeks before the elections and two days after Prime Minister Menachem Begin met with Egyptian president Anwar Sadat at Sharm el Sheikh in the southern Sinai, Israeli warplanes, in a meticulously planned and executed operation, crossed the airspace and air defense systems of Saudi Arabia and Jordan and, with pinpoint bombing, destroyed the core of the nuclear reactor Iraq was building near Baghdad, then returned safely to Israel. Prime Minister Begin had repeatedly charged that Iraqi dictator Saddam Hussein wanted the facility for the production of nuclear weapons, and had warned him and other Arab leaders that Israel would not only not tolerate any such development but would act to prevent it. The bombing of the Baghdad reactor was thus a clear indication that the government was ready to take other extreme unilateral actions against threats to Israel's existence, even if they were perceived to be looming in the distant future.

There was no doubt in the minds of the overwhelming majority of Israelis that Iraq was on the way to acquiring nuclear weaponry that would threaten Israel. The reactor, of the Osirak type, was

71

supplied by France; French technicians were completing its construction. Under considerable economic pressure, French president Giscard d'Estaing had agreed to provide the Iraqis with "weaponable" grade instead of "caramel" nuclear fuel. Caramel would have been equally useful for the proclaimed peaceful purpose of the reactor, but is specially treated to prevent its transformation for use in a nuclear explosive device. Inspections by the International Atomic Agency were intended to provide a safeguard but these were later exposed as inadequate if not a sham. They were, moreover, under pretext of the war with Iran, prevented for a long time by the Iraqis. More ominous, Iraq had been secretly buying German-patented components, mostly from Italy and Brazil, for the construction of facilities to extract weapon-grade uranium from the fuel supplied by the French. At the same time, Iraqi agents had been purchasing components, mostly in Italy, for the construction of medium-range missiles suitable for the delivery of nuclear warheads. Iraqi newspapers went out of their way to reassure Teheran that Iran had no reason to fear Iraq's nuclear capability. There was no doubt about the target: it was "the Zionist enemy" who should take fright.

Israel had tried to persuade France and Italy to withhold the sale to Iraq of instruments, equipment and other material suitable for nuclear weapon production, but to no avail. Two reactor cores were sabotaged mysteriously in the French plant, just as they were ready for shipment to Baghdad. Two nuclear specialists working for the Iraqi project died in Europe, in equally mysterious circumstances. Still, the Iraqis pushed on. Israel finally took direct action, explaining that, had the bombing been ordered a few months later, when the reactor would have been operational, radiation would have been likely to endanger Baghdad's civilian population.

The refusal of the European countries to risk financial consequences, even at the cost of nuclear proliferation and mortal threat to Israel, reinforced Prime Minister Begin's deep-seated "Holocaust complex" and his conviction that, where matters of Israel's existence are involved, Israel must act alone when necessary.

There was, of course, from all over the world negative public reaction to the attack. Yet the daring to penetrate Iraqi airspace and the spectacular accuracy of the Israeli bombing of the reactor was, in private, respected and admired, even by many Arab countries and other states usually very critical of Israel.

In Israel the operation met with criticism from a few, and with approval from many. It certainly helped Begin regain votes from an Opposition hurt by Peres's criticism of the bombing.

The first Begin cabinet was insecure, not quite sure of its brief. But after the elections in the summer of 1981, the Likud, far more confident, began to assert itself. Now sure of popular backing, no longer caretakers, they intended to rule in the fullest sense of the word. The message quickly got around: from now on, the Likud would brook no interference.

And yet it would be wrong to assume that the Likud government that was formed in 1981 was an ordinary majority government. Many old suspicions remained. The hard-core Herut party members, centered around Begin, habitually distrust all outsiders—members of the Opposition and, probably, a considerable number of members of other parties in their own coalition. In some ways, the situation calls to mind Richard Nixon's frequent sense of beleaguerment. Even in his heyday, the president never believed he could really rely on more than a small minority of his party. He developed various defensive gambits to protect himself against his political enemies. Similarly, Begin acted, in many respects, as if he were the head of a minority government, supported by what he still believed to be a fickle popular majority. He rarely came into contact with the public and maintained no intellectual rapport with them.

In spite of his gradual retreat from the public eye, culminating when he finally tendered his resignation in September 1983, his followers continued to admire him. Most of his supporters did not seem to expect him to show a physical interest in them. Although he paid a brief visit to the once menacing PLO base of Beaufort Castle soon after it had been taken by the IDF, he did not set foot in Lebanon again. Nor did he visit any combat troops or any of the more than 500 bereaved families whose sons, husbands, and fathers were killed in the campaign. In spite of his pride in the settlement of the West Bank, he hardly ever crossed the Green Line (the pre-1967 border) into Judea or Samaria, to encourage the settlers or review progress.

Only in part may this be attributed to the fact that, since assuming office, the prime minister had been under constant medical supervision, fearful for his health. The truth is that Menachem Begin was an unusual person of many parts. When he resigned, very frail, in his seventy-first year, he was still the born leader, idolized by immigrants from Moslem countries and their children who had come to form Israel's majority. By others, he was loathed with equal emotion. He was respected but disliked by many of the American leaders and senior civil servants he had encountered since 1977.

With the pettyfogging discipline of his legal training he could be pedantic, precise, or long-winded. Electioneering or speaking in the Knesset, he was sometimes a rabble-rouser, at times a great orator. He cared deeply about his country and its people and saw the nation's security problems against the trauma of the Holocaust of European Jewry. Yet his main support came from the communities who immigrated to Israel from North Africa and Asia and who never experienced the Nazi menace.

He was the classic product of prewar East European urban culture. His roots still determined many of his political and social concepts, including the nature of the autonomy he offered to the Palestinians. His after-office hours were dedicated to his family, to the study of politics, and to reading the press. His close political allies, staff, and personal friends were all of Polish origin. Although before the establishment of the state in 1948 he was the commander in chief of the Irgun Zvai Leumi, the right-wing armed underground, he had little military training and was visibly awed by senior military officers; he clearly felt inferior in their company.

Having been for decades an Opposition leader, often ostracized, even boycotted, he remained ill at ease in the role of leader of the national majority. A committed democrat, his respect for the Israeli Knesset (parliament), of which he had been a member since it first convened in January 1949, was profound. As was evident when he appeared before the Kahn Commission of Inquiry into the Sabra and Shatila massacres, he had a similar veneration for the Israeli judiciary.

He had often shown more respect for form than for content, and could be swayed by it. Free with superlatives, he described Presi-

dent Jimmy Carter as the second greatest person he has ever met—
the first being his mentor, Jabotinsky. (To judge from his autobiography, it is interesting to note, Carter took an intense personal
dislike to Begin.) He considered Ronald Reagan one of Israel's best
friends. Yet, when U.S. Ambassador Samuel Lewis came to him on
September 1, 1982, with the president's new peace plan, Begin said
this was "the saddest day" in his life.

He paid lip service to the need to give Israel's Arabs complete
equality and to ensure a fair deal for the Palestinians. But he was
not fully interested in the fate of either, nor did he follow up on his
verbal commitments for their equality.

By constantly comparing the PLO to the Nazis and overusing the
term "Holocaust," he perhaps unwittingly devalued the memory
and the meaning of that catastrophe. To the end, Begin remained
uncomfortable in the company of Gentiles and seemed to have little
compassion for Diaspora Jewry.

Totally uninstructed in the mechanism of government, confident
that things will "work out," he had little patience with the techni-
calities of office. Except for populist sentiments, he showed very
little interest in economic matters; some of his most extraordinary
statements related to bilateral international negotiations in which
he committed Israel to totally unnecessary giveaways. For instance,
during the long period from President Sadat's arrival in Jerusalem
in November 1977 through the Camp David proceedings in September 1978 to the final peace treaty in March 1979, the American
government was prepared to share financially in the peace process.
Yet Begin insisted that Israel would accept no grant but would
repay every dollar it was lent by the United States.

His foreign policy was almost completely determined by internal
politics. He addressed himself to his domestic supporters with little,
if any, regard for the impression he may have created abroad. From
the declaratory unification of Jerusalem in 1980, which did no more
than proclaim what had been the de facto situation since the
summer of 1967, to the imposition of Israeli law on the Golan
Heights in fall 1981, he seemed to ignore world opinion.

In return, no Israeli leader had ever been so disliked abroad. Both
the foreign press and the Western TV networks frequently vilified
him; many of the leaders of European democracies avoided and

loathed him. Israelis traveling abroad found themselves repeatedly on the defensive on this score.

During Begin's tenure in office, there had been a widespread emergence of anti-Zionism, which in many cases was a thinly disguised form of latter-day anti-Semitism. In turn this nourished Begin's long-standing fears and phobias. He had a tendency to stir up issues long dormant, such as the legitimacy of Israel's West Bank settlement policy and even its very presence in Jerusalem. In a way no premier had before him, Menachem Begin thrived by polarizing the issues, placing himself squarely at one end of the spectrum, sharpening domestic disputes and international controversies, rather than striving for true consensus and compromise.

Over the years, Begin had often seemed captive to the power of his own rhetoric: committed to some of his eloquent promises, forgetful of others. Relying uncritically on the judgment of their leader, his supporters were rarely bothered by his rhetorical ambiguities.

Yet, in times of internal stress, the prime minister all but disappeared. Since autumn 1982 he became even more remote. He appeared to have lost his zest for living nor did he seem to enjoy confrontation with the opposition at home and abroad. He avoided the representatives of the press and rarely appeared in public. When ethnic tensions grew stronger and some Sephardim who felt themselves socially deprived voiced the most violent feelings against Ashkenazi leaders, no guiding, moderating voice was heard from Menachem Begin. But then, even when still stronger, in better health, he had not come forth to encourage, calm, and lead his divided and bitter people through the last stage of the peace treaty with Egypt, when settlers in Yamit and a dozen Sinai villages had to be forced to evacuate their homesteads.

One of the most dramatic events leading to the war in Lebanon occurred at the other end of Israel, in Sinai, south of the Gaza Strip. According to the Israel-Egypt peace treaty, April 26, 1982, was the final date for the evacuation from the remaining outposts held by Israel in the Sinai. For months the Movement Against the Withdrawal had been gathering strength, with increasingly overt help from official quarters, including tacit encouragement from Defense Minister Sharon. The goal of the movement was to try to hold on to the town of Yamit, as well as nearly a dozen villages in the north-eastern corner of the Rafiah Salient, which Israelis had settled over the previous twelve years. The government remained passive almost to the end and thus encouraged even further the right-wing elements who began to occupy farms and homes vacated, for huge compensation payments, by the settlers.

Toward the end of March, however, the prime minister ordered the army to evacuate the squatters and those recalcitrant settlers who were still in the area. The final confrontation took place in Yamit, a small model town built several years earlier by Israel on the white sands of the Mediterranean coast. The clash, on April 22, 23, and 24, two days before the deadline, was bitter and violent. It was brought into every Israeli home, live, on television. Although the young soldiers sealing up the houses and dragging the resisting settlers away behaved with admirable coolness and self-restraint, the scenes had a traumatic effect, especially on the nationalistic supporters of the government.

One of the major aims of the show of stiff resistance by the Sinai settlers, as well as of the exorbitant amounts of compensation willingly paid to them by the government, was to impress upon the world how excruciatingly painful it is to remove Jews from their land. But when the dust had settled on the ruins of Yamit (razed to the ground on April 25 by Israeli bulldozers) and after the settlers had collected their compensation, when the chips were down the Begin government lived up to its obligations; it handed over the vacant territories. This, some commentators pointed out, proved that when Begin wanted to, there was nothing sacrosanct about Jewish settlements that protects them from being uprooted. Begin partisans would have replied that those settlements were not within the boundaries of Eretz Yisrael, the Land of Israel.

The Sinai evacuation might easily have become an encouragement to the Palestine Liberation Organization and its supporters in the West Bank, and could have made the West Bank population even more susceptible to PLO influence from Beirut. It was important to show the government's determination to prevent such developments and to demonstrate that whatever happened in Sinai could have no parallel on the West Bank and with the Palestine question.

Since the signing of the Camp David agreements, Begin's opponents on the right had charged that he was giving up the Sinai, vital to Israel's security, for a series of undertakings that were not worth the paper they were written on and that could, and would, be violated by Egypt. It was clear that a war to destroy the PLO in Lebanon would create immense pressure on Cairo. If Egypt resisted the pressure, it would prove to the government and to its critics that the first real peace treaty test had been passed. This, by itself, was no reason to go to war in Lebanon, only a welcome by-product. But the extreme eagerness with which the government rediscovered the PLO threat in southern Lebanon was born out of the desire, some suspected, to distract public attention from the dismal handling of the Sinai evacuation.

5

One War, Three Battles

My generation, dear Ron, swore on the Altar of God that whoever proclaims the intent to destroy the Jewish state or the
Jewish people, or both, seals his fate.—Prime Minister Menachem Begin in a letter to President Reagan[1]

ON November 11, 1982, the building which the Israel Defense
Forces had made their headquarters in Tyre exploded and
collapsed. The seven stories crumbled, killing seventy-five Israeli
soldiers and policemen as well as fourteen Palestinians who were
being held as suspected PLO terrorists. Although the origin of the
blast was not immediately apparent, most Israelis promptly assumed that a terrorist's bomb had caused the destruction. An inves-
tigating committee later determined that the explosion of leaking
gas plus criminally faulty construction had combined to cause the
disaster. But the first gut feeling of many Israelis was that the main
goal of the invasion of southern Lebanon, to destroy the PLO and the
threat they posed for Israel, had been shown to have failed dismally.

The question of whether the PLO could be overcome by military
means had been argued in Israel at least since the summer of 1976,
in the wake of the Entebbe raid. Despite the dramatically successful
release of the victims of that hijack, terrorist acts continued.
Twenty-six people were wounded in a bloody attack on El Al pas-

sengers queuing up in Istanbul airport to board a plane to Israel. In a rare appearance a few days later, the then chief of intelligence, Major General Shlomo Gazit, analyzed the phenomenon of the PLO as a terror organization: he argued that though it can be contained with a reasonable degree of effectiveness, it cannot be completely destroyed; a political solution, he stated, is the only means of stopping it.

Menachem Begin, at that time still leader of the Opposition, was vocally upset by the general's thesis and was quite testy with him in subsequent meetings. The debate took on a new dimension after Begin won the general elections in 1977 and the hawks were in the driver's seat.

The first attempt to destroy the PLO bases in southern Lebanon took place in March 1978, following the terrorist attack outside the Tel Aviv Country Club, in which a bus full of holidaying Israelis was hijacked. The Litani operation that followed this massacre was of a far more limited nature than the campaign of 1982 was to be; it aimed only at destroying the PLO bases south of the Litani River. In the 1978 operation Israel forces occupied the whole of southern Lebanon except the town of Tyre and its immediate surroundings. Seen with hindsight, it is not considered a successful campaign. The Israelis moved forward too cautiously and unimaginatively, deploying a relatively large number of troops and using a heavy amount of firepower. The PLO fighters, more agile than anticipated, succeeded in escaping to the northern banks of the river. Soon afterward, Israel transferred control of the region to the UNIFIL troops. The PLO units returned to their old bases and set up new ones, right under the noses of the United Nations forces.

Shortly after the campaign, in April 1978, General Rafael Eitan became chief of staff, and in August 1981 ex-major general Ariel Sharon became minister of defense. Both men favored not waiting for a political solution to the problem of the terror organization: a military campaign, linking up, for instance, with the Phalange forces as far as Beirut, would destroy the PLO once and for all. As early as the year before Operation Peace for Galilee they were voicing their doctrine with persistence and growing vigor.

In spring 1981 the city of Zahle was besieged by the Syrians, who had sent more than a dozen SA-6 surface-to-air missile batteries into the Al-Bika'a valley: the threat to the Christian Lebanese Front was evident. Prime Minister (and then also acting Minister of Defense) Begin promised his Lebanese friends to try to relieve the pressure on Zahle. For a few weeks late in April and throughout most of May, Israeli fighter bombers were on standby, waiting for the order to destroy the missile sites. Only strong American pressure persuaded the Israelis to hold back.

The situation worsened early in July, when the PLO in southern Lebanon used their modern 130 mm. artillery and 120 mm. Katyusha rocket launchers to bombard northern Israel and the Galilee "Finger," or Panhandle, in a massive ten-day attack, forcing 60,000 inhabitants of the area into their underground shelters. Many of them found the tension hard to bear and fled to safer parts of the country. Israeli refugees in Israel was a new situation, politically and socially unacceptable. The time had come to move into southern Lebanon to destroy the PLO bases, at least as far north as Sidon, insisted Chief of Staff Eitan. Begin agreed in principle, but again under considerable pressure from the Americans, he ended by agreeing to a cease-fire, against the advice of most of his military aides, who protested that Ambassador Philip Habib had "cheated" Israel out of a necessary war. The PLO, who won a political achievement by forcing the United States and Israel to indirectly negotiate with them, now accelerated their arms procurement program.

To bolster morale in the Galilee Finger, Begin made a public appearance in the northern town of Kiryat Shmona. He promised his listeners that "never again" would they have to go down into their underground shelters.

Through late 1981 and early 1982 the influence of the doves in the government gradually weakened as the voices in favor of an attack gathered strength. Prime Minister Begin, a hawk but heretofore very careful when it came to the use of force, could no longer stand up to the single-minded pressure of his defense minister. "Arik" Sharon played on the prime minister's well-known awe of Israeli generals and, after a prolonged personal campaign, convinced Begin of the benefits of a war to wipe out the PLO. On earlier occasions— several times late in the winter, then on the eve of Passover in April 1982, then again in early May—Sharon had sought cabinet approval to commence the operation. But it took the attempt on the life of Israel's ambassador to Britain to persuade the prime minister and his colleagues to approve Sharon's plans, if in a limited version. On June 6, 1982, Israeli tanks crossed the Lebanese border and the war began.

When he appointed Sharon as his minister of defense, Menachem Begin made it clear that he wished Eitan to remain chief of staff at least until the end of 1982, although he was aware that since the Sinai campaign back in October 1956 there had been little love lost between the two men. Eitan had been one of the first officers to join Sharon in 1953, when he headed a small commando unit conducting reprisal raids behind enemy lines. Both had grown up in *moshavim* (cooperative villages), "Arik" in Kfar Malal on the Sharon plain, "Raful" Eitan in Tel Adashim in the heart of the Jezreel valley. Arik had the ingenuity and imagination, the self-assurance and charisma to make men follow him. Raful, a simpler person, was physically courageous and could lead men to their deaths yet be adored by those who survived. An earthy, dedicated, no-nonsense farmer, he always seemed excited and envigorated by danger and the smell of gunpowder.

In the Suez Campaign of 1956, both men participated in the Battle of Mitla Pass. Looking back, it seems to have been a reckless and unnecessary engagement, causing too many casualties. There were recriminations, although they were kept discreet, but Arik's main lieutenants—Mordechai "Motta" Gur, who later preceded Raful as chief of staff, Yitzhak "Chaka" Hofi, commander of the northern front in the Yom Kippur War and later to head Israel's Mossad (Secret Service) for eight years, as well as Raful himself—kept silent. They expressed their feelings by refusing to serve under Sharon, whom, in private, they accused of lack of courage and of duplicity.

Sharon in turn made it plain that he regarded Eitan as a person of limited intelligence. In his eagerness to become minister of defense, however, Sharon accepted Eitan as the prime minister's condition. Now the two men found common ground in their aim of getting government approval to move the Israel Defense Forces into Lebanon and wage a campaign against the PLO.

Eitan instructed his staff officers to begin preparing the first plans for "Operation Oranim" (pine trees) as early as 1979. The plans were updated, improved, and changed periodically, providing several options. They included a minimalist concept of moving approximately as far north as Sidon, as well as a more ambitious option to reach the metropolitan area of Beirut and link up with the Lebanese Phalangist forces, headed by Bashir Gemayel. In late spring of 1981, after the Syrian army had occupied Zahle and moved land-to-air missiles into the Al-Bika'a valley, it became clear to the military command in Israel that the invasion of southern Lebanon was inevitable; the only question was when it would take place. Sharon learned of the plans soon after he became defense minister and approved them in principle. He worked on technical details, shelved the more moderate options, and helped improve the more ambitious, far-reaching ones.

Operation Peace for Galilee finally begin on Sunday morning, June 6, at eleven A.M., shortly after the cabinet had approved it. In their meeting that morning, the government authorized the Defense Forces to move up to a line along the El Awali River basin, just beyond the city of Sidon, some 25 miles north of the border. Heading the column that moved along the coast was thirty-two-year-old Colonel Eli Geva with his tank brigade. Later, he was removed from his post for having warned his commanders that, if ordered to attack the inner city of Beirut, he would refuse to obey.

At about twelve o'clock on Sunday night, an amphibious force composed of paratroopers and fifteen tanks landed at the mouth of the El Awali River. Reinforcements landed during the night and the body proceeded north, to Damour and Beirut. In the south, the tanks moving up along the coast encountered PLO resistance, mainly in the refugee camps of Rashadieh and El Baz on the outskirts of Tyre and in Ein Al Hilwe, close to Sidon. Both there and at Rashadieh, there was considerable fighting, for six days.

A second column crossed into Lebanon through Metulla, in the eastern sector and, by midnight, Beaufort Castle had been captured. Set atop a hill commanding the Galilee Finger, the Beaufort, a structure dating from Crusader times, had for years, served as a PLO fortress from which Katyusha attacks regularly hit the Israeli towns and settlements below.

On Monday evening another column began to move, this one along the very narrow road to Jezzine, in the Al-Shouf Mountains. By Tuesday, some of the troops at the head of the most westerly column had crossed the 25-mile line and were coming close to Damour, on the road to Beirut.

A major characteristic of the battles along the coastal road was that opposition was never allowed to hold back the advancing columns. Some of the troops were left behind to fight and take the resisting stronghold, but the main force pushed on. Accordingly, the infantry were ordered to handle the resistance at Rashadieh, while the main armored columns proceeded north.

The toughest battle took place in Ein Al Hilwe, where the PLO had based their southern command. Heading the PLO resisters was a Shi'ite zealot by the name of Haj Ibrahim Rannem, who fought savagely and with much cruelty. He held several hundred Palestinians hostage and, when the Israelis sent Palestinian prisoners to plead with him to free the hostages, he had the prisoners shot dead. He had all the hostages, including the women and children, killed before the camp was finally occupied by the Israelis.

It was already clear that the PLO forces had taken a severe beating. Apart from those encircled in the refugee camps near Tyre and Sidon and still battling in Damour, what was left of their forces on the hills of Nabatieh and, to the north, toward Jezzine and the southern part of the Al-Bika'a, could no longer effectively interfere with the Israeli advance.

At the end of the week's fighting, on Saturday night Israeli troops reached the Beirut suburb of Baabda, where the Presidential Palace is located, and cut the Beirut-Damascus road. They now had also established a firm link on land with their Phalange allies.

Official overall command of the Israeli forces was in the hands of Major General Amir Drori, commanding officer of the northern front, but chief of staff Eitan was constantly with the troops on the front lines, assessing progress, giving orders, changing targets, improvising and inspecting. Back at the command post, Sharon assumed his favorite role, that of a kind of super chief of staff, fully involved in the battle, directing its main moves.

Fighting the PLO in the south and west represented one of what turned out to be two different wars in Lebanon. The other war was the confrontation with the Syrians. Intelligence assessments had indicated that the Syrian army would prefer to avoid confrontation with the Israelis, and early plans of operation were accordingly drawn up so as to prevent the spread of the armed conflict into territory held by the Syrians. It was, however, clear that if the Syrian command felt that the Israeli moves threatened their forces in Lebanon, they would give battle. It was generally agreed that even if that were to be the case, the Syrians would try to limit the hostilities to Lebanon, and be careful not to extend them to the Golan Heights. Certainly, they would not want the fighting to spill over into Syria and threaten Damascus, barely 45 miles from the Israeli positions on the Golan and half that distance from the front in the Al-Bika'a Valley.

On Monday, June 7, in the early morning, Israeli forces occupied the predominantly Druse town of Hasbaya, on the northwest slopes of Mt. Hermon, facing the southern part of the Al-Bika'a Valley below. The Syrians stayed put but later the same day they sent a tank unit from the Damascus-Beirut road to reinforce the PLO farther west, south of Jezzine.

Then, on Tuesday, the third day of the war, it became clear at the headquarters of the Israeli Northern Command, where Sharon was spending most of his time, that he was itching to engage the Syrians as soon as possible. Sharon was careful to have on record government approval of every major move he made, but rather than present an overall plan for the entire campaign, which the cabinet probably would not have approved, he requested clearance one step at a time. On Tuesday evening, for example, when they met, the government still had no inkling that Sharon's intention was to reach Beirut, cut the road to Damascus, and make contact with Bashir Gemayel and his Lebanese forces. All Sharon had been authorized to do was to engage the Syrians and destroy their missile positions in the Al-Bika'a.

The commander delegated to move north on the eastern front was Major General "Yanosh" Bengal. Until late in 1981, he had been commander of the northern front and had now returned from a sabbatical in the United States. In the Yom Kippur War, Bengal had been commander of the Seventh Brigade, the most prestigious armored brigade of the Israeli army, the one that made the crucial contribution to stopping the Syrians on the Golan and a few days later pushing them back toward Damascus.

A considerable part of the invading force were now under Bengal's command. They started to move early on Wednesday morning. In the subsequent fifty-plus hours before the cease-fire on Friday noon, the Israeli tanks maintained close contact with the Syrians, who were in a fairly orderly retreat. With approximately 1,000 soldiers killed and as many as 300 tanks destroyed or damaged, the Syrians suffered heavy casualties. Nevertheless, they managed to carry out local counterattacks, two of which, south of Lake Karoun and in Ein Zahalta, were costly to the Israelis.

This was a war in which the quantitative superiority of the Israel forces was not realized in the actual battles. Although huge numbers of armored vehicles were introduced, the terrain, especially in the eastern sector, often necessitated single-file movement of tanks, armored personnel carriers, and even foot patrols. Thus the confrontation was, with the few exceptions in which whole brigades were involved, a war of small units, often aided by the helicopter gunships, which proved themselves efficient adjuncts to ground fighting.

When the cease-fire took effect on Friday noon, the Israelis were close to the town of Shtura, where, until the middle of the week, the Syrian forces had had their Lebanese headquarters.

The confrontation with the Syrians was not limited to ground forces. On Monday and again on Tuesday, Israeli planes encountered the Syrians in the air. On Wednesday morning, they attacked the Syrian missiles in the Al-Bika'a. Thirteen batteries of Soviet SAM-3 and SAM-6 missiles had been brought into the valley in April 1981, causing a crisis for Israel. In 1982, despite Israeli warnings, they had been reinforced, so that by June 9 there were a total of nineteen batteries in the valley. When the Israeli air attack began, the Syrians sent up 100 fighter planes to block it, but they failed. By the end of the day, seventeen Syrian batteries had been totally destroyed and twenty MiGs had been shot down. The remaining two batteries were destroyed the following day. Altogether, the Israelis shot down eighty-six fighters during the war, all MiG-21s and supermodern MiG-23s, and MiG-25s as well as six Gazelle helicopters. The Israelis lost one Skyhawk fighter and one Cobra helicopter, both shot down by the PLO in the south, but came out of the air-to-air battles unscathed.*

(In July, one Phantom reconnaissance plane was shot down by a Syrian surface-to-air missile. Soon afterward, eleven Soviet specialists arrived at the site of the downed plane in Syrian-controlled Lebanon to extract some of the secret Israeli electronic equipment from the wreckage. The Israeli air force, determined that the enemy not gain any intelligence benefit, bombed the Phantom into scrap. The technicians were all killed.[2])

The Israeli air force achieved its stunning kill ratio thanks to superior electronic vision and targeting capabilities which enabled the Israeli planes to fire while still beyond the horizon.

By the weekend, the first main phase of the invasion had been completed. It was evident that the army had moved farther than necessary to secure the immediate safety of the Galilee. The Israelis had destroyed the PLO and its infrastructure south of Beirut, had administered a shock and a thrashing to the Syrian army, and had linked up with the Christian Lebanese forces in East Beirut.

In the Syrian and PLO headquarters and command posts Israeli intelligence found documentation confirming previous information that the Syrians were preparing for a new strike against Israel sometime before 1985. Modernized tank corps were to join twenty-eight commando battalions, supported by their air force. The Syrians fought well in this brief war but their casualties were considerable. They have since refurbished their arsenal (see Chapter 7).

Ever since 1967, Arab-Israel wars have been the testing ground for new first-line Soviet and Western armaments. New weapons are, of course, tried out in other places as well. French missile sales, for instance, were boosted by the much-publicized successful use by the Argentinians of the air-to-sea Exocet in the Falkland Islands in 1982. But it is in the Middle East that most arms are bought for actual use, rather than for deterrent effect.

---

*In the past twenty years, in its confrontations with the Israelis, the Syrian air force has lost some 600 first-line fighter planes. Syrian pilots have shown remarkable tenacity, constantly coming back to fight the Israelis despite the odds against them.

There was one discovery that worried the Israelis: the weakness of their armored personnel carriers (APC's) against the rocket-propelled grenades (RPGs) of the PLO and Syria. During the preceding decade, virtually all Israeli infantry and paratroopers had been trained to move into battle on the thousands of APC's Israel had acquired over the years. The APC was an essential piece of equipment for the highly mobility-oriented Israeli military command. In the fighting in Lebanon, however, it was shown that a determined opponent, whether an individual Syrian or a PLO infantryman, could, with a single well-aimed RPG shot, destroy an APC. The vehicle would often burst into flame, killing or seriously wounding the troops inside. It was an ominous threat for the modern, mobile Israeli armored infantry, which will have to find better protection if it ever has to move into battle zones again.[3]

Possibly the biggest success of the Lebanon war was achieved by the Israeli weapons industry. In 1973, approximately half of Israel's weapons were locally made. By 1982, the proportion had risen to over two-thirds. The war tested and showed the superiority of several new locally produced systems: the Merkava (Chariot) tank, armor-piercing ammunition, and pilotless Remotely Piloted Vehicles (RPV), or drones. The last caused a major revolution in air-to-ground warfare, especially in the elimination of antiaircraft missiles.

The Israeli generals, and especially General Israel Tal, Israel's "Mr. Armor," who conceived the elements of the Merkava Mark I tank, singlemindedly pushed to develop and produce it. He and his associates invented specific gadgets for it while bullying, cajoling, and persuading the ministers of defense and finance to provide the necessary funds; they were justly proud of its performance. In battle along the coast road and especially in confrontation with Syrian armor, including the Soviet-made T-72, the high survival rate of the tank and its crew was amply demonstrated. So were its powers of negotiating difficult terrain and its effective gun that, with its high firepower and accuracy, achieved through a sophisticated fire control system, proved capable of penetrating the very good Soviet armor.

It had been rumored that the new Soviet T-72 tank was made of superhard metal invulnerable to Western firepower, but the Israelis scored some dozen direct hits, damaging the tank and destroying the myth of its invincibility. Their success was due in part to the new Hetz 105 mm. armor-piercing, fin-stabilized ammunition adopted by the Israeli tank corps for standard use. Concentrating all its energy into a small projectile, it can penetrate thicker armor plate than conventional NATO ammunition can.

The Syrian antiaircraft defense system was based on a configuration of SA-6 missiles and 250 ZSU-23/4 quadruple 23 mm. automatic cannon. Both are mounted on tracked vehicles and controlled by radar. The Israeli air force had suffered considerable losses when it first encountered these missiles in the early days of the Yom Kippur War in 1973. Later in that war it captured quite a few of them and had since studied them in detail and learned how they work.

The confrontation over the missile batteries was probably the first battle in history waged by electronic means. As such, it was a clear victory for American-Israeli know-how, supported by excellent Israeli air force training and careful coordination. Her "Drones" (RPV's) were used as decoys and provided instant ground intelligence in conjunction with the equipment installed on the American-built E-2C Hawkeye that can track up to 250 enemy aircraft, as far as 185 miles away. Israel used two types of RPV, the Tadiran Mastiff, launched from the F-4 Phantom; and the Israel Aviation Industry's Scout, launched from the ground. Both are equipped with radar reflectors that magnify them to make them appear as large as fighter planes. (They can carry out multiple-purpose chores and, with receivers, they can tune in to radar transmitters. Some carry radar transmitters as well. Having an endurance flying time of over seven hours, they relay back in "real time" a complete view of the area patrolled.)

The Israeli command could, with all this radar and electronic equipment, scan the entire aerial battlefield and could thus enjoy total air superiority. American military specialists believe that at least one EC-135, a modified Boeing 707, was used as an electronic countermeasure (ECM) platform to jam radar and communications at the Soviet missile batteries. To ferret out the Syrian defenses, a cluster of RPV's were sent out to the missile battery enclave. The

Syrians, believing they were being attacked, turned the radar of both the missiles and the cannon on the drones. The Israeli fighter planes then came in.[4]

It is thought that the F-15 and F-16 planes used the "Wild Weasel" electronic system, which not only can disrupt the radar of the SAM but can also, in certain situations, redirect the missile, turning it into a latter-day boomerang. To these devices were added the CH-53 helicopter, which carried radar-jamming equipment to complement the land-based jammers stationed on the hilltops overlooking the Al-Bika'a Valley. When the Syrians started working their radar, they were detected by the EC-135 and the jammers went into action; the Israelis then sent in their Phantoms and, mainly with cluster bombs, blasted the blinded missiles and cannon. In one day, June 9, 1982, the Israelis obliterated more SAM batteries than had been fielded by both the Syrians and Egyptians together during the entire Yom Kippur War. When, a few days later, the Russians brought some SAM-8s (nicknamed "Geckos" in the West) and SAM-9s into the Al-Bika'a, they, too, were destroyed by the Israelis.[5]

One result of the destruction of the missiles in the Al-Bika'a Valley was the mutual disappointment of the Soviets and the Syrians with each other. It was not until nearly the end of November 1982, almost six months after the war, that Syrian President Hafez al-Assad had some warm words to say about the military support he had received from the Russians. Privately, it could not have escaped the Syrians that their Soviet equipment was inferior to its American counterparts. The Soviets, for their part, have increasingly had no kind words for the Arabs in general and the Syrians in particular, claiming that they cannot be trusted to do anything right and are both incompetent and cowardly.

For sheer numbers of aircraft and firepower, the air battles on June 9 around the missile sites were as intensive as any in aviation history. It was clear that the Syrian command was making a desperate but futile attempt to save the missile batteries. With their ground forces, both armor and commando, their tactics were more careful: when faced with overwhelming power, they retreated in as orderly a fashion as possible, maximizing the discomfort and damage to the enemy, while incurring minimum casualties themselves. There was no evidence in this combat that the Syrian army had changed since the Yom Kippur War. They were still stubborn fighters, but lacked any grasp of or talent for improvisation and, therefore, reacted poorly to surprise, failing to develop fully their counterattacks.

The Israeli forces fighting the PLO had a more complex and difficult task. The enemy had concentrated its more powerful bases in densely populated civilian centers, in the towns and villages, and on the crossroads. Preliminary intelligence had located most such PLO centers and they were known to the advancing army. With the aim of minimizing the number of civilian casualties, the Israelis gave warning by dropping leaflets as well as by radio and loudspeaker several hours before they struck against the PLO, advising the local population to move out, preferably to the nearby citrus groves or to the beaches.

To ensure bombing accuracy and reduce the number of civilian casualties to the very minimum, each pilot was assigned one target only and allowed to drop only one bomb on each run. The ground forces had to be careful to aim only at buildings from which shots were being fired; before attacking a house, it had to be checked to make sure that there were no civilians inside.

Many innocent lives were thus saved, but this caution gave the PLO time to prepare for the attack. The Israelis did not have the advantage of surprise, which would have shortened the actual engagement and reduced their own casualties. (After the war, there was considerable criticism from some of the more hawkish elements in Israel on this score; they charged that the IDF had suffered too many casualties because of these precautions.)

The battle damage to civilian centers was compounded by the PLO habit of establishing combat positions among the general population. Hundreds of such incidents were reported. The story of one middle-aged, middle-class woman, reported in the London *Times*, was typical: "When the Israelis came," she said, "the Palestinian fighters took their guns and placed them next to our homes, next to apartment blocks and hospitals and schools. They thought this would protect them. We pleaded with them to take their guns away, but they refused. So when they fired at the Israelis, the planes came and bombed our homes."[6]

The reporter continued:

> The director of one Sidon hospital still seemed to disbelieve his
> own words as he described how the guerrillas deliberately set up
> their anti-aircraft guns around his clinic. And, a few kilometers
> away, at a refugee camp, the Palestinians actually put their guns on
> the roof of the hospital. As another doctor put it: "The guerrillas
> knew what would happen. The Israeli planes came and bombed the
> hospital. Everyone there died—the sick, the wounded, the fighters
> with them."
> This was also the fate of the elementary school off the Jezzine
> Road. The people clustered in the basement for protection—most of
> them refugees from Tyre—although the Palestinians had put a gun
> mounted on a jeep beside the building. The vehicle lies there still, its
> gun barrels absurdly twisted by the explosions that followed. The
> Palestinians used the school for cover, so the Israelis employed
> equally savage retaliation. They bombed the school.[7]

In the early reports, the extent of destruction on the coast road
leading to Beirut was grossly exaggerated. One Western observer
reported:

> Expecting to find the major cities completely devastated by the
> bombing, it was surprising to see so many buildings still erect. In
> Sidon, for example, there were at least ten buildings totally levelled,
> but it was not the Dresden-like landscape I thought I would see.
> Churches and mosques were largely untouched. It was also appar-
> ent that much of the destruction had accrued over time: the result of
> internal warfare. Even to the untrained eye, it was clear that many
> of the buildings were victims of decay and neglect resulting from
> previous battles.[8]

The massive artillery attacks on Kiryat Shmona and other places
in the Galilee Finger in July 1981, which turned many of the local
Jewish population into temporary refugees, were followed by information originating at PLO headquarters that an accelerated arms
procurement program, including tanks and artillery, was meant to
transform their forces into a modern army. These developments

pushed the Israelis into their invasion. Yet, when captured, the PLO combat equipment indicated that the purchasing program had no central planning and that its importance had been exaggerated. According to Israel Defense Forces spokesmen, the inventory captured as of October 13, 1982, after the end of the fighting and the Israeli evacuation of West Beirut, included:

> 1,320 armored combat vehicles and other vehicles (243 in West Beirut), including several hundred T-34, T-55, and T-62 tanks, some damaged.
>
> 82 field artillery pieces—122 mm., 130 mm., 155 mm., and 25-pound guns (12 in West Beirut).
>
> 62 Katyusha rocket launchers (6 in West Beirut).
>
> 215 mortars—60 mm., 81 mm., 82 mm., 120 mm., and 150 mm. (13 in West Beirut).
>
> 196 antiaircraft weapons, including 43 AA machine guns and 153 AA guns—20 mm., 23 mm., 30 mm., 37 mm., 40 mm., 57 mm., and 100 mm. (38 in West Beirut).
>
> 1,352 antitank weapons, including 1,099 personal weapons, 27 antitank missile launchers, 138 recoilless rifles, and 88 antitank guns (159 in West Beirut).
>
> 33,303 small arms (4,999 in West Beirut).

Thousands of pieces of communications and optical equipment were captured as well. Altogether, it was a large amount of equipment for a hostile force but hardly a serious military threat, especially as much of it was mismatched and haphazardly assembled.

As the first stage of the war ended, with Israel occupying all of southern Lebanon, preliminary conclusions began to emerge about the PLO as a fighting force. They often fought well, sometimes desperately. Their preference for choosing positions on central crossroads or in the heart of a built-up area was correct from their point of view and made the Israeli task more difficult. From their dugouts some of them held out tenaciously against all odds, but the efficiency of their chain of command was weak. In no case did they launch a counterattack; rarely did they operate in groups larger than half a dozen. Often courageous in their fixed positions, there were few individual cases of offensive daring. The squad of three

PLO men who penetrated the Israeli lines to take a prisoner were an exception to the rule.

The war showed that the PLO ambition to build a modern army that would gradually replace the guerrilla and terrorist units was a tragic miscalculation. They were neither technically nor psychologically ready for the changeover. However, by amassing arms on such a large scale and training in their use, they undoubtedly hastened the Israeli decision to destroy their power base. At their most effective they operated in this war as a guerrilla organization should, making the life of the much stronger opposing army difficult and making IDF operations more costly than any regular army the size of the PLO force could have done.

The complex job of fighting the PLO could have proved more embarrassing and costly had the PLO been able to develop tactical coordination among its units. Even with the benefit of hindsight, there is no satisfactory explanation why, at the same time as it was arming in substantial quantities and training many thousands of young fighters, the PLO was devoting so little thought to how to make the best use of all its potential.

When the Israeli government ordered the army into Lebanon, it was reacting to the power being amassed by the PLO. Whether or not Israel's own use of force was overdone, whether or not the campaign was really a series of repeated overkills, as it appeared to some people, including U.S. ambassador Philip Habib, it was, to a large extent, a response to the growing PLO pretensions. Yet by March 1983, it was clear that Israel had not seen the last of the PLO. Sporadic PLO terror against civilians in Israel and against the IDF in Lebanon was becoming more frequent. At the same time, the possibility of the PLO's putting together a regular army seemed more remote than ever.

The Lebanon war gave Israel a fresh opportunity to test its soldiers and officers once more under fire. There were few acts of heroism and little bravura. The moves were made by experienced, sober officers, bent on carrying out their mission with minimum casualties. At times, this slowed the pace. But in general, the IDF gave an impressive professional performance.

When the war was over, criticism was voiced of the unimaginative battle plan. It was asserted that, with so much time available in which to plan the campaign, it could have been devised differently. Rather than launching the offensive by attempting to seize the Beirut-Damascus highway, the IDF could have threatened southern Lebanon by invading it from "the rear," possibly by landing forces in friendly Junieh and setting forth from there. The IDF would almost certainly have saved many lives by using its paratroopers in an airborne role rather than as "leg" infantrymen.

It is ironic that Defense Minister Sharon, once considered perhaps the most original of Israeli generals, was hamstrung by his own devious political relationships and his need to cajole the government. Because he knew he did not have cabinet support for his whole campaign, Sharon was prevented from making such imaginative and strategic tactical moves and had to settle for the duller, slower, more costly, essentially frontal push forward.

The size of the army at the disposal of Sharon and Eitan was substantially larger than the force that had engaged the Egyptians during the Yom Kippur War. Including the reserves, not only did the Israeli generals command more forces than did the PLO leadership but also more than the Syrians had available for confrontation with Israel. Rarely had so great a power been concentrated in such a rugged and confined area of less than 1,000 square miles. One explanation why so many men were brought in was to give as many officers as possible an opportunity to take part in the action. With the narrow roads in the hills, long traffic jams became inevitable, slowing down the pace of the campaign. In the informal debriefings later, there were those who argued that the desired results could have been obtained sooner had the number of troops and vehicles been only one-third to one-half of that which actually crossed into Lebanon.

Argument on this point was most heated in relation to the tank corps. These units performed in the central theater and, to a lesser degree, in the eastern area, leading up to the Al-Bika'a where, armor strategists say, they had no business to be. Their involvement was quite possibly decisive, but all too often they moved as a column, with only the three tanks up front actually fighting the enemy. The rest, by their sheer number, congested the poor, narrow roads, which also took a severe beating from the sheer weight of these modern dinosaurs. Many tanks lost their traction and slipped, stopping the advance of entire convoys and slowing down combat progress.

For Israel, the cost of the war was considerable. The number of casualties was high: more than 500 men killed, and close to 3,000 wounded by the end of the first year after the invasion and the numbers still rising as sporadic PLO ambushes of small Israeli units continued. There was, from a strictly military point of view, also the cost of military secrets revealed—an inevitable outcome of their application.

More than ever before, waging a successful war depends today on the element of surprise. The more "conventional" type of surprise, such as mounting an unexpected attack on a supposedly impenetrable fortification in impossible weather, is still effective. "You can only do an Entebbe once," as one Israeli general remarked. But to this should be added the surprise of military technology being used for the first time, before any counterdevice has yet been introduced.

> The central theme—the very core—of the decisive air battle in Lebanon was electronic combat . . . [it] was the war of the future—a war in which electronic combat was a central and dominant theme . . . as successful as it was, the Israeli electronic combat . . . is only a harbinger of things to come. . . .[9]

Modern warfare cannot be waged without taking the wraps off equipment, inventions, and new battle gambits, which until that moment were top secret. Should the gadgets used to destroy the missile sites have been revealed? Should the armor-piercing capabilities of the Hetz have been exposed? Ferocity of battle, threat to the state, and the perceived need to implement cost-saving measures are all factors that go into deciding which new technological developments to disclose and when to disclose them.

After the Lebanese invasion, the price paid by making new equipment public knowledge was argued with passion among those involved in matters of defense. Still, it could not be denied that the Lebanon war was an impressive victory for Israeli forces and hardware.

6
Beirut, the Hostage City

THE siege of Beirut, like the campaign as a whole, had not been planned in detail. There was an underlying idea: to destroy the PLO as a military force and to prevent its reorganization by expelling the surviving terrorists from southern Lebanon, thereby also helping the Lebanese Christians reassert control over the whole of that country. The actual battle, however, as it took shape, was a series of military improvisations, with Prime Minister Begin and his government having little to say in the decisions of Minister of Defense Sharon.

For the first time in many wars, Israeli soldiers felt that they were welcome in their role. On their way north and on the outskirts of Beirut itself, they were greeted with smiles, flowers, and bowls of rice. Only Raymond Ede, son of a former Lebanese president and himself a perennial candidate for the presidency, who after three assassination attempts against him in the mid-1970s had decided to live abroad, commented that the Syrians, too, had been heartily welcomed when they first arrived, in the summer of 1976, but by the autumn, the Lebanese had come to loathe them. He predicted that the same would happen to the Israelis. Yet in those warm, lush June days, few Lebanese along the coast or in the Al-Shouf Mountains agreed with him. The average Lebanese who met the Israeli found that these soldiers were different: unpolished perhaps, but relaxed and smiling; correct, even eager to make friends; never requisitioning stores but always paying for anything they needed.

As the IDF came closer to Beirut, the local people described to them again and again, almost compulsively, the horrors and atrocities they had suffered at the hands of the PLO. In the suburbs, the residents kept urging the Israelis to finish the job and occupy the ultimate PLO stronghold—the city itself. After the expulsion of the PLO and the retreat of the Syrians, they trusted that the Israelis, too, would go back across the border. Then the Lebanese, so they repeatedly explained, would reassess their national priorities and reestablish lawful, active government, free from outside pressure.

Neither in the first half of June 1982 nor later did the Israeli government seriously study what the consequences might be of applying the military force that ultimately offered the PLO no alternative but to defend West Beirut. With the exception of one or two ministers, the cabinet was never given the information or the tools necessary to evaluate the path the war was taking or the military decisions that were being made. Had the government had a clearer picture on June 6 and known that Sharon intended to occupy Beirut, or had it been warned that the Israel Defense Forces might still be in Lebanon in 1983, it undoubtedly would not have approved the initial plan for an operation that was scheduled to be completed within forty-eight hours. The government certainly did not envision that, in its desire to save the lives of hundreds of Israeli soldiers by avoiding street-to-street fighting in densely populated urban areas, Israel would enter a two-month siege of Beirut that would estrange world opinion and even alienate many of Israel's closest friends in the American administration and Congress.

Not only were Sharon's overall battle plans not laid before the Israeli cabinet for advance approval, but politically sensitive military moves were only brought to its attention *ex post facto*. Only on Sunday, June 13, after the Israelis had already made contact with the Christian Lebanese forces in East Beirut, was the government told that the city had been surrounded.

There is no evidence that the cabinet approved the heavy air attack on Beirut that preceded the strike against the Syrian forces on the Beirut-Damascus road on June 22, or even that the cabinet approved the offensive itself. The government was not told of the plan for the big call-up of reservists at the end of July nor of the heaviest of all air raids on Beirut, on August 11 and 12. Begin later explained ironically how he was made aware of all the military decisions taken: some he was asked to approve in advance; others he heard of after they had been executed.

On Sunday, June 13, 1982, the Israeli government decided not to resort to occupation in order to expel the PLO from Beirut. Begin informed the Knesset Foreign Affairs and Defense Committee accordingly, and announced that Israel's intention was to apply sufficient pressure to expel all PLO fighters and to have the Syrians withdraw from Lebanon. Only when the IDF had thus secured the safety of Galilee and completed its mission would the government order Israeli troops home. The prime minister offered the PLO safe conduct out of Beirut, but warned that if they did not leave the city voluntarily, force would be used to get them out. He added that Israel had no intention of occupying West Beirut.

Two days before this announcement, Israeli troops had made contact with the Christian Lebanese Forces on the outskirts of Beirut and by Saturday night they had moved beyond Baabdeh and were in control of several miles of the Damascus road. Beirut Airport had suspended operation and Israeli units were stationed at the southern end of its runways. From the sea, Israeli patrol vessels, gunboats, and missile boats now kept watch over the city. West Beirut was under siege and the PLO command was encircled.

Begin's statement that Beirut would not be occupied came as a lifesaver to Yasser Arafat and his surrounded PLO fighters. They reacted in a way the prime minister had not foreseen, and their reaction in turn affected what happened next to West Beirut. Realizing that here was a political opportunity to be exploited, Arafat called on his beleaguered forces to reorganize themselves and continue their resistance. His propagandists claimed that Beirut would be the Arab Stalingrad, the graveyard of the invader. To an American journalist, a PLO officer said, "We have grown up fighting in the streets of Beirut. It is what we do best."[1] And thus began a two-month war of attrition, the kind of combat Israel likes least. Thousands of Palestinian and Lebanese civilians were killed, along with a painful toll of Israeli soldiers, while the West became impatient and angry with Israel for what it saw every night on its

99

television screens as lack of compassion for the many hundreds of thousands of Lebanese civilian hostages suffering under the siege.

After the first week of the war, Israel had several options in order to benefit from its military achievement, other than laying siege to West Beirut or storming it. Israel could, for instance, have tried to seek an understanding with Syria's President Assad or could have approached the Egyptians, who were scrupulously observing the recently implemented peace treaty. Israel could have suggested that Egypt act as go-between to convince the PLO command to move its troops out of Lebanon. But the Israeli cabinet and its three leading ministers did not show any imagination. They reacted with suspicion to any opinion from outside their circle, any voice that warned them against occupying a major Arab capital. Begin, careful by nature and too detached from the battlefield, seemed to see nothing but his own commitment to destroy the PLO. Foreign Minister Yitzhak Shamir displayed trust in no one, certainly no foreigner. Sharon's record showed that he was never comfortable in the give-and-take of negotiation. Not one of this triumvirate seemed capable of risking the fruits of military victory for something less tangible or of entertaining any new, untried avenues.

It is true that to do so, to seek an alternative settlement, Israel would have had to renege on a series of verbal commitments and understandings with the Kataeb and the Lebanese Forces. But instead of engaging the PLO as they were expected to by Israel, these Christian elements had so far remained relatively inactive during the fighting; they seemed to confirm suspicions that, when under pressure, they were not to be trusted as allies.

Thus a dramatic negotiating initiative was never really considered. Instead, expelling the PLO from Beirut became the focus of Israel's policy. Yet an immediate assault on West Beirut seemed likely to be too costly militarily and too dangerous politically. The siege, with all its tragic consequences, began. The United States, Britain, and France closed their embassies in West Beirut and offered to ship their citizens home.

For the advancing Israeli troops, their mid-June encounters with members of the Christian Lebanese forces had been encouraging. Here were Arabs who were warm, friendly, welcoming, and intelligent and who, despite the chaos prevailing in their country, appeared to keep daily life going more or less normally.

Later, some uncomfortable questions were asked: Why did the Christian Lebanese forces never join the IDF, not even in the battles at the approaches to Beirut? What held their leaders back from publicly welcoming the Israelis as their allies against the occupying PLO and Syrians? And finally, what prevented them from reasserting their independence?

The political arm of the Kataeb offered some answers to these questions. They did not have the modern arms or the training necessary to fight alongside the Israelis, they said, but would try to help wherever possible. The question about the public welcome evidently bothered them and, after careful study, they issued cautious statements about the urgent need to expel all foreign forces from Lebanon.

The views of Bashir Gemayel became clear by June 24, when he paid a one-day visit to King Fahd of Saudi Arabia. Together they charted the short-term limits of fraternization with Israel. They provided for informal contacts but did not permit the signing of a peace treaty. It should have been obvious to the Israeli government that however grateful Gemayel might be, he was determined to head all of Lebanon and its ethnic groups, including the Moslem half, which had little sympathy for Israel. The Lebanese Forces under his command had to plan for this unified future and thus play down the Israeli connection. The Israelis should have understood that the Lebanese Christians, and their candidate for president, would have to live with the Moslems after the war was over.

At the same time, however, almost everybody in the Christian community was urging the Israelis to complete the task of eliminating the PLO and to occupy West Beirut. The PLO would never give up of its own free will, the Christian argument ran. Whenever an Israeli official countered that such a battle would cause many casualties, not only to the terrorists but also to Lebanese civilians and Israeli soldiers, the free Lebanese would reply that the Israelis were clever enough to find a way. Some Christians were shockingly indifferent to loss of life, if not downright bloodthirsty. In private encounters, such as one over a pleasant lunch in an East Beirut high-rise building, within 200 yards of the line dividing the city, the hostess, a brilliant teacher and poet, expressed the opinion that the Israeli fighter pilots were wrong to take pride in their precision bombing and that they wasted time in circling their targets to identify them before they hit. This only gave people an opportunity to run for shelter and hence the number of casualties was too small, she said.

Only token fire was exchanged between the PLO and the Israelis in Beirut during the middle of June. The official Israeli position was still that its troops were in the suburbs but had not actually entered the city proper. Israeli soldiers drove through the eastern sector of the city, more as sightseers than as an occupying force.

As they had done along the coast during the first week of the operation, Israeli fighter planes began flying over West Beirut, dropping leaflets calling on the inhabitants to leave. Lest they be misunderstood, the pilots then drove their message home with sonic booms, many of them in sleep-shattering night flights.

By the end of the second week of the invasion of Lebanon, tens of thousands of Beirutis and Palestinians had begun to move out of the western sector and the nearby camps. All in all, more than 100,000 people left the city, many of them Shiites from southern Lebanon who had taken refuge in Beirut between 1976 and 1981. Most of those who elected to leave turned south, to their old hometowns and to the safety of territories now under Israeli control. It was a strange sight to those Westerners who had read, before coming to Lebanon, about streams of refugees fleeing away from the Israelis.

By the third week, it became clear to the Israeli command that the PLO was showing no signs of capitulation. The stalemate was finally broken in the eastern suburb of Aley. Syrian forces were stationed there and Ariel Sharon was waiting for a chance to push them out. Following a local exchange of small arms fire, hardly noticeable in the normal course of events, he ordered the Israel Defense Forces to occupy both the suburb and the mountain ridge above it, up to Bahamdoun, which overlooked the Damascus Road.

It was a bloody battle. Israeli armor and incessant air attacks inflicted heavy casualties on the Syrians. In Beit Morry, about a mile north of the fighting, thousands of Lebanese could be seen standing about in the streets, sitting on the balconies of private homes nestling on the hillside, or calmly eating shishkebab on the terraces of local restaurants, watching two sets of foreigners killing each other. The whole scene took on an odd, surrealistic air.

By the weekend, Sharon had achieved his objective.* The Israelis had suffered some thirty dead but the Syrians had been pushed some 15 miles out of the beleaguered city. The PLO, 12,000 of them or more, were encircled in Beirut and some 2,000 Syrian troops were also trapped.

With the closing of the American Embassy in West Beirut, the ambassador's residence in Ba'abdeh, barely 150 yards from the mansion of the Lebanese president, became the center of American life in the area. There were no restrictions on movement (even in West Beirut most Lebanese went about freely), but American diplomats, remembering previous ambushes and assassinations, preferred to stay indoors. It was a hot, humid summer and, in addition to Ambassador James Dillon, his personal staff, and the guards, the building hosted U.S. special envoy Philip Habib and his entourage. For more than two months, some thirty to forty Americans were stuck in the compound in a self-imposed state of siege. Gradually, the nervous strain began to tell. The place was crowded; it afforded little if any privacy. Although Ba'abdeh was fired at rarely, the acoustics of this hill suburb are excellent and the amplified noise of shells falling on Beirut made everyone nervous. Many of those in the residence felt they were in a front-line fortification. As in most of Beirut, there were repeated power cuts; the air conditioners kept breaking down. There was a shortage of some fresh foodstuffs and it was hard to get exercise. Habib himself was eating too much, nervously putting on weight and showing signs of frustration with the stop-and-go character of negotiations between the Israelis and the many Lebanese factions, as well as with the indirect nature of the only contact he was authorized to have with the Palestinians.

---

*It was, however, after this battle, which was opposed by many of the IDF reserve officers and soldiers who took part, that the fragile Israeli consensus broke down. The following weekend, an ad hoc group called Soldiers Against Silence, together with the Peace Now movement, organized an antiwar demonstration in Tel Aviv. Some 100,000 attended.

The choice of Philip Habib as mediator was sound. His parents were Lebanese Christians who had emigrated to the United States early in the century, before he was born. He still had family in Lebanon, including an old uncle in the village of Ein Arab, in the northwest reaches of the Hermon mountain range, overlooking the Al-Bika'a Valley. He had grown up in the foreign service but had had little exposure to the Middle East until the 1970s, when he had acted as assistant to Secretary of State Henry Kissinger. At the age of sixty, with a history of severe heart attacks, Habib had retired to California. There, he was retained as a part-time consultant by George Schultz, soon to be recalled to Washington as secretary of state but at that time president of Bechtel Corporation, the huge international construction firm with extensive operations in Saudi Arabia.

Philip Habib had first been called by President Reagan to act as his special ambassador in the Lebanon crisis of spring 1981. The Syrians had brought their SAM missiles into the Al-Bika'a Valley and the Israelis had warned that if the Syrians did not remove them, they would. Habib failed to persuade the Syrians but he did succeed with the Israelis. They held their fire for over a year, until the June 1982 Peace for Galilee operation. Although Habib's intervention appeared to offer a good way out for Prime Minister Begin, the fact that the ambassador had failed with the Syrians was remembered by the Israelis and did not make his task easier when he returned to the Middle East on the eve of the siege of Beirut.

Habib felt comfortable in the Middle East. Although Ariel Sharon was not always cordial and occasionally went out of his way to be rude, turning his personal grievances into a political issue, other Israelis respected and liked Habib, enjoying his sense of humor and his wisdom. At the ambassador's residence he also received an ongoing stream of Lebanese visitors, Christian and Moslem alike. Apart from Elias Sarkis, the lame-duck president whom Habib saw almost daily, and Shafik al-Wazzan, the prime minister who had officially resigned but who was actually still at work and the main intermediary with the PLO, there was ex-premier Saib Slaam, the respected veteran Moslem leader, still running his medical practice and his hospital. With little personal ambition left but with the wisdom of age, Slaam was a Moslem moderate and Habib enjoyed his homilies, anecdotes, and jokes. More heavy going were the younger visitors like Walid Junblatt, the feudal but leftist Druse chieftain, and Bashir Gemayel, commander of the Christian Kataeb militia, whose visits were more formal. There were also visitors from the States. The American press came and received "in-depth" backgrounders which, they were told, were "not for attribution"; they never let Habib down. There were also senators and congressmen who flew in and out on brief study missions.

Also involved were the particular interests of Damascus; those fluctuated as the Syrians studied the meaning of the Israeli offensive, evaluated the damage they had suffered, and reassessed their policy in Lebanon.

Finally, there were the Lebanese Christians—charming, cruel, insecure, indecisive, difficult, and sometimes impossible to deal with. They were led by young Bashir Gemayel, who seemed suspect to the Americans and was unpopular with them.

Habib's mission was to prevent the occupation of West Beirut. It was a long-drawn-out, exhausting effort and possibly would not have succeeded without the pressure of Israeli bombardment of West Beirut. It intensified toward the end of July and continued, with short lulls, until the PLO finally agreed to pull out.

Habib spent most of his time at his "command post" on the embassy grounds. The Lebanese who acted as intermediaries between the United States and the PLO—Saib Slaam, Shafik al-Wazzan, and Walid Junblatt—were not as experienced in such matters as are some Western diplomats, and each of these Lebanese had his own political interests to serve. The PLO leadership, never a monolith, is at its best when dealing with generalities, so it found the discipline of a specific technical compromise hard to deal with. From mid-June to early August they vacillated. The Israelis were also slow. Their representatives, either Sharon or Foreign Ministry Director General David Kimche, accompanied by Sharon's right-hand man, Major General Avraham Tamir, or Chief of Military Intelligence Major General Yehoshua Saguy, commuted from Jerusalem, and every step was referred to their government for approval.

Reporters covering Ambassador Habib in Beirut in the summer of 1982 were of the opinion that the negotiations for the evacuation of the PLO from Beirut would have been completed faster if he had been able to talk directly to the PLO leadership. Habib, it was felt, would have been much more persuasive than the Moslem Lebanese intermediaries in making clear to the PLO that there was no alternative but to leave. The Lebanese, and especially Prime Minister Shafik al-Wazzan, were believed to fear the PLO chieftains; they seemed to prefer to water down some of the facts, never fully spelling out the options as clearly as Habib would have presented them. They allowed the leaders of the PLO to harbor their illusions too long. The Lebanese also slowed down Habib's negotiations in other ways; when the bombing became heavy they would refuse to travel into West Beirut and talks were halted for a day or two.

More significantly, although the later air raids proved an important incentive in convincing the PLO to depart, the earlier strikes had the opposite effect. Habib is said to believe that the actual decision to quit was deferred several times following Israeli bombing spasms that elicited suicidal "we're staying put" declarations from the PLO. Yet progress was made in these cumbersome and indirect negotiations. Although some important points remained open until the second week of August, many items concerning the banishment of the PLO troops were settled before the final agreement was reached.

As time passed, the senior Israeli field officers lost whatever enthusiasm they might have had on June 13 or 14 for the idea of taking West Beirut in battle. The opportunity, they felt, had been missed. The PLO was now well entrenched and an all-out offensive would be too costly.

Fighting in a built-up area would be totally different from a campaign in the desert or even in mountainous terrain, where armor can be maneuvered imaginatively. In house-to-house, street-to-street combat, the attacking force loses many of the advantages it enjoys in open country. In a city, with its virtually endless maze of walls, houses, and streets to be crossed, artillery and air support are less effective and armor is far more exposed to ambush and its movement necessarily constrained. The infantryman is called upon to move step by step in a series of one-to-one encounters that work to the benefit of a defender who, on other counts, cannot measure up to his antagonist.

Until the end of July, when the Israeli troops attacked and occupied Beirut Airport and nearby Palestinian camps, there was no substantial ground movement in Beirut. Israeli artillery and naval shelling, however, accompanied by aerial bombardment, had made life in the besieged city unpleasant, to say the least. The artillery would begin in the early afternoon, then the naval guns would join in. Toward late afternoon the air force would appear and add to the destruction while the artillery continued its bombardment. Occasionally the supply of electricity or water would be cut off, adding to the pressure and discomfort. Periodically the PLO or Syrians would retaliate with a single salvo or with several rounds. But most of the smoke came from the PLO-held southern suburbs of West Beirut, where fires broke out sporadically.

The American government became increasingly embarrassed by the daily television reports of bombardments on Beirut and on July 18 suspended temporarily the shipment of 5,000 cluster bombs to Israel.

The PLO leaders had been shocked by the almost total detachment with which the Arab nations reacted to their predicament; they saw that the other Arabs were unenthusiastic about the possibility that the terrorist fighters might be evacuated to their own countries. But now, at least, the PLO began to feel increasingly confident that the Israelis had lost their zest for battle and would not dare enter West Beirut. They were also encouraged by sympathy from the West and by the way so much of the media blamed the Israelis for the plight of the besieged population.

Meanwhile, on July 22, following steady infiltration of PLO troops through the Syrian lines in the Al-Bika'a Valley, Israel launched a sudden artillery attack, destroying possibly more than seventy Syrian tanks. That day, the volume of shooting in Beirut quickened, to continue almost uninterruptedly until July 27. The PLO retaliated by firing their larger "Grad" Katyushas, mainly at the Christian suburbs. They also hit the port of Junieh and caused minor damage to a Red Cross ship anchored there. The next day, all parties agreed to a cease-fire, which was promptly broken in the afternoon of July 30.

It gradually became clear that the Israelis had little desire to expose their soldiers to the risks of storming West Beirut. The battles along the highway leading to the city had shown to what unusual lengths the PLO would go to shelter their positions behind civilian populations. Intelligence indicated that, in the area now under siege, the terrorists would expand this tactic. At the end of July the PLO had no intention of moving out voluntarily, yet Begin's government was committed to removing them. Entrenched among the civilians of Beirut, should the PLO be immune to attack? A majority of the Israeli government did not think so. Thousands of reservists in crack combat units were recalled. A coordinated tank and infantry attack was imminent.

On August 1, a few days after the sudden call-up of the reserves, the Israeli troops began moving toward Beirut. Careful not to attack the city itself, they took up positions in the airport buildings and in El Ouzan, northwest of the airport; they also encircled the Palestinian camp of Bourj el Barajne. To strengthen the pressure, a second force crossed the dividing line between the two sectors of the city, close to the parliament building. This second force came in from East Beirut, occupied the Museum, and reached the Hippodrome, the racetrack on the way to the Corniche el Mazra'a. As the battle moved into the built-up area on August 4, the number of Israeli casualties mounted; on that day, eighteen men were killed and seventy-six wounded. The number of PLO and Lebanese victims was considerably larger. The PLO let it be known that they had decided it was time to get out.

On Thursday, August 5, Habib told a visiting congressman that while he could not condone any form of bombardment, if ever there was an air raid with a message, the Israeli bombing of Beirut the day before was it. And Arafat and his colleagues had read the message. Habib was confident that the PLO would begin to leave the city within days.

But they now raised technical questions about their departure. Sharon suspected that the PLO was procrastinating, playing for time or better terms, and ordered the fire to continue.

The final bombing lasted for two violent days, August 11 and 12. The Israeli air force attacked not only the camps sheltering fighters, but also high-rise buildings in the center of the city, which, it was claimed, housed the offices of the various PLO factions. It was the heaviest, most concentrated air onslaught since the war began, carried out on the orders of Ariel Sharon, without prior approval by the Israeli cabinet or prime minister.*

The attack ended the battle of Beirut. As the dust settled, nearly half a million people were still in the war-torn city and the camps bordering it. They had repeatedly been urged to leave and had always been allowed to do so. But seeing the pilferage of the property of those who did abandon their homes, most preferred to stay with the bombs.

Later interviews with PLO officers confirmed that in the cumbersome, indirect negotiations between the Israelis and the PLO, via the Americans via the Lebanese, the bombings of August 11 and 12 had been crucial to the PLO decision finally to abandon Beirut.

Yasser Arafat and his lieutenants clearly realized that they had suffered a devastating military setback. They were overawed by the Israeli air raids and artillery bombardments. These were not World War II-style wholesale repeat poundings of a wide general target, but strikes precisely aimed at concentrations of PLO fighters and at their offices. The accuracy and unrelenting attrition of the fire had a cumulative effect.

Added to the continuous bombings had been the psychological warfare: the supersonic planes that went boom in the night as well as the on-again, off-again interruptions of water and electricity supply. And rumor, always a powerful weapon in the Middle East, was now skillfully wielded by the Israelis.

Until the second week of August, Arafat had been holding out for political concessions. Always brilliant with the media, he convinced many of his listeners that there was no precedent for his two-month stand against the powerful Israeli army. But he wanted more than glory. Yet Arafat had totally failed to establish the modern army he was so fond of boasting about. Well trained, motivated, at times courageous, the terrorists lacked the training and leadership to counterattack the Israelis in an organized force of any size.

Whatever discreet private meetings may have taken place

---

*The American administration had rarely been so angry with Israel as when they learned, on Thursday, August 12, of the scope of the bombing of the past two days. Their disenchantment with Sharon seemed to be complete.

109

between the PLO and American officials, the U.S. administration had always been careful not to overtly break its promise to the Israelis on this vital point.* Now, Arafat wanted some form of official recognition from the United States. He did not get it. In spite of the impression he had made on the Western media and public, the American administration continued, until the end of the siege, to maintain only indirect contact with Yasser Arafat.

Such was the climate in the summer of 1982 in Beirut, that within weeks would breed the assassination of the Lebanese president-elect and the revenge massacres. Yet for the moment, with the PLO fighters agreeing to depart, an important stage in the conflict had ended.

---

*Arafat had met with U.S. congressmen from time to time. There was the famous meeting of late July 1982 with a delegation that included Paul N. McCloskey of California. After some noisy publicity and implications of vague recognition of Israel by the PLO, when the PLO leader's words were deciphered it became clear that the congressmen had been taken for a ride.

7

Moscow Was Slow to React

I T is the assessment of many sovietologists that in recent years Moscow has come to realize that its position in the Middle East and its capacity to influence events there are impaired by its lack of diplomatic relations with Israel. In a demonstrative act of anger, Russia had recalled its ambassador to Israel at the outset of the Six Day War in June 1967 and had cut off diplomatic relations with the Jewish state. There was very little contact, and usually indirect at that, between Moscow and Jerusalem during the following fifteen years. Some years passed before the Soviets realized how advantageous this decision was for the Americans, giving them the frequent opportunity to act as sole arbiter between Israel and the Arab countries. Now, with the strong Israeli presence in Lebanon, the United States was diplomatically well positioned, determined to widen its sphere of influence and to gain further benefit from the vacuum left by the Soviet Union.

Moscow was in a quandary. Any country can sever contact with another state in a huff, but even a great power needs a good reason and a face-saver to explain to friends in the Arab world why it has decided to renew its relations with a despised "lackey of imperialism" such as Israel. The embarrassment is greater when, as in this case, Russia has hardly been encouraged to make friendly overtures in recent years by Begin and his cabinet. Until envoys are exchanged, the Soviets will remain handicapped in their ability to influence the course of events in the Middle East.

The invasion of southern Lebanon in June 1982 came at what was clearly an unpropitious time for the Soviets. The crisis in Poland, following the suppression of Solidarity and the arrest of Lech Walesa, had not yet been defused. There were no signs of an end to the war in Afghanistan, where more and more Soviet troops were mired by the local guerrillas. In Washington, President Ronald Reagan's hard-line attitude toward the USSR had been reinforced in sensitive areas, among them disarmament, by Secretary of State Alexander Haig. The Soviets appeared overextended and some observers believed that this fact, along with the division in the Arab world engendered by the Iran-Iraq war, might have been one of Israel's major considerations for the timing of the Lebanon invasion.

Since the economic revolution caused by the oil-rich Arab countries after the 1973 Yom Kippur War, the Soviets had been discreetly trying to improve relations with Saudi Arabia and also Kuwait, doubtless hoping, through increased trade, to enjoy some of the new Arab wealth. When the Saudis agreed to finance Syrian arms purchases from Russia, in the later 1970s and early 1980s, Moscow seemed to have made some progress. Diplomatic contacts with the Arab monarchies, although still limited, were far less hostile than they had been ten years earlier. The Russians noted with some appreciation that the Arabs showed little enthusiasm for the new American administration's attempt to strengthen an anti-Communist alliance. Troubled by the confrontation in Afghanistan, the Kremlin must have wished to avoid any new Middle East eruption.

It was against this background that one of the more interesting events in Soviet Middle East diplomacy, scheduled for the first ten days of the Lebanon war, did *not* take place. A delegation of Arab League foreign ministers who had gone to Moscow to enlist Soviet intervention, and who talked to Foreign Minister Andrei Gromyko and other top officials, were not received by Chairman Leonid Brezhnev. The failing health of the aging leader was the official explanation and could have been one of the reasons. But Brezhnev's absence from the talks probably also indicated that Moscow was at a loss about how to respond to developments in Lebanon; in such cases the Kremlin prefers to delay any commitment on the part of its top leaders. It was more than a week after the invasion of Lebanon before Tass, the official Soviet news agency, published an official warning to Israel, on behalf of the Soviet government. Even then, the message was relatively mild, pointing out that since the Middle East lies close to its southern border, developments there "cannot but affect the interests of the USSR."

Another reason for keeping a relatively low profile during the war in Lebanon was less abstruse and closer to home. The Kremlin was still in the midst of the maneuvering for Chairman Brezhnev's successor. This demanded the full-time attention of the topmost contenders for the post. Intervention in a Middle East crisis is not the type of action a lesser bureaucrat would dare to take on his own responsibility, especially not in a period of transition. The severe Soviet economic problems, too, in these circumstances would take priority over any Middle East initiative. There was speculation that the passivity of the Kremlin indicated that the successor to Brezhnev had already emerged, before the death of the ailing leader, and that the indifference to the war in Lebanon was already a reflection of the Middle East policies of the new leader. The contradictory reports that circulated afterward about Yuri Andropov's views on the Moslem world and the Arab-Israeli conflict as well as the lack of substantive post-Brezhnev statements in the first few months after his death on these issues permitted speculation to continue as to what the Soviet-Arab considerations really were.

As so often happens when the Kremlin has not yet made up its mind, Moscow left it to the Soviet media to comment. They predictably repeated the usual charges that Israel was acting in the service of American imperialism (a charge which, incidentally, again raised the question of whether crimes committed on behalf of an imperialist superpower are more or less cardinal than sins committed in one's own name). Related commentary by Tass left no doubts about the subjects of Soviet fears: "Israel and the United States seek . . . the division of Lebanon and the formation of a puppet government obedient to the American-Israeli *diktat*. In other words, attempts are being made to consolidate, through the hands of Israeli gendarmes, American imperialism's rule in the Middle East."

Brezhnev sent a letter of "firm support" to Yasser Arafat—but nothing more. And the two letters sent by the Soviet leader to restrain Israel, although uncouth by international standards, did not go beyond language used by Moscow against Israel in the past; some experts even felt that the remonstrations sounded relatively moderate. All this contrasted strongly with events in the Yom Kippur War. In October 1973, trying to recoup some of the influence he had lost with Anwar Sadat a year earlier, Brezhnev had sent President Richard Nixon a warning of "unilateral steps" that the USSR would take if the United States did not compel Israel to lift the siege of the Egyptian Third Army. There were no such threats from Moscow in the summer of 1982. Nor were there ostentatious alerts of Soviet airborne divisions or moves of Soviet warships in the Mediterranean.

The PLO under siege in Beirut sent desperate calls to the Soviets to come to their aid, but to no avail. When it was learned that Soviet arms had failed in confrontation with American arms, the Kremlin dispatched a three-star general to Damascus. This might have suggested plans for a major resupply of equipment lost by the Syrians, but it added up to only a few planeloads, insignificant compared to the daily airlifts of 1973, when the Syrian army was replenished and modernized within a matter of weeks.

This was all the more remarkable since the Israeli invasion was badly hurting Moscow's two closest allies in the Middle East: Syria, whose air force and antiaircraft batteries were being hit, and the PLO, whose infrastructure was destroyed in the rapid drive north and in the ensuing two-month period of attrition.

As in every war between surrogates, the prestige of the principals involved was an important issue; this time the upper hand of America was clear. Washington emerged as the determinant power in the area, underscoring even more Syria's isolation in its ties with both Moscow and Teheran. In the eyes of many Arabs, Moscow acquired some of the attributes of a paper tiger, and its most important tool of influence, the supply of arms and military advisers, depreciated considerably in value.

Of special interest to all concerned was the question of how Moscow would interpret its obligation under the Soviet-Syrian friendship pact. The events did not provide conclusive answers. Israel had speculated that the Russians would not feel bound to rush to the aid of Damascus when Syrian troops came under Israeli attack in Lebanon, an area outside the borders of Syria and therefore not within the bounds of the Soviet commitment.

Moscow and Damascus obviously differ in their understanding of their mutual obligations stemming from the Soviet-Syrian Friendship Treaty, Article 6 of which states that in the event of crisis the two sides would cooperate "to remove the threat that has arisen and to restore peace." The Syrians made it clear that the Israeli invasion of Lebanon required, in their opinion, much greater Soviet involvement. Syrian Information Minister Ahmad Iskendar Ahmad, in a *Pravda* interview in mid-June, went so far as to call for a "strategic union" between the two countries. Moscow privately (and somewhat vaguely) is said to have assured Damascus that if Israel attacked Syrian territory directly, "Syrians would not fight alone." In public, however, Moscow carefully avoided speaking of any commitment under the friendship treaty. Some Israelis interpreted certain Syrian expressions as hints that even deeper attacks would not elicit a direct Soviet reaction. But Israel preferred not to test this assumption and scrupulously abstained from attacking SAM batteries on the Syrian side of the border, even though on at least one occasion they fired on Israeli planes flying in Lebanese airspace.

No less notable was the fact that the Soviets abstained from any material support of the PLO. President Brezhnev's two letters to President Reagan spoke of the "barbarous extermination of Lebanese and Palestinian children, women, and old people" but made no mention of the PLO or even of Palestinian combatants. PLO officials repeatedly appealed to Alexander Soldatov, Soviet ambassador to Lebanon; he always promised to cable Moscow forthwith, but Moscow seemed never to respond to the appeals.

For Begin and most of his cabinet, destroying the PLO infrastructure was the main purpose of the Lebanon war. But there is more than a whiff of suspicion that Defense Minister Sharon was not averse to the idea of using the opportunity to thrash the Syrians and thus demonstrate Israel's usefulness as America's surrogate power and give a boost to his ideas of "U.S.-Israel strategic cooperation vis-à-vis the Soviet Union." Once it became clear that the West was not using the fall of West Beirut as an opportunity to eliminate the PLO as the major source of international terror, the clash with the Syrians emerged as the most important part of the Lebanon war, as far as the West is concerned. Mainly for political purposes, Israelis probably exaggerated the importance for the Pentagon of their victories over Syria's Russian-supplied weapons. But there is no question of the great military importance of the defeat of the major Soviet weapons systems—the MiG-23 and -25 fighter-bomber planes, the T-72 tanks, and most striking, the various configurations of SAM-6 to SAM-9 antiaircraft missile batteries.

The MiG-23 was no newcomer to East-West confrontations; a sample aircraft had already been examined in detail by the Americans, and there has been more than one opportunity for Western military and weapons experts to evaluate the quality of the plane and its performance capabilities. This, however, was the first major opportunity to test the Russian planes against their Western counterparts in combat conditions. Even assuming that Moscow did not let Syria have the latest version of the aircraft nor all the most sophisticated electronic gear at its disposal, the results of the air encounters were stunning: eighty-six Syrian planes downed without the loss of a single Israeli aircraft. The superior performance of the Israeli pilots was of crucial importance but there were two other contributing factors: the superiority of the airplanes—F-15s and F-16s, Phantoms and Israeli-made Kfirs—flown by the Israelis and the combat tactics and the electronic devices developed by them for over-the-horizon combat.

The T-72 tank has been touted as the most advanced of modern heavy battle tanks, especially impressive because of its armor, which is impervious to NATO tank weaponry. Unlike planes, there are no exact figures for the T-72s lost nor did the Israelis reveal the number of their own tanks destroyed. But battlefield experience has shown that the T-72 is far from invulnerable; its armor is clearly penetrable and it also has some serious operational problems. In comparison, the Israeli Merkava, also in action for the first time in this war, justified the high hopes that its design—low profile and rear entry—would provide much better protection for its crew; the tank also proved its attack capabilities.

During the Yom Kippur War, the Israeli air force suffered heavy losses from Egypt's Soviet-made SAM antiaircraft missile system and especially from the SAM-6 batteries. Finding an answer to this critical problem was the major challenge facing the air force as well as the military research and development teams. As stated in Chapter 5, the results were highly successful. All SAM batteries, including the new, extremely mobile SAM-9s, with which Israel and the West had little experience, and which were introduced into Lebanon by Syria and Libya, were destroyed without the loss of a single Israeli warplane. On June 9 alone, the critical day of the SAM battle, seventeen batteries were totally destroyed and several more put out of action. Israel declared that it would not tolerate the stationing of Syrian SAM on Lebanese territory, and even after the cease-fire, until the end of the summer whenever a SAM battery was moved onto Lebanese soil, the Israeli warplanes promptly destroyed it.

The faltering performance of their weapons systems was a serious blow to the Soviet image. While the aircraft losses appeared to be primarily a question of sophisticated combat tactics and gadgetry, the matter of the T-72 and of the SAMs' vulnerability was a shock to Moscow. Tank warfare is even more central to Soviet military doctrine than to the West, while the air defense system of the Soviet Union rests almost entirely on the SAM systems. As soon as the scope of the losses and their complete disproportion became known in Moscow, high-powered Soviet military delegations, led by Deputy Chief of the Air Force General Yevgeni Syurasov, arrived in Damascus to investigate. Within a few weeks, several hundred Soviet experts, reportedly including the chief of staff of the Soviet armed forces, Marshal Nicolai V. Ogarkov, were engaged in the investigations. The Russians debriefed Syrian pilots who had managed to survive the encounters and studied damaged parts of their aircraft to discover more about Israeli weapons and tactics. That they were especially anxious to find out how the Israelis had outwitted the SAM systems is demonstrated by their advancing batteries provocatively several times inside Lebanese territory—accompanied by Soviet experts whose task it was to observe Israeli methods of attack.

Both the Soviets and the Israelis were equally anxious to prevent new information from falling into enemy hands. The Syrians went to extraordinary lengths and quickly removed any immobilized

117

T-72 so that, despite considerable efforts, the Israelis failed to capture any of them. The best the Israelis could do was to obtain pieces of the special armor developed by the Russians and to accumulate precise data on the performance and points of vulnerability of the Soviet tank. On the other hand, the Russians tried hard to lay their hands on the electronic gear in the Israeli planes—and the Israelis were just as determined to prevent that from happening. It was reported that after one Israeli plane was downed by Syrian antiaircraft fire, eleven high-ranking Soviet officers rushed to the scene—bringing along, according to one version, two captured Israeli pilots, in the hope of locating the most sensitive instruments quickly. But the Israeli air force, probably unaware that its own members were also present, attacked the wreckage and destroyed it completely before anything could be recovered. (See also Chapter 5.)

The discovery of just how vulnerable the SAM systems are was a bitter pill for Moscow. While Russia's own air defenses are certainly more dense, modern, and elaborate, the complete destruction of the SAMs put into action by the Syrians has to be taken as proof of basic weaknesses in the system. Some reports went as far as to claim that Russia now felt obliged to rebuild its air defense system from scratch, assuming that instruments and tactics known to the Israelis would be available also to the Americans. This would entail a multibillion-dollar program and considerable long-term investment in research, development, and new manufacture, spread over several years.

A related development was the amount of military information that suddenly fell into Israeli (and, presumably, American) hands for the first time—from operational SAM-9 systems to pieces of Soviet composite armor. The opportunity to test them and to observe, at first hand, their performance under actual battle conditions was of extremely high value. Should Moscow or Washington (or both) come to the conclusion that the SAM system is, indeed, to a large extent ineffective, it may have a profound effect on East-West relations.

Doubts about the SAMs and other Soviet weapons systems also affected Moscow's allies and customers. Syria and Iraq must have wondered how well their hinterland and their capitals are protected by Soviet air defense systems against potential Israeli or Iranian attack, respectively. Talk of a major Soviet arms deal with Jordan diminished after the start of the Lebanon war, and items in the press indicated that Russian arms salesmen were in trouble in various Third World countries.

Moscow, stung by Arab criticism, went so far as to charge that it was the divisions within the Arab world that were the main cause of their defeats. "Where are you, Arabs? What have you done for your Palestinian brothers?" Radio Moscow lamented in mid-June. Later, Soviet diplomats were quoted as saying with derision, "Six weeks after the start of Israeli aggression, the Arab countries have not yet succeeded in agreeing on a summit conference."

The Soviet press tried to improve the picture by reporting nonexistent successes in Israeli-Syrian air and armor battles. But Moscow did not hide its anger over the disgrace suffered by Soviet weapons in Arab hands. Many a Moscow cocktail party produced its report of some high-ranking officer or bureaucrat telling Western and Third World diplomats how inept the Arabs were in handling Soviet weapons and in learning from their own mistakes. The Russians claimed that the Syrian pilots took off with a "loser mentality," behaved accordingly in battle, and were therefore shot down. "The Arabs expect the USSR to work miracles for them," was the frequent refrain.

Similar criticism appeared in the Soviet press, which went out of its way to denounce as "malicious Western lies" reports about the superiority of Western armaments. Tass noted with approval an article in the Jordan newspaper *El Rai*, which had pointed out that the same Soviet weapons and even less advanced ones had brought victory to the North Vietnamese people over the mighty American forces. Even when the United States bombed Communist North Vietnam, the Soviet Union was never expected to fight alongside the liberation movements, Tass quoted.

One of the practical conclusions for Moscow seems to have been that in the circumstances, there was no need then to replenish Syrian and PLO arsenals with emergency shipments of more sophisticated weapons.

Dissatisfaction with the Syrian and PLO protégés was one, but not necessarily the most important, reason for Moscow's clear reluctance to rush to their aid when the Israelis moved into Lebanon. The Soviets also seemed to have realized that, whatever steps they might take, they would only be helping a clearly losing cause. Moscow let it be known that it saw little hope for an Arab victory without Arab unity. The Soviets do not like to get involved in conflicts in which they will have little influence not only over the opponents of their allies but over their allies, too. The Syrians and expecially the PLO appeared unpredictable. Moreover, the Soviets could not overlook the overall genuine Arab reluctance to support Hafez al-Assad and Yasser Arafat. Yet to some Western diplomats in Moscow the relative passivity of the Kremlin also appeared to reflect the assumption or at least the hope that, in the long run, the Soviet Union could profit most from the war in Lebanon by waiting it out on the sidelines. Israeli intransigance, so ran the argument, would sooner or later change sentiments in Lebanon and convince pro-Western Arab countries to back Syria once again.

Another reason for Soviet caution in Lebanon was in the realm of superpower relations. The suppression of Solidarity in Poland and the invasion of Afghanistan were already exacerbating American-Soviet tensions. There was no advantage for Moscow in stretching such tensions too far, especially over an issue that was not seen as vital to its interests. Moscow could not know how far Washington supported the Israeli action and how firmly it would back it up if the Soviet Union went beyond verbal denunciation.

As early as the second day of the war the Kremlin must have realized that the only cause that could prevent the defeat of the PLO forces and heavy Syrian losses might require direct Soviet military intervention. This would entail the risk of direct confrontation with the United States. The danger, in Moscow's eyes, did not disappear even after the resignation of Alexander Haig as secretary of state. The Soviets could not fail to note that the American veto of the Security Council resolution demanding the withdrawal of Israel from Lebanon was cast *after* George Shultz replaced Haig toward the end of June. This demonstrated, in the words of Tass, that "unconditional support of the U.S. strategic ally, Israel, has been and remains the cornerstone of the U.S. political course in the Middle East."

In 1982, Moscow was far more skeptical about its chances of regaining in the Middle East the dominant position it had held before 15,000 Soviet advisers were ordered out of Egypt by President Sadat in 1972. Since the Yom Kippur War, Moscow has held a second rank in the Middle East while Washington has assumed the role of principal power. The Russians apparently still see little chance of changing this situation by the injection of force, without running the risk of an armed clash with the Americans. The alternative is to use all possible means to prevent local or regional settlements from being reached without Russian participation.

At the close of autumn, positions began to change. Yuri Andropov's rule became more firmly established in Moscow. Washington then reverted to its attempt to be all things to all people in the Middle East, giving the Soviets a new opportunity to try to rebuild their position in the region. Their chosen instrument continued to be Syria and the means again were primarily arms shipments and military assistance.

In the late fall of 1982, it has been ascertained, the Russians supplied Damascus with a number of SS-(SAM)-5 batteries, manned exclusively by Soviet crews and reportedly out of bounds for Syrians. The total number of Soviet personnel in Syria was also said to have increased from 3,500 to more than 5,000. In the first months of 1983 they issued a number of warnings, ostensibly to deter an Israeli attack on Syria.

The increased Soviet involvement led to talk of a new round of fighting between Israel and an emboldened Syria. By the late spring of 1983, however, it was still being debated whether Moscow indeed wanted military escalation or was merely trying to accumulate political capital and was in fact restraining the Syrians. The SAM-5 missiles, although of the older generation, are a vital part of the air defense system of the Soviet Union and have never before been stationed outside the Warsaw Pact countries. One cannot exclude the possibility that the Kremlin generals would like to test these missiles against Western electronic capabilities, as represented in Israel's arsenal; but one should not dismiss the political risks Moscow would assume if the test failed, as was the case with the SAM-6s in 1982.

The central message of the Soviet moves appeared thus to be

addressed to Washington rather than to Jerusalem. Although the SAM-5s, with a range of 180 miles, can reach beyond Beersheva in southern Israel from the Syrian positions, they can also hit targets in the eastern Mediterranean, where the American Sixth Fleet sails. Moscow's moves reaffirmed the long-standing assumption that the Soviets would intervene to protect Damascus if strategic targets inside Syria were attacked by the Israelis; yet the wider aim appeared to be to signal that the Kremlin was back in the Middle East game and wanted Washington's recognition that no settlement in the region could be achieved without its participation.

President Assad of Syria was obviously aware of his mandate to prevent a Lebanon settlement undesirable to Moscow—and aware of the extra leverage this gave him vis-à-vis the Soviets. This, in turn, increased the danger that Damascus would try to drag the Soviets into the confrontation further than they originally intended.

The American failure to foresee how firmly Syria would reject any Israel-Lebanon understanding inadvertently abetted Soviet efforts to stage a comeback to the center of the Middle East scene.

8

An Arab Maze

F OR the Arab world, the war in Lebanon was the culmination of a decade of high hopes and deep disenchantments. Conflicts between the traditional Arab-Moslem values and modern technological society were a central theme of the Arab quest for identity, especially after their defeat by the nascent Israel in 1948. Each subsequent Israeli victory has deepened the frustration and self-doubt.

The 1973 Yom Kippur War and its consequences seemed to break the evil spell: the military victories in the first days of that war, followed by the newly acquired oil weapon, revived Arab dreams of again becoming a great power, restoring their ancient glory and, perhaps, even their supremacy, not only over Israel but also over the Christian world.

Before that decade was over, with Camp David and the Israel-Egyptian peace treaty, followed by the Gulf war between Iran and Iraq, the Soviet invasion of Afghanistan, the acceleration of Israeli settlement of the West Bank, and the Israeli bombing of the nuclear facilities near Baghdad, the dream had begun to fade. The pattern of Arab impotence repeated itself when Israel entered Lebanon to destroy the PLO infrastructure: Syria even found it necessary to indicate that it would not seriously interfere with Israeli operations in southern Lebanon if Israel did not attack Syrian positions in the

Al-Bika'a valley. No other Arab country even contemplated coming to the aid of the Palestinians.

Thus, when the fighting in Lebanon was over, two seemingly conflicting sentiments were felt in many Arab countries: there was renewed anger and hatred of Israel, often expressed—even in Egypt—in an anti-Semitic (i.e., anti-Jewish) terms. At the same time there appeared a sense of relief at not having been dragged into the armed conflict with Israel.

The familiar agonizing questions were occasionally asked by the Arab media: Why were the Arabs apparently so powerless? Was there something inherently lacking in Arab culture or society that caused its weakness? Was it, perhaps, the lack of political freedom?

Despite their low profile during the war, or perhaps because of it, events in Lebanon sent shock waves through the Arab world. The tremors were weaker than those after the Six Day War, the Yom Kippur War and the OPEC oil embargo, President Anwar Sadat's visit to Jerusalem, or the Egypt-Israel peace treaty. But the effect was potentially almost as significant, especially if it ultimately results in major changes in the PLO structure and its attitude toward recognition of Israel.

Their passivity during the war in Lebanon was also an expression of the deep divisions in the Arab countries: those who could have come to the aid of the PLO preferred not to; the few who were ready to help were in no position to do so. For most Israelis, and certainly for the Israeli government, it was a confirmation of their long-held belief that the Arabs pay lip service to the PLO more out of fear than love and that many of them would not be distressed to see it cut down to size, even by Israel.

Second only to Lebanon, Egypt was probably the major Arab beneficiary of the Israeli move. True, the military action encouraged extremists in the Middle East to attack once again the peace treaty without which, they claimed, the Israelis would not have dared to leave their southern front uncovered and, with only a partial mobilization of reserves, mount the offensive in the north. This argument, however, was easily overbalanced by the fact that those who denounced Egypt actually did even less for the PLO than did Cairo. The Egyptians protested directly to Jerusalem and, later, after the

Phalangist massacre in Sabra and Shatilla in September, recalled Ambassador Said Mourtada "for consultations," indicating that he would not return to Tel Aviv until all Israeli troops were out of Lebanon.

At the time of his succession to power, President Husni Mubarak assured both the Egyptians and his contacts abroad that he would adhere to the foreign policies established by his assassinated predecessor and maintain the new relationship with Israel. Two years after the death of Sadat, he had formally done so, but in practice it has become a frosty, sterile peace. The ex-pilot lacks the flair that his more imaginative precursor had and there was little chemistry or respect between the Israeli premier and the new Egyptian president.

Egypt, in the post-Sadat era of the early 1980s, is a sobered country, craving to return to the arms of its Arab brethren. Many Egyptians suspect that the aid promised by America and Europe will not be enough to solve their enormous economic problems. They are generally disappointed with the way the country is handling its own affairs and skeptical whether the peace process with Israel was worth the effort and political sacrifice of recent years.

One way in which Egyptians let off steam is through their publications. These, in the days following the invasion of Lebanon, poured out a nonstop tirade of vile anti-Jewish articles and cartoons, seldom matched in recent years. Prime Minister Begin was depicted as hideous a villain as can be imagined. At first, the Israeli leadership, fully engrossed in the campaign, was unaware of this ugly anti-Israel publicity attack.

In mid-June, however, the government realized that it was remiss in neglecting its Egyptian neighbor and considered sending a senior representative, possibly a high-ranking cabinet minister, to brief the Egyptian leaders on the campaign and plans for the future. The prime minister had one of his periodic meetings with President Yitzhak Navon, who is fluent in Arabic and, having more time on his hands, had been reading the Egyptian dailies and weeklies. The president reported in some detail to Begin on the recent wave of hostility, following which the prime minister, insulted and angry, gave orders to cancel any government initiative toward a visit to Egypt and to reduce contacts to the very minimum. The Egyptian government reciprocated by discouraging opportunities for direct commercial relations.

Egypt's role after the fighting in Lebanon remained ambiguous. President Mubarak claimed credit for softening the position of Iraq, which for the first time publicly indicated the possibility of recognition of Israel and even the necessity to consider Israel's security requirements. This was a startling hint from the country that has been more virulently hostile to Israel than any except Colonel Muammar al-Qadaffi's Libya. Iraq participated in the 1948 Arab attack on the new Israel but, unlike Lebanon, Syria, Jordan, and Egypt, has since refused to sign an armistice agreement so as "not to sully its hands."

No great favor to Israel was meant by Iraq's expressions in 1982, but it indicates that tactical needs can impose even on the most hostile Arab countries a measure of flexibility. Iraq, deeply enmeshed in its war with Iran, needs Egypt's and Jordan's help, has been discreetly vying for American aid, and apparently feels that it must show consideration for their policies vis-à-vis Israel. More important, Iraq wants all Arab efforts to concentrate on the Persian Gulf conflict and not be split between Iran and Israel.

Egypt blamed Israel's invasion of Lebanon as the major cause for the weakening of the fragile social and economic relations between the two countries. But there was also the Taba irritant. On the 650-yard-long bay of Taba, just south of Eilat, a 600-room Sonesta Hotel, constructed by Israeli entrepreneurs, was close to completion when the peace treaty was put into effect early in 1982. The area involved about one square mile, compared to the 22,000 square miles of the Sinai given back to Egypt. The Egyptians claimed Taba Bay as their own but the Israelis put their foot down, asserting that the maps of the area drawn close to the turn of the last century definitely show Taba outside the Sinai. International legal experts privately consulted conceded Israel had a case, but the position was not completely clear, which did not contribute to the harmony between the two countries. With increasing personal hostility between the leaders of Israel and Egypt and their inherent obstinacy, the Taba Bay question could become dangerous.

Some Israelis suspected that the recall of the Egyptian ambassador provided an opportunity for President Mubarak to more or less permanently downgrade the level of diplomatic representation in Israel, abetting his effort to rejoin the Arab family. Certainly, Egypt's endeavor to get back into the fold was facilitated by the war between Iraq and Iran. Continuing the policy initiated by Sadat, Mubarak provided the Iraqis with arms and other military assistance. Baghdad, in return, praised Egypt and even hinted about a renewal of diplomatic relations, broken off after the peace with Israel was signed. But the fact that the Lebanon war showed the Arab world's lack of any possible concerted effort was probably the biggest factor in improving Egypt's position. At the peak of the bombardment of West Beirut, even Yasser Arafat appealed to Mubarak to use his relations with Israel to persuade Begin to desist from "these barbarous attacks." It must have given the Egyptian government some sense of satisfaction to fulfil Arafat's request.

Egypt maintained a strongly critical stance toward Israel after the cease-fire and during the negotiations on the future of Israel-Lebanon relations. At the same time, Mubarak urged Arafat to recognize Israel unilaterally, so as to gain American recognition and put the blame for the lack of progress in the peace process entirely on Israel. Arafat, in turn, said that he would not embarrass Egypt by calling for the cancellation of the Camp David agreement but that Cairo should stop embarrassing the PLO by calls for recognition of Israel.

Mubarak's efforts to bring about the PLO's approval for Jordan-Israel negotiations go beyond an obvious interest in seeing the Sadat initiative and the Camp David process vindicated. Any moderation of Arab hostility toward Israel also means lessening Arab condemnation of Egypt's peace treaty with its eastern neighbor. Even more important, Mubarak probably realizes that the present freeze in economic and cultural relations between Israel and Egypt will ultimately also endanger formal diplomatic relations. Egyptian newspapers make it clear why the government is worried about such a development: in articles responding to the hawks who demand that Egypt sever its ties with Israel completely, the papers warn that such a move would serve as an excuse for the Israeli government to start hostilities against the Arabs.

Saudi Arabia can also write the war in Lebanon on the credit side of its political ledger. Throughout the war, it played a central role in the diplomatic efforts on behalf of the PLO and, after the war, on behalf of the Moslem elements in Lebanon which were interested in restricting the scope of normalization with Israel. Saudi Arabia claimed, with some justification, to have successfully applied its influence with the United States to counter Secretary of State Haig's anti-PLO policies and, after his replacement by George Shultz, to get them altered.

American policy in Saudi Arabia has for decades been based on a mixture of naiveté, oriental romanticism, and outright wishful thinking.[1] This combination was evident anew in the American assumption that the Saudis would help Lebanon sell to the PLO and Syria the American-mediated agreement with Israel—an agreement which provided for the withdrawal of all non-Lebanese forces. After three months of gentle but fruitless pressure, Washington seemed surprised to find that Saudi assistance was clearly not forthcoming. It is still not evident that Washington now understood that Saudi Arabia's leverage with other Arab countries has repeatedly proved to be close to zero. Saudi Arabia failed to dissuade Egypt from its commitment to the Camp David peace process, was unable to persuade the PLO to join King Hussein and take up Reagan's Peace Plan and, in spite of Syria's need for Saudi funding, failed to influence Damascus on any issue. In general, the Saudis may be effective in squeezing concessions and goodwill from the United States but they have repeatedly failed to deliver. In spite of their wealth, grants, and subsidies to various poorer countries in the Arab world, they have little clout outside their own country. The Americans apparently found it hard to accept that King Fahd of Saudi Arabia is a dull, hesitant statesman, far more adept in dealing with his tribes and clans than in operating on the world stage. The Saudis counseled the Lebanese not to agree to any normalization with Israel that would imply peace on terms other than those laid down at the Arab summit conference held in Fez, Morocco, in mid-September 1982. One of the Lebanese negotiators was quoted as saying that the Saudis told them explicitly to give Israel whatever is necessary for security but nothing more.

From the beginning, Saudi involvement in Lebanon against normalization of relations with Israel was greater than realized in the West. Their acceptance of Bashir Gemayel and then his brother as president was made dependent on the Gemayels maintaining a sensible distance from the Israelis. It was made clear that the Lebanese and their economy could continue to depend on the Saudi funding of their financial institutions and real estate projects as well as industrial development and tourist and entertainment facilities. But no financial aid for reconstruction would be forthcoming until all Israeli forces were withdrawn; nor, on the other hand, would the Saudis support the Lebanese if relations with Israel were placed on a completely normal footing.

The war also benefited Jordan. In the years of civil strife and the PLO and Syrian occupation of Lebanon, Amman had replaced Beirut as the regional headquarters for several international companies. Its stability, in contrast to the warring in Lebanon, the unrest in Syria, and the fighting between Iraq and Iran, enhanced the economic boom in the country. Syria was in no position to engage in much troublemaking in Jordan, while the PLO, expelled from Beirut, had to be thankful for King Hussein's hospitality on his own terms.

After the war, Jordan became the focus of American efforts to use the events to revive and expand the Camp David process; a weakened PLO, it was believed, could consent to be represented by Jordan in the talks on the future of the West Bank. Under the momentum of the settlement in Lebanon, Israel would, so Washington expected, agree to such talks and to the indirect PLO representation.

King Hussein, however, in the winter of 1982 and early in 1983, met difficulties in his talks with the PLO about obtaining its approval for Jordan to stand in for the Palestinians in negotiations with Israel; he was therefore reluctant to do so. Washington was led to believe that it had to convince the king and prove that, once the negotiations began, it would be able to oblige Israel to make major concessions on the West Bank. Cutting down Israeli demands in Lebanon was thus presented as the test of American ability to twist Israel's arm on the terms of Palestinian autonomy. "Hussein wants to see whether there is water in the pool before he dives in; Washington is pumping water from Lebanon to convince him to jump," an Israeli government radio commentator explained.

Earlier, in the fall of 1982, the king of Jordan was on the road or, rather, in the air, for much of the time, flying from one Arab capital to the next for consultations. Ostensibly he was reporting to his fellow rulers on his visits with the Arab League delegation to Washington, Tokyo, and several West European capitals, the purpose of which was to explain the decisions of the Arab summit held in Fez. At the same time, however, the king was sounding out and seeking support for the idea of entering into negotiations with Israel in terms of the American proposals.

The reason for Hussein's interest in negotiating seems obvious: Israel was and still is busy rapidly establishing new settlements on the West Bank and if negotiations were postponed much longer there might not be much left to negotiate about. (Indeed, President Mubarak of Egypt, urging Yasser Arafat to recognize Israel unilaterally and offer to join the talks with Israel, is said to have used the same argument.) But the Jordanian king had an even more pressing reason. He clearly realized that, no matter what other gains it derived from the 1982 war, Israel will never again permit southern Lebanon to become a base for PLO operations. In the absence of a negotiating process, however, the PLO is likely to attempt to resume such operations; with Lebanon out of bounds, they may try to shift their bases to Jordan. Such a move, as Israel has warned in the past, would invite Israeli retaliation and turn Jordan into a battle area— and what that could mean was starkly demonstrated in Lebanon.

King Hussein is first and foremost adept in the art of survival. No ruler in Asia, Europe, or the Americas (except President Alfredo Stroessner of Paraguay) has been in office longer than the Hashemite monarch, who ascended the throne in 1952. With few exceptions, such as joining President Gamal Abdel Nasser of Egypt in the Six Day War in 1967 and expelling the PLO from his country in September 1970, the most enduring and possibly underrated characteristic of his whole tenure has been timidity. As American pressure grew in the fall and winter of 1982 to 1983, King Hussein's caution reasserted itself and he opted once again to try to ride out the storms of the region. He obviously was unwilling to expose himself and risk his life for what he must have considered a thankless task.

Syria has played a central role in igniting most of the Israel-Arab wars for many years. In the mid-1950s, the Damascus-initiated contacts between virulently anti-Israel Syria and Soviet-equipped revolutionary Egypt created in Israel an unbearable sense of imminent attack. This was a psychologically contributing cause of Israel's joining Britain and France in the 1956 Suez campaign.

In the spring of 1967, it was Soviet-Syrian collusion about a (nonexistent) "massing of thirteen Israeli brigades on the Syrian border" that encouraged President Nasser to escalate his belligerency in a series of acts which culminated in the Six Day War.

Again in 1973, collusion between Syria and Egypt made it possible to launch the Yom Kippur War. Though the Egyptian crossing of the Suez Canal was the more spectacular start to that war, it was the advance of Syrian tanks through the Golan Heights toward the Galilee that was more menacing to the survival of Israel.

The Israeli involvement leading to the war in Lebanon was also tied to Syria: the 1981 advance of Syrian SAM batteries into Lebanon posed a threat to Israeli air surveillance of PLO activities in southern Lebanon and strengthened the feeling in the Israeli military command that Syria and the PLO were preparing another surprise attack against Israel.

The Syrian Ba'ath regime that faced Israel in the spring and summer of 1982 was in a vastly different position from when it attacked Israel in October 1973. Gone was the self-assuredness that had enabled President Hafez al-Assad to send his best troops, including the presidential guard, to fight on the Golan Heights. This time it was an uncertain regime which had only recently killed some 10,000 of its own citizens in Hama and destroyed most of its mosques to suppress the swelling Moslem Brotherhood opposition. The Syrian regime was isolated in the Arab world because its hatred of the Iraqi Ba'arth leadership under Saddam Hussein had led it to side with Iran and Ayatollah Ruhollah Khomeini in the Gulf war. After the confrontation in Lebanon, Syria still had the healthy respect for Israel's military power that had been one of the main lessons learned by Damascus from the outcome of the Yom Kippur War.

Except for Lebanon itself, Syria is the Arab country most affected by the recent war. Damascus never fully recognized the independence of Lebanon, which it considers to this day part of Greater Syria. No Syrian ambassador resides in Beirut. "Whereas Israel has designs on Lebanon for the purposes of its own security, Syria has designs on Lebanon full point," as a British newspaper put it.[2]

Consequently, Syria's interest in Lebanon is twofold. Syria's first objective is to assert its influence on the internal affairs of Lebanon, reflecting its presumptive special status in that country. These interests inevitably also enmesh Syria in the religious and communal strife of Lebanon as well as in the conflicts engendered by the PLO occupation of that country.

Naturally, the Syrians have more affinity for and closer ties to the Lebanese Moslems than to the country's Christians. On various occasions, however, Damascus has sided with some sectors of the Christian community. Over the years, as a result of personal vendettas and murderous feuds between heads of Lebanese clans, it became common for some Christian leaders to turn into temporary allies of the Syrians. Such was the case of ex-president Suleiman Franjieh, who upon the murder of his son Toni by aides of Bashir Gemayel became a supporter of Syria.

In the civil war of the late 1970s, when the PLO threatened to overwhelm the Christian forces, the Syrian troops first sided with the Kataeb Phalange militias, administering a crushing defeat to the Palestinians at Tel el-Za'atar. Later, however, they shifted their support back to the PLO and were their allies when the Israelis arrived to destroy the PLO infrastructure in southern Lebanon.

Syria's second interest in Lebanon is security related. Damascus considers the Al-Bika'a valley in southeast Lebanon, almost within artillery range of Damascus, as part of Syria's defense zone. Long before the 1982 war, the spread of some 30,000 to 40,000 men of the Arab Deterrent Force in Lebanon had become a military burden on Syria. Yet Damascus, seeing itself as the main bulwark of Arab resistance to Israel, was convinced that Israel was determined to destroy the Syrian regime. Thus, Syria considered its continued presence in Lebanon vital, both to prevent Beirut from following Egypt's example in making peace with Israel and to protect Damascus from Israeli attack via the Al-Bika'a. Accordingly, a considerable part of the Dissuasion Force sent by Syria in the name of the Arab League to put an end to the civil war was actually stationed in the Al-Bika'a as an advance Syrian defense line.

After the war, Damascus concentrated on salvaging some military presence in that area, even after any general withdrawal of foreign troops from Lebanon. As the talks between Israel and Lebanon commenced in December 1982, Syria made it clear that whatever special security arrangements might be agreed upon between the two countries, Damascus would claim the same rights for itself. If nothing else, this proved an effective hindrance to a quick Beirut-Jerusalem agreement, especially since the United States preferred to have Israel give up many of its demands rather than have Syria gain the same presence on a permanent basis.

The Syrian position hardened when the Israel-Lebanon agreement was reached in mid-May. Ignoring Lebanese requests and American approaches, it showed, in public at least, no intention of redeploying its troops or evacuating them from Lebanon. Nor did it appear interested in an Israeli withdrawal. In part this was rationalized by one Arab who knew President Assad well and noted that "by their being fifteen and a half miles away from Damascus, the Israeli troops' threat from the Al-Bika'a forms a cohesive influence, deflecting Syrian opposing factions who might otherwise have threatened the regime from organizing themselves." And a Syrian minister added recently, "In the past they never respected Lebanon's integrity, regarding it as a region of Syria, and also, in our age, Lebanon and Syria are one people in one country who were coerced into partition."[3]

Syria considers itself the cradle and the heart of Arab nationalism, and the effort to live up to this title serves the regime in Damascus as justification for its undertakings for the protection of its own rule. In this self-proclaimed role the Syrians support some of the Arab terror organizations and stand in the forefront of the hard-line Arab states which refuse to consider a negotiated settlement of the Arab-Israel conflict. Besides housing a number of PLO offices, Damascus is headquarters to the extreme leftist Popular Front for the Liberation of Palestine of George Habash, the Democratic Front for the Liberation of Palestine of Naif Hawatmeh, and the Popular Front—General Command of Ahmad Jibril. Although weaker than it was in the early 1970s, there is also Syria's "Palestinian" armed group, Al-Saika, which is for all practical purposes under the direct command of Damascus. All through the civil war and during the Israeli invasion of Lebanon, Al-Saika also served as a Syrian instrument to raise tensions with Israel, where needed, by creating incidents.

After the cease-fire, Syria continued to maintain forces in Lebanon. It assisted Al-Saika and other elements in crossing the lines to attack Israeli units. With the aim of putting indirect political pressure on Israel, it has also fostered Lebanese communal warfare. In Tripoli, in the north, Syria backed the Alawi community (the minority subsect of the Shiite Moslems to which most of the ruling military clique in Damascus belong) fighting the PLO units; in the Al-Shouf mountains, southeast of Beirut, the Syrians backed the fighters belonging to feudal leftist Druse chieftain Walid Junblatt against the Christian militias. The Syrian assumption was that prolonged communal warfare would accelerate the American push for a settlement in Lebanon and strengthen the pressure on Israel to withdraw without achieving the military and especially the political aims of its war. Most of all, Damascus wanted to prevent progress toward an Israel-Jordan agreement on the West Bank. Any agreement that would normalize relations between Israel and Jordan and defuse the Palestine powder keg would leave Syria isolated in the Middle East and bereft of any leverage in the Arab world.

Syria's involvement became more intensive in the summer of 1983. Several veteran Fatah officers refused to accept Arafat's appointment of three discredited PLO officers to new senior field posts. Damascus seized upon the demoralization in the PLO and moved to turn the general resentment into a full-blown revolt against Arafat. It was obvious that in doing so Damascus was hoping to make the PLO totally subservient to itself. It certainly contributed to a crippling division inside the PLO.

The Arab world is again in a state of flux. The overall weakening effect of its splits and divisions has again been demonstrated, but unlike previous collective defeats, this one has so far not produced any major shift toward national or religious extremism. Fear of religious fanaticism—as personified by the fundamentalists in Iran—has had a sobering effect on most Arab leaders, and the danger of a trend in this direction has lessened as the world moves into the 1980s. The realization has also been brought home that there are other threats, real and imaginary, facing the Arab world besides the dangers of Zionism. A division of Arab efforts between the Gulf and Palestine could be more threatening than the existence of the State of Israel. This discovery could even bring about a new Arab maturity and willingness to face reality—including the reality of Israel.

The
Tarnished
Image

In most of the stories television cares to cover there is always "the right bit"—the most violent, the most bloody, the most pathetic, the most tragic, the most wonderful, the most awful moment. Getting the effective bit [on film] is what television news is about. It is the bit . . . you will go through just about anything to get because it means success and missing it consistently means you'd better look for a job other than a TV correspondent.—Robert MacNeil of the "MacNeil-Lehrer Report."[1]

In Operation Peace for Galilee, the image of Israel suffered more damage than at any time in its history. The coverage by the foreign media became a major issue in Israel's domestic debate about the rights and wrongs of the war. The Opposition saw in the bad press, exaggerated though it was, a reflection of the wrong decisions taken by the government, while the government pointed to the more glaring examples of irresponsible journalism to uphold its claim that the criticism originated in prejudice and not in any fault or wrongdoing of its own.

The coverage also elicited from a number of thoughtful journalists some of the harshest criticism ever rendered of the professional abuses committed by their colleagues. In a letter to the British magazine *The Economist,* for instance, Melvin J. Lasky, editor of

Encounter, wrote: "The accounts [of our free Western press] offered of the Lebanese tragedy of 1982 often touched the nadir of twentieth-century journalistic misdemeanours."[2] But that was later.

The images of the war in Lebanon had been preceded by the impression of continuous use of force by the Israelis. Reports of more West Bank settlements, declared "unconducive to peace" by the United States and other governments, were followed by announcements of violent clashes between Palestinians and Israeli security forces. Arab students protested, universities were closed down, and there were confrontations in the streets resulting in occasional casualties and even deaths.

All these were among the contributing factors that enabled the perceived roles of David and Goliath to be reversed. Now the underdogs were the Palestinians, attracting the bias of favoritism reserved by the media for the Third World. And to this were added the prejudice-inspiring caricature drawings and narrative presentations of Prime Minister Begin. Together, they form the background for the presentation and perception of the war in Lebanon by the media and their audience.

TV Guide remarked early in 1982 that "what the television industry needs is a good war to boost its image." The war in Lebanon was made for television, as TV correspondents remarked happily. Their home offices had a clear idea of what a war, and especially a war of this type, should look like and adhered to it in preparing their next edition.

Unlike the newspaper reader who can skip the stories that do not interest him, the uninstructed television viewer is part of a captive audience; he absorbs images and sounds that do not relate to previous knowledge and he forms his opinions on the basis of superficial or fleeting impressions.

On the very first day of the war, the Israeli government departed in two ways from public relations policy of previous wars: it announced what the limits of the advance would be—40 kilometers (25 miles)—and it forbade correspondents to join the advancing troops. The government predicted an outcome and then prevented it from being witnessed. The first departure came home to roost the day Israel's tanks moved on beyond the 40-kilometer line. This badly damaged Israeli credibility, both objectively and by giving many correspondents the feeling that they were personally cheated. The ban on journalists hurt Israel from the beginning, since correspondents stationed in Beirut were under no such constraint and had no difficulty in reporting the war as seen from the Arab side or in enlarging upon the PLO communiqués.

The ban soon had to be lifted and a daily press routine developed. Each morning, groups of correspondents gathered in the dining room of the Gesher HaZiv kibbutz guesthouse, near the coastal highway, and at the Arazim Hotel in Metullah, just south of the Lebanese border. This was where the forward headquarters of the Israeli Army Spokesman were located and where daily permits for entry into Lebanon were issued. The correspondents provided their own transportation, traveling two to four per car, and the Army Spokesman's office furnished the escort officers whose task it was to explain, to facilitate movement, to make sure that the groups did not inadvertently cross the lines and fall into PLO or Syrian hands, and to get them back to Israel by nightfall.

Until mid-June, Tyre and Sidon were the main attractions, as they provided the opportunity to report and, in particular, to film the destruction in the two city centers and adjoining refugee camps. This proved to be a war in which tank and aircraft battles provided far less dramatic photo opportunities than did urban areas and Palestinian camps; curiosity about the eastern front, where the real war was being fought and where Israel's American and locally made weapons confronted Syria's Russian arms, seemed less pronounced. When the Israeli troops reached Beirut and made contact with the Christian forces east of the city, Beirut became the focus of most foreign correspondents.

There were two important consequences of the pattern of commuting by car between Israel and East Beirut, avoiding the sniping from the Western part of the city. First, it forced a very tight timetable on everybody. With the heavy military traffic on the coastal highway, correspondents leaving Gesher HaZiv between 7:30 and 9:00 A.M. could pay only short visits to Tyre and Sidon before hurrying on north to the Beirut area. After two to three hours there, they had to rush back to Israel and to the television studios in

Herzlia to be in time for the satellite transmission of films for the evening shows in America. This left little time for in-depth investigation, especially when "meeting the guys from the other side" was one of the major purposes of the Beirut visit. These were the correspondents stationed in West Beirut, who usually stayed at the Commodore Hotel and who had little difficulty crossing the lines into East Beirut, where the Alexander Hotel was the favorite press location. Here the visiting correspondent, just arrived from the home office to cover the war from the Israeli side, was briefed by his veteran counterpart, who was usually well versed in the PLO arguments.

This was the first modern war in which dozens of newsmen crossed the combat lines while the fighting was going on and covered the battleground from both sides, practically simultaneously. One of the more unusual consequences of this unique situation was that press facilities set up by the Israeli Defense Forces also served correspondents reporting from the other side. The satellite transmitter in West Beirut was knocked out in the first days of the war and soon there was a daily taxi service which took video tapes from the Commodore to the Alexander, to be relayed via the satellite station in Israel. Later, when the Israeli authorities became less cooperative, films were occasionally sent via Damascus (sometimes by the same taxi) or even by express boat to Cyprus, but much of the material transmitted to the West from PLO sources went through Israeli facilities.

When the Israeli Army Spokesman later established his office in East Beirut, the phones there provided direct dialing both to the Commodore Hotel in West Beirut and through the Israeli telephone network. Thus, newspapermen in Beirut were able to call their offices in New York or London via Tel Aviv. The first reports on the Sabra and Shatilla massacre by the Christian militias were sent to the West by phone from this Israeli army press office.

There was a vastly exaggerated presentation of the destruction and devastation of the cities of Sidon, Nabatieh, and Damour, occupied by the Israelis in the first stages of the war. There was also repeated implication that this damage had been inflicted wantonly and unnecessarily. In Tyre, Sidon, and Nabatieh much of the destruction was on the main street, along which most of the through traffic, including newsmen and television crews, passed. Here stood the buildings in various stages of the civil strife that preceded this war. Focusing their cameras on destroyed buildings, without showing the untouched houses nearby or even next door, the photographers and especially the electronic journalists created for the viewer an image of almost total devastation. (The badly damaged block in the center of Sidon came to be referred to by local citizens as Television Avenue.)

Much of the ruin shown originated from previous hostilities, years before the Israeli invasion. Occasionally, a tree growing out of the rubble or thick weeds covering the stones betrayed the real age of the damage, if not its origin. Less often but common enough was the misrepresentation in a photograph, such as one that appeared in the August 2, 1982, issue of *U.S. News and World Report,* showing a woman mourning at a graveside in Beirut. Only those who read Arabic could see from the date on the tombstone that the deceased had died on August 10, 1980, which was almost two years before the invasion. More publicity was given to the picture filed from Beirut of a heavily bandaged "small girl who had lost both hands." The picture was cited by President Reagan in connection with the Israeli bombardment of *West* Beirut but the Israelis located the victim, who turned out to be a boy, in *East* Beirut, i.e., in the sector held by the Christians with Israeli presence and bombarded by the PLO and the Syrians; happily, he had not lost any limbs but had suffered burns which were practically healed by the time he was found. Usually, however, there was no such explanation for the attentive reader or viewer. More often unintentionally than otherwise, the visual media gave even less balanced coverage than the written reporting.

One of the most violent and distorted reports about the war to appear in the United States was written by Jacobo Timmerman, the former Buenos Aires Jewish newspaper editor who became famous through the international campaign to release him from imprisonment by the Argentine junta. When he was freed, he moved to Israel, where he resides part of the time and where, after a brief visit to Lebanon late in June, he wrote a series of articles for *The New Yorker,* later published in book form. Typical of his reporting were the incessantly repeated assertions about "the ruins of Tyre and Sidon," the "burned and destroyed cities," "the rubble that was

139

Tyre," and the like. Israelis who read these *Reflections* were shocked by the patent falsehood of Timmerman's claims that he had witnessed such sights and by other allegations he made. They were also shocked that such a respected magazine had printed his charges although the truth of the matter was by then generally known and had already been published.

Another part of the anti-Israel impact was caused by a surprising recklessness with figures and the evaluation of the sources from which they originated. The major U.S. networks and their European counterparts spoke repeatedly of "600,000 homeless refugees" in southern Lebanon—an area the *total* population of which was 500,000. The erroneous and misleading figure was first put into circulation by correspondents stationed in Beirut; they certainly should have known it was farfetched. The International Red Cross was quoted as the source who first used the figure of 300,000; this, too, was exaggerated at least by a multiple of four, as later reports indicated. It was hardly noted that at the same time that many people abandoned their homes, more than 120,000 veteran refugees from PLO terror could, and did, at long last return from Beirut to their homes in the towns and villages of southern Lebanon.

Similarly, early reports of as many as 6,000 civilian casualties in the south were a grave exaggeration. The figures were attributed, if at all, to the "Palestinian Red Crescent," creating the impression of a reliable source, somewhat like the Red Cross. Few, if any, of the media pointed out that the Palestinian Red Crescent was an arm of the PLO headed by Dr. Fathi Arafat, brother of PLO chief Yasser Arafat.

Much of the information concerning the alleged number of victims emanated from a spokesman of WAFA, the PLO news agency, who would arrive at the Commodore Hotel the day after bombardments to show selected journalists "the damage caused by the enemy."

"The 'Lebanese Police,' so often quoted in this context, ceased to function in West Beirut early in the siege. With deadlines to meet and under the risk of falling bombs, most journalists were content with what they got," reported American novelist Kenneth R. Timmerman, who has written a book on the war in Lebanon and his experience in the prisons of the PLO.[3]

The initial cavalier attitude toward facts had begun to improve somewhat late in June, then the siege of West Beirut intensified. While the cumulative damage to some parts of the city was considerable, other sections, where the PLO was absent, did not suffer. Yet the picture relayed by most of the media was of an entire city living in hell. On August 13, 1982, the *Washington Post* without comment quoted a PLO spokesman in New York that on the previous day 42,000 shells had been fired on West Beirut. In the eleven hours of the reported shelling, that would have meant 3,800 shells per hour and 64 shells per minute, without a single interruption. Even more absurd was a report quoting a PLO communiqué (again without comment) in the August 14 *International Herald-Tribune,* that Israeli warplanes had dropped 44,000 bombs and that some 700 houses had collapsed. The Israel Air Force is reported to have some 600 fighter-bombers; even if half the entire force were to be engaged and each plane made three combat sorties, carrying four bombs on each run, it would still only add up to some 3,600 bombs, less than one-tenth the number uncritically quoted in the Western media.

A major controversy developed in the U.S. over the use of American-made cluster bombs. Israel maintained that these bombs were used only against military targets. The American press, however, reported that Israel had used the bombs in violation of U.S. laws, and the supply of this weapon was suspended. In mid-October, the *Washington Post* admitted that its source on the cluster bombs had been one Franklin Pierce Lamb, self-styled "expert" and "specialist in international law," who has been involved in previous charges of misrepresentation, dating back to March 1980, when he reportedly claimed to be a member of Senator Edward Kennedy's campaign staff and issued unauthorized statements (carried by *The New York Times*). It was the same F. P. Lamb who was the source of a widely quoted UPI dispatch that Israel had used an American "vacuum bomb" to flatten an eight-story building in West Beirut. The Pentagon afterward denied that such a bomb even existed. All this, however, did not prevent the Western press from being duped again by the same Mr. Lamb, after the Sabra and Shatilla massacres, when he sold two stories to foreign journalists. One was the photograph of a military identity card, belonging to an Israeli soldier allegedly killed in the Sabra camp, and the other a report that the bodies of three of the refugees killed in Sabra had been found booby-trapped with American cluster bombs. The Israeli Commission of Inquiry located the "dead" soldier in a military hospital, where he testified that he had lost both of his feet and all of his personal effects when his vehicle was hit miles east of those camps. Questioning Lamb directly about the alleged booby-trapped bodies, the commission elicited his answer that they had been "seen" only by one of his "assistants."

On the other hand, the media at first hardly reported the fact that Israeli troops were welcomed by the Lebanese population as the ones who would put an end to the PLO rule of terror. Seldom was it mentioned that the PLO deliberately positioned their guns and command posts among the civilian population in order to protect themselves from Israeli attack or at least to provide pictures of innocent casualties. Correspondents and free-lancers have reported that their home offices failed to use material about PLO destruction of churches, hospitals, and the like, even in cases when they purchased such photos or films. But the most distorting omission was that the fighting was rarely viewed against the framework of the seven-year-long civil war which had produced not only much of the destruction shown on the screens and in the newspapers but also the hatreds which animated relations between the various factions in Lebanon.

Even some Israeli journalists were surprised by the amount of firepower employed and the extent of destruction they encountered in southern Lebanon. They, too, often failed to distinguish between old ruins and new. But after the initial dismay, both Israel and its friends abroad, especially in the United States, began to react to the bias displayed by the media. The networks and the newspapers—again, more in America than in Europe—did have second thoughts and began to provide a more balanced coverage. Thus, when the Phalangist massacre of refugees occurred in the Sabra and Shatilla camps, most Western media were careful to distinguish between charges of Israeli negligence and Phalange participation. Still, while Prime Minister Begin was castigated for his reluctance to appoint a commission of inquiry, little, if any, attention was given to the lack of effort among the Lebanese Christians to find the culprits in their ranks.

The relationship between representatives of the free press in

Beirut and the terrorists was one of the less glorious chapters of Western journalism. Cooperative correspondents were provided not only with information and access to "sources" but also with physical protection that often seemed essential in the lawless conditions in the PLO- and Syrian-controlled areas. Those who failed to cooperate were warned and at times quickly removed by their organizations. Others were less lucky and paid with their lives.

Silencing the press with gun and dynamite is a time-tested method of the terrorists in Lebanon:

> On April 1, 1975, an explosion destroyed the offices of the weekly *Al Jamhoud*.
>
> On May 5, 1975, an explosion in the daily *Al Mouhared* destroyed the entire building.
>
> On May 20, 1975, an explosion destroyed the Sadr printing plant, which served a variety of newspapers.
>
> On August 8, 1975, the daily *Al Moustagbal* received threats that its building would be blown up. It was closed down and its offices moved to Paris.
>
> On August 26, 1975, the offices of the weekly *Al Hawadith* were set on fire and burned down; the editorial, administrative, and printing staff moved to London.
>
> In September 1976, Edouard Saab, editor-in-chief of *L'Orient du Jour* (and also the Beirut correspondent of *Le Monde* in Paris), was murdered.
>
> On March 20, 1980, Salim Lawzi, editor of *Al Hawadith,* who had returned to Lebanon from London for a family visit under a safe-conduct from Lebanese Prime Minister Salim el Huss, was kidnapped. His mutilated body was later found in a Fatah torture cellar near Beirut.
>
> On July 20, 1980, Riad Taha, president of the Beirut Publishers' Union, was shot from an ambush.
>
> On November 1, 1981, there was an explosion in the printing plant of the daily *Al Safir*.
>
> On Nobember 9, 1981, an explosion destroyed the offices of the daily *Al Liwa'a*.

The Western media, which later played up Israel's military censorship of the Lebanese invasion, very rarely hinted at this more effective form of censorship employed by the terrorists. And they refrained from telling their public how many Western correspondents whose reporting the terrorists disliked had been murdered in the preceding years: Larry Buchman, of the ABC television network; Marc Tryon, of the Free Belgium radio station; Robert Pfeffer, correspondent for Germany's *Der Spiegel* and Italy's *Unita*; Italian journalists Tony Italo and Gracielle di Faco; Sean Toolan, of ABC; and Jean Lugeau, of France's TV Number One. The eighth Western victim was Edouard Saab, listed above.

Nor did the Western press corps report the existence of terrorist prisons. Each of the fifteen organizations making up the PLO had its own prison in Beirut. When an American writer, released after being held for twenty-four days underground, approached a well-known wire service with his story, they declined to handle it for fear of putting their men in West Beirut in jeopardy.

The stick-and-carrot technique was sufficient to assure a pro-Palestinian bias in the dispatches. In 1980, for example, the *Washington Post* had published a four-part series about Lebanon. There was nothing in it about the PLO ministate and what it was doing to the people. The incredible, almost total absence of reporting about the PLO ministate in southern Lebanon seems, in retrospect, quite understandable. The story of the reign of terror against the local population and of the atrocities perpetrated against the Christians in PLO areas seldom, if ever, reached Western screens or newspapers. Israeli government circles, upon discovering the extent of the selectivity in reporting from West Beirut, claimed that some of the same old Beirut hands who had previously engaged in the conspiracy of silence about the PLO in southern Lebanon were the ones now setting the tone of the coverage about the Israeli invasion. Their tendentious reporting was a direct consequence of their earlier cover-up, the Israelis charged.

One can argue with the generalization implicit in the charges made by Zeev Chefetz, former head of the Israeli Government Press Office, in February 1982 that Western media representatives in Lebanon "fear or respect Arab terror but take for granted and abuse the freedom [of Israeli society]." However, the effects of PLO intimidation of Western journalists are indeed embarrassing. ABC's "20/20" program of July 1981, one of the most friendly to the PLO until the siege of Beirut, was prepared after the killing of ABC's Beirut correspondent in retaliation for the network's previously critical reports on PLO activities.

Nor was it coincidence that when the PLO kidnapped and threatened four Western correspondents (including representatives of the *New York Times* and the *Washington Post*), not a word about it appeared in their papers until the story was disclosed by the Israelis.

Later, when West Beirut was under Israeli attack, such attitudes were reinforced by the "Stockholm syndrome," the tendency of hostages to develop sympathy with their captors and even to defend them after liberation.

Many of the old hands stationed in Beirut, or coming in regularly to cover the PLO, did not need to be convinced by such crude methods. Kenneth Timmerman reported:

> Much more important were the direct means employed by the PLO to control the journalists present in West Beirut, and the indirect means used to intimidate them.
>
> First there was the press pass issued by WAFA with the bearer's photograph, a duplicate of which remained in WAFA's offices. Without this pass, no journalist could hope to circulate in West Beirut; caught photographing, or taking notes, he would be immediately arrested if not shot on sight.
>
> No newspaper or other medium would commit the error of sending in to West Beirut someone who had adversely reported in the past on the activities of the PLO or the Syrians, for fear of his simply disappearing. Thus a first "selection" of journalists was made by the PLO: there simply were no unfriendly journalists operating in the besieged city."[4]

Unbalanced reporting from biased sources was compounded by instances of unfair editing. Although security censorship of military information exists in many other countries, the American networks "punished" Israel for its censorship; not only did they show a "censored" sign on a black screen whenever material had been eliminated, but on many occasions they superimposed the words "Passed by Israeli censors" over the material shown. For this, there was no precedent in modern reporting. No such method was used, a few weeks earlier, with pictures from the Falklands, where British censorship was actually much tighter. Another technique, obviously misleading to the public, was to use new information as voice-over, with repeats of older film clips of spectacular violence.

Conservative commentators in the United States charged that liberals in the American press were again fighting the Vietnam War, this time their target being Israel. But Israelis were much more disturbed by the feeling, nourished by some of the terminology being used, that the Western European media were being influenced, perhaps subconsciously, by a subtle echo of traditional anti-Semitism.

Beyond the issues specific to the war and to the fact that one of the opposing sides was the Jewish state, the story of the media in the 1982 war in Lebanon has wider significance. It illustrates the invidious results when the built-in distortions of television presentation combine with the requirements of haste in electronic journalism and with a deep-rooted or newly acquired bias. Focus on the visually dramatic reinforces the loss of perspective, while the lack of time for verification supports the tendency to back whoever is considered to be the underdog.

The public relations mistakes of the Israeli government doubtless contributed to the negative image created by the media. Also, some of the probable or possible fundamental causes of the negative image, such as anti-Zionism being a latter-day version of age-old anti-Semitism (in its traditional meaning of anti-Jewish prejudice), are specific to the Israel-Arab dispute. Yet, all things considered, the resulting distortions exceeded what could be explained by specific elements. They indicate that more general causes were at work, which might reappear, under similar conditions elsewhere, and that in the aggregate, they could be characterized as factors contributing to substandard professionalism.

Analyzing the causes of Israel's confrontation with the media, one can divide them along two axes: the first separating mistakes made in good faith from those made malevolently; the second separating mistakes specifically attributable to Israel from those attributable also to other conflicts.

Among the bona fide errors attributable to Israel, one can list the cumulative impact of some of the stories that preceded the war, such as violence during the evacuation of Yamit and the clashes with Arab youths on the West Bank. One should add here the influence of the mostly anti-Begin Israeli press, read by foreign correspondents and quoted extensively abroad.

The most obvious of the malevolent causes specific to the coverage of Israel is anti-Semitism, mostly latent. It was reflected in the frequent use of matching Holocaust imagery. NBC was among the first to claim that Israel was striving for a "final solution" of the Palestine problem in Lebanon. The London *Spectator* coined the charge that Israel was "pounding the star of David into swastikas." The New York *Village Voice* described a refugee camp on the West Bank as a "concentration camp," and various media items compared the shelling of West Beirut to the destruction of the Warsaw Ghetto or even of Lidice by the Nazis. It appeared as a catharsis of accumulated hatred of the Jews that the West had always wanted to express since 1945 but never dared to.

Some of the malevolent causes may appear specifically Israel related but are, in fact, universally applicable. Expensive pro-Arab (or pro-PLO) advertisements in the American press, less disguised than in the campaign waged in 1981 in favor of selling AWACS planes to Saudi Arabia, were in this case directed against Israel; but the same petrodollar effort may tomorrow be directed against Western interests. The commentary on and treatment of the news from Lebanon in the American media showed clear State Department orientation, not to say influence, which, similarly, one day could just as well be directed against, say, France, Turkey, or Japan.

Many of the journalists were still operating under the Vietnam syndrome of suspecting everything official and believing almost anything that came from those whom they identified as the underdog. After Vietnam and Watergate were disposed of, new traditionally respectable targets were needed; Israel fitted the bill perfectly.

Perhaps the most disturbing manifestation of this form of journalism is the use of a double standard in evaluating the behavior of the two opposing sides. It may sound flattering that the West expects much higher moral standards of behavior from Israel than it does from the Syrians or the PLO. But is such an expectation

147

legitimate? Does not the setting up of very high criteria ensure that those measured against them will fail? Do not double standards automatically give license to the less moral to behave less morally?

Is it not reminiscent of the double standards often used by Western media in measuring Soviet and Third World behavior as against that of the West? These are not just philosophical questions. As in the case of Israel, the double standard, even if dressed in complimentary justifying language, actually serves those who act in accordance with lower standards.

The most universal implications of Israel's media experiences in Lebanon stem from the consequences of modern mass-communication reporting from an open society. There were no restrictions on the number of newsmen who rushed in to Israel to cover the war. Every public figure in the country was approachable, and after brief initial hurdles the war zone was, practically speaking, wide open to the press.

Consequently, some of the reporting suffered from a lack of professional standards and expertise. Approximately 1,500 journalists came and went in the three months of active warfare. (In comparison, in the entire Soviet Union there are only about twenty-six accredited American correspondents and about the same number of other Western correspondents.) Some correspondents stayed for several weeks, but most spent only a few days in the region. A few were old Middle East hands, but for many others, it was their first assignment in the area. This accounted for their lack of background knowledge, their superficiality, and the unusual credulity displayed by a great many of them. It probably was no coincidence that veteran reporters and commentators were considerably more restrained in chastising Israel. Similarly, by and large correspondents who had served in the Soviet Union or in Southeast Asia and who had experience with the press restrictions of totalitarian regimes, on the one hand, and the sufferings caused by war and terror, on the other, were the most careful to check their facts and their emotions when reporting from Lebanon.

The ignorance of the newcomers and the bad conscience over their past silence of the old Beirut hands perhaps explains the fact that while Israeli military censorship was emphasized constantly, the "censorship of exclusion" practiced in PLO-controlled areas, though much more effective, was left practically unmentioned. With a little cheating, every reporter could easily avoid Israeli censorship, and many did. But, as in the Soviet Union or Red China, very few correspondents in PLO-controlled areas dared go where the authorities did not want them to go nor did they see what officials did not want them to see.

This is particularly important in our age of electronic journalism. Unlike the newspaperman or even the radio correspondent who reports his observations and conclusions (the differences between the two still being observed by many), television reporters can film—and their audience can see—only where the authorities enable them to set up their bulky equipment. Nobody filmed the thousands of victims of Syrian vengeance in the city of Hama in February 1982, when President Hafez al-Hassad destroyed all the mosques in the city center and ordered not only the killing of rebel Moslem Brotherhood members but also of thousands of innocent civilians. Nor has anyone filmed the two million people or so living in the *gulags* of Communist China, or the tens of thousands killed in the Iraq-Iran war. The rulers of Damascus, Peking, Baghdad, and Teheran simply do not permit journalists to roam about their countryside, carrying cameras. In the electronic age, free societies are thus confronted with a crucial dilemma: restrict the freedom of the press or help distort the balance of perception in favor of the totalitarians who do not allow the world to see the facts.

Never before have viewers in every corner of the world been able to receive such a stream of images direct from the battlefield "where it happens, when it happens" as they did during the war in Lebanon. Never before has this immediacy created so many distortions and potentially long-lasting political consequences. With the new communications technologies, this represents additional potential for manipulating public opinion and limiting its independence of judgment.

It is not only the general public which is thus superficially impressed. Secretary of State George Shultz remarked during the siege of Beirut that "the administration has seen the pictures and has been affected by them." Thus, we come close to completing the vicious circle: a retired film actor, elected president with the help of the visual art of electronics, is making his decisions on the basis of what he is shown (or not shown) by the electronic media. What is seen on the TV screen exists for decision-making purposes; what is not seen may or may not exist.

It raises some crucial questions: Are the democracies being disarmed by their natural revulsion for images of war in their living rooms? Can an open society, any open society, wage a just but protracted war in an age of instant electronic media, or is this ultimate instrument of politics now reserved for dictatorships? Was the Lebanese war the last in which the electronic media were allowed to watch and report fully and freely?

10

The Longest Night

Nobody supposes that the State of Israel is, or can be expected to be perfect. Some see it, none the less, as "the start of the beginning of salvation." And then came Lebanon. The shock expressed by Jews worldwide was not just one of human decency, nor its effect merely a temporary rift with Jewry. This was also a religious shock. Because, although Jews have recently made this complaint, it is not really the rest of the world that applies higher standards to Israel, but Jewry itself.

— The Economist[1]

THERE was a certain inevitability as the tragedies of the wars of the Palestinians, the Lebanese, and the Israelis suddenly fused in the cruelty of the Phalangist massacre of residents of the Sabra and Shatilla camps in Beirut, shattering the long hours from early Thursday, September 16, to Saturday, September 18. For the Palestinians it was the culmination of the long tragedy of defenseless official "refugee" status and of protection and domination by the PLO. For the Lebanese it was the tragedy of hatred and lack of self-restraint that had led them into the bloody civil war, losing control over their own country and destiny. For the Israelis it demonstrated the consequences of domination over others and its insidious impact on the values of the nation.

The events in Sabra and Shatilla were not the first massacre in the seven years of civil war in Lebanon. In January 1976 the Christian city of Damour was captured and destroyed by Palestinian terrorists who slaughtered many of its civilian population. (Damour subsequently became one of the main bases of the PLO.) In August 1976 the Christian forces captured the refugee camp of Tel el-Za'ater in Beirut, which was one of the major Palestinian terrorist strongholds in Lebanon. Thousands of Palestinians were butchered then. Other massacres followed on both sides of the amorphous and shifting front line. The strategy of the Palestinian terrorists, organizing and entrenching themselves in the civilian population, both in the camps and in certain sectors of many Lebanese towns and cities, contributed significantly to the high number of noncombatant victims of the civil wars and of the Israeli attacks on the terrorists. The number of victims of the various hostilities has been estimated at some 100,000 killed, most of them civilians, including women and children.

The events leading directly to the massacre in Sabra and Shatilla began in the afternoon of Tuesday, September 14, 1982, at the headquarters of the Phalangists in the Ashrafiah suburb of Beirut. There, president-elect and Phalangist chief Bashir Gemayel was in conference with top leaders of his organization. A huge quantity of explosives—planted, according to most assumptions—by Syrian-inspired and -financed elements, suddenly ripped through the building, destroying several floors and burying Bashir Gemayel and some two dozen of his followers under the rubble. The U.S. marines and the French and Italian troops who had come to Lebanon in the third week of August to help stabilize the atmosphere and maintain some order while the PLO and the Syrian troops moved out of West Beirut had already embarked for home. In a conference between Defense Minister Sharon and Chief of Staff Eitan, the dispatch of Phalangist units, rather than Israelis, to clean the refugee camps of PLO terrorists was among the decisions taken. Shortly before midnight, the death of Bashir Gemayel was confirmed and Sharon received Begin's final approval for Israeli troops to move into West Beirut, on the pretext of ensuring that a semblance of law and order be maintained.

On Wednesday, September 15, the Israeli soldiers under the

command of Brigadier General Amos Yaron completed their occupation of West Beirut, but they quite clearly made a point of not entering the refugee camps. Major General Amir Drori, in charge of the Northern Command, tried in vain to persuade the Lebanese regular army to move into the camps.

On Thursday, September 16, the commander of Israeli troops in Beirut met with the head of the Phalangists for a final discussion about the entry of the Phalange into the two camps. At 6 P.M., the Lebanese Phalangist forces moved in, and at 7:30 P.M., an hour and a half later, the Israeli cabinet was informed of the action. Half an hour after that, Israeli soldiers listening in on the Kataeb radio first heard remarks indicating that there were civilian victims of the action against the terrorists in the camps.

Early on the morning of Friday, September 17, Israelis learned from reports by Phalangist officers in the camps that about 300 people "including terrorists and civilians" had been killed. The information reached General Drori, who ordered General Yaron to stop any further movement of the Lebanese inside the camps. He again tried to convince the Lebanese regular army command to send its troops into the camps, but to no avail. In the afternoon, Chief of Staff Eitan visited Phalangist headquarters in Beirut and authorized them to continue mop-up operations in the camps until 5 A.M. the next morning. Between 8 and 9 P.M., Eitan phoned Sharon to say that "the Christians have gone too far" in their action.

Early Saturday morning, September 18, the Phalangists entered the Gaza Hospital and evacuated the foreign medical personnel who, on their way out, saw many corpses in the streets. General Yaron, informed that the Kataeb were still in the camps, ordered them to leave immediately. They complied. In the afternoon, foreign journalists in Beirut heard of the events and the BBC carried the first report of the massacre. In the evening a shocked Israeli public heard from the radio for the first time what had happened in Sabra and Shatilla.

The Jewish New Year occurred the weekend beginning Friday afternoon, September 17, through Sunday evening, September 19. All businesses, public offices, and newspapers in Israel were closed, and radio and television were being manned by a skeleton staff. Yet

153

as early as Friday morning, in Tel Aviv, Zeev Schiff, military editor of *Ha'aretz,* Israel's leading daily paper, received a telephone call from one of his informants that "there was killing in the refugee camps in Beirut." Shortly afterward, he had a meeting with Communications Minister (former deputy minister of defense) Mordechai Zipori and informed him of the disquieting reports. Zipori tried to call the chief of Military Intelligence, Major General Yehoshua Saguy, but could not locate him and spoke instead to Foreign Minister Yitzhak Shamir, who he knew was due to confer later in the morning with Defense Minister Sharon and U.S. special envoy Morris Draper. Shamir failed to inquire about or follow up on the information. On Friday evening, Ron Ben Yishai, the military correspondent of Israel Television, called Sharon at his home and asked him about rumors of a Phalangist massacre in Sabra and Shatilla. Sharon replied that he had heard the rumors but he failed to add anything; he, too, apparently, took no action.

And so it was only on Saturday afternoon, from the BBC broadcast, that Prime Minister Begin first learned of the consequences of General Sharon's decision to send the Phalangists to clean out the nests of terrorists in the refugee camps. Sunday was still a holiday but foreign and domestic TV and radio reports of the massacre were the only topic being discussed in thousands of synagogues and homes throughout the country. On Monday, horrified editorials in all the morning papers called for an immediate investigation. Public pressure began to build, demanding the establishment of a full commission of inquiry to look into Israel's possible responsibility for not preventing the tragedy. The prime minister rejected the demands, stating in a righteous manner that, as in earlier waves of anti-Semitism, "Gentiles kill Gentiles and the Jews are blamed." The remark was echoed in considerable sections of the Israeli public, especially when it later became apparent that the media abroad focused their denunciations more on Israel than on the Christian Lebanese who had actually perpetrated the atrocity against the Palestinians.

As more details—and pictures—of the events reached the public, pressure mounted for the establishment of an inquiry commission. A call by a large group of law professors was followed by a strong plea from Professor Ephraim Urbach, a leading biblical scholar and president of the Israel Academy of Sciences; there were demonstrations in the streets of Tel Aviv and Jerusalem. Ultimately, President Yitzhak Navon made a television appearance urging "a full and authoritative inquiry." Giving ground reluctantly, the prime minister suggested a governmental inquiry (which would not have had subpoena and other judicial authority) and announced that he had asked Chief Justice Yitzhak Kahan to undertake such an investigation. To Begin's embarrassment Justice Kahan declined.

The following night, on the eve of the weekly cabinet meeting, an estimated 400,000 people—more than 10 percent of the population of the country—assembled in Tel Aviv's main square and demanded a full judicial inquiry. In its size and structure, it was a demonstration unprecedented in the history of Israel, and it convinced several members of Begin's government to join the pressure on the Likud leader to agree to set up a commission of inquiry. The next day the prime minister gave in and on September 28, 1982, ten days after the massacre, a commission was constituted, consisting of Chief Justice Kahan, Supreme Court Justice Aharon Barak, and Major General (Reserve) Yona Efrat.

It was an impressive team with impeccable credentials from every point of view. Justice Kahan was not only the president of the supreme court of the land but also an observant Jew of highly traditional views, coming from an Orthodox rabbinical family. Due to retire in 1983 after decades of service on the bench, he was unknown to the general public but well respected in his profession. Justice Barak, much younger, had proved his lack of bias when, as attorney general early in 1977, he went ahead with the prosecution of the wife of then prime minister Yitzhak Rabin for illegal possession of a bank account in America, thus bringing about her husband's resignation. Both Prime Minister Begin and President Jimmy Carter were impressed by Barak's contribution to the successful culmination of the Camp David negotiations in the fall of 1978. Shortly afterward he was appointed to the supreme court. Reserve Major General Yona Efrat had a distinguished record; he had served on various military commissions and enjoyed the respect of the top echelons of the officer corps.

Meeting in a building set aside for the purpose on the campus of

155

the Hebrew University in Jerusalem, the commission heard testimony from 60 persons and visited Beirut, while its staff of lawyers and investigators took 180 statements from another 163 witnesses. The principal figures investigated, including the prime minister and the ministers of defense and foreign affairs, as well as the chief of staff and several of his top generals, appeared in open session, while others were interrogated by the staff. Some of the testimony was given *in camera,* to protect sensitive security matters.

Although there were indications leading the general public to expect that the report of the commission would be tough, when it was finally published early in February 1983 its severity impressed all Israelis. The report stated unequivocally that the massacre had been perpetrated by Lebanese Phalangist forces and that no Israelis had either participated in or been directly responsible for the crime. But it stated with equal definitiveness that Israel, as the power in control of the camps at the time, bore the indirect responsibility of not having prevented the tragedy.

In the long run, the most important section of the report, also likely to have a lasting impact in other civilized democracies, deals not with personalities but with principles; with the indirect responsibility of an occupying power that must not only abstain from acts against the civilian population but is also obliged to prevent others from committing such crimes in the area under its control:

> If it indeed becomes clear that those who decided on the entry of the Phalangists into the camps should have foreseen . . . that there was danger of a massacre and no steps were taken which might have prevented this danger or at least greatly reduced the possibility that deeds of this type might be done, then those who made the decisions and those who implemented them are indirectly responsible for what ultimately occurred, even if they did not intend this to happen and merely disregarded the anticipated danger. A similar indirect responsibility also falls on those who knew of the decision; it was their duty, by virtue of their position and their office, to warn of the danger and they did not fulfil this duty. It is also not possible to absolve of such indirect responsibility those persons who, when they received the first reports of what was happening in the camps, did not rush to prevent the continuation of the Phalangist actions and did not do everything in their power to stop them.

> We concur that special caution is required so as not to fall into the hindsight trap, but that caution does not exempt us from the obligation to examine whether persons acting and thinking rationally were duty bound, when the decision was taken to have the Phalangists enter the camps, to foresee, according to the information each of them possessed and according to public knowledge, that the entry of the Phalangists into the camps held out the danger of a massacre and that no small possibility existed that it would in fact occur.[2]

This is the central moral and normative message of the commission's report. It set out new rules for combatants and occupying powers that in the past were not codified. It establishes the obligation of the occupying power: (1) to foresee danger to civilian population; (2) to warn of the danger; and (3) to act to prevent it or reduce the possibility of its happening. Moreover, the criterion of the responsibility of the occupying power's obligations is not only actual specific information in his possession, but also public knowledge of the existing danger.

The ten main chapters of the report,* which were published in the *Jerusalem Post* and *The New York Times,* commence with a detailed description of the events immediately preceding and following the assassination of Lebanese president-elect Bashir Gemayel. The longest chapter is devoted to an elucidation of events in the camps from the time the Phalangists entered on the evening of Thursday, September 16, until their evacuation on Saturday, September 18, in the early morning. The report leaves no doubt that it was Defense Minister Sharon's decision to send in the Phalangist militias to clean out the terrorists who were hiding in the camps, having stayed behind in Beirut in contravention of the agreement for the complete evacuation of all PLO combatants. Sharon was motivated not only by his desire to keep Israeli forces out of the camps—to save lives—but also by his wish to respond to criticism inside Israel that the Phalangists were shirking their share in the fighting in Lebanon.

Although Israel authorities made repeated efforts to convince the commanders of the Lebanese regular army, instead of the Kataeb, to

---

*About ten pages, dealing with confidential intelligence matters, were not released for publication.

move into the camps, the Lebanese government, presumably acting under American advice not to talk to the Israelis, refused.

The report also shows that some of the Israeli officers stationed outside the camps had grave suspicions, as early as Thursday night, that something had gone wrong with the Phalangist operation, but that they did not know the extent of the killings. Yet neither they nor their superiors acted then to get the Lebanese forces out of the camps.

The report hints that the commission was in doubt concerning the truth of parts of the testimony given by Foreign Minister Shamir, Chief of Staff Eitan, and intelligence chief Saguy, but apparently did not have sufficient proof to indict them for perjury.

On the institutional level, the report reveals that Defense Minister Sharon took vital decisions on his own, without consulting the prime minister, and that he gained Begin's or the government's approval only *after* events had been set in motion. Nor, according to the report, did Sharon hurry to inform the prime minister of results. For his part, Begin's attention to essential matters appears to have been inadequate. Concerning these three critical days in September, the commission, in its findings, lends credence to the Opposition's charges of improper functioning on the part of the cabinet during the initial stages of the Lebanon war.

Nine of the Israeli leadership in charge during the three critical days were earlier warned, as required by law, that the commission might find against them. Of the nine, two were, in the end, not faulted: Sharon's personal assistant Avi Dudai and the head of the Mossad (Secret Service). Three more were severely criticized but no recommendations were made against them. Thus Major General Drori of the Northern Command had reported by telephone to Chief of Staff Eitan that "the Phalangists have gone too far," had ordered the cessation of Phalangist activities in the camps, and had repeatedly asked the Lebanese regular army to move in. But when the chief of staff arrived in Beirut, Drori did not sufficiently stress the gravity of the situation to him. Nor, the report found, as was his duty as the area commander, did he oppose General Eitan's decision to permit the Phalangists to stay in the camp for another day. Balancing what Drori did correctly with the points where he was at fault, the commission found it sufficient to define his degree of responsibility without recommending further action.

Foreign Minister Shamir was blamed for failing to take seriously the information he received from Communications Minister Zipori about the reports of killings in the camps. But the commission gave him the benefit of the doubt concerning his assertion that, over the telephone, he heard the word "unruliness" and not "slaughter."

Nor were steps recommended by the commission against Prime Minister Begin, who, they found, "was not a party to the decision to have the Phalangists move into the camps." His overall behavior in the affair, however, was severely censured. "We are unable to accept the Prime Minister's remarks that he was absolutely unaware of [the] danger to the civilians in the camps," stated the report. "We are unable to accept the position of the Prime Minister that no one imagined that what happened could have happened." The commission, however, noted "the rosy reports" Begin had received from Sharon and Eitan indicating that everything was proceeding smoothly in West Beirut. Yet,

> We find no reason to exempt the Prime Minister from responsibility for not having evinced . . . any interest in the Phalangist actions in the camps. . . . It may be assumed that a manifestation of interest by him . . . would have increased the alertness of the Defense Minister and the Chief of Staff to the need to take appropriate measures to meet the expected danger.[3]

More than specific charges relating to the massacre, it was the general picture of lack of interest, lack of attention, and lack of control over crucial events that was the most damaging aspect of the sections dealing with the prime minister.

The most severe criticisms in the report were directed at the minister of defense and three officers: Brigadier General Amos Yaron, division commander in the Sabra and Shatilla sections of Beirut; Major General Yehoshua Saguy, chief of Military Intelligence; and Chief of Staff General Rafael Eitan.

The report stated that General Yaron had heard that "the Phalangists were perpetrating acts of killing which went beyond combat operations and were killing women and children as well," but he did not pass on this information to his superiors.

> A number of times, Brigadier General Yaron approached the Phalangist officers who were in the forward command post, including one of their veteran leaders, Eli Hobeika, and repeated the admonition not to do harm to women and children; but other than this he did not take any initiative and only suggested that the Phalangists be ordered not to advance. . . . [That] did not ensure an end to the killing.[4]

Some of the harshest words of the commission were reserved for chief of Intelligence Saguy. That was although, or rather because, he and Military Intelligence in general had in the past opposed close operation with the Lebanese forces. Intelligence had considered the Phalangists undisciplined, unreliable, and unwilling to get involved in any serious fighting. Defense Minister Sharon, however, had disregarded this evaluation and relied on that of the Mossad, who cooperated closely with the Phalangists. As a result Saguy, instead of redoubling his efforts to warn the minister of his suspicions, reacted by simply stepping aside, acting as an insulted party. "The fear that his words would not receive sufficient attention does not justify total inaction. This inaction constitutes breach of duty,"[5] the report stated, and recommended that Saguy be relieved of his post.

Chief of Staff Eitan was viewed by the commission as a partner in Sharon's decision to send the Phalangists into the camps. "Even if the experts did not fulfill their obligation [to warn against the Phalangist entry], this does not absolve the Chief of Staff of responsibility." In one of the most stinging sentences, the report says that "the Chief of Staff ignored this danger [to the civilian population] out of an awareness that there were great advantages to sending the Phalangists into the camps and perhaps also out of hope that in the final analysis, the Phalangist excesses would not be on a large scale. . . ." Moreover, after General Drori issued an order to halt the advance of the Phalangists because of reports of the killings, "not only did the Chief of Staff not raise the subject of the Phalangists' behavior when he met their leaders afterward . . . but expressed satisfaction with the Phalangist operation." As a result, "the Phalangist commanders could have gotten the impression . . . that no reports of the excesses had reached the Israel Defense Forces—and if they had reached the IDF, they had not aroused any sharp reaction." General Eitan's behavior constituted "a breach of duty and a dereliction of duty incumbent upon the Chief of Staff," the commission stated, adding that only because he was due to complete his term of service two months later (in April 1983), recommending his removal would not have been "of practical significance."[6]

Finally, Defense Minister Ariel Sharon was found responsible for "having disregarded the danger of acts of vengeance and bloodshed by the Phalangists against the population of the refugee camps, and having failed to take this danger into account when he decided to have the Phalangists enter the camps. In addition, responsibility is to be imputed to the Minister of Defense for not ordering appropriate measures for preventing or reducing the danger of massacre. . . . These blunders constitute the nonfulfilment of a duty. . . ." Consequently,

> The Minister of Defense bears personal responsibility. In our opinion, it is fitting that the Minister of Defense draw the appropriate personal conclusions . . . and if necessary the Prime Minister consider whether he should exercise his authority . . . according to which, the Prime Minister may, after informing the Cabinet of his intention to do so, remove a Minister from office.[7]

These recommendations became the center of the political storm that broke in Israel immediately after the publication of the report.

In the war that had mushroomed out of proportion and beyond control, Sabra and Shatilla was a calamity. Of the three peoples concerned—the Palestinians, the Lebanese, and the Israelis—only the last and the least involved has dared so far, to make a public reckoning. In the aftermath, Begin's coalition government survived three no-confidence motions in the Knesset with a safe margin and public opinion polls showed that, if new elections were held after the report was published, the Likud alliance would have been reelected with a respectable majority. Indeed, the polls indicated that even if retiring president Yitzhak Navon had headed the Labor list, as many opponents of Begin had hoped and expected, Labor would have had a very hard time supplanting the Likud.

Yet beyond the superficial familiarity, after the publication of the Inquiry Commission Report, the political landscape had changed and tremors continued to shake Israel.

The commission, doubtless drawing on its knowledge of Defense Minister Sharon and his testimony before their body, had clearly stated that if he did not act as they recommended, the prime minister should consider applying Article 21 of the Basic Law to remove him. While the cabinet was still discussing the matter, Sharon went to a meeting of the General Staff of the Israel Defense Forces and initiated talk of the commission's report. He then proceeded to the cabinet and told his colleagues about the "bitterness" in the General Staff at the commission's recommendations (a representation that was misleading as far as Sharon's removal was concerned). Sharon's bull-in-a-china-shop manner was obviously intended to convince the cabinet that the army was against the recommendations. "There was a whiff of 'putsch' in the air," Interior Minister Yosef Burg said at the third consecutive cabinet meeting held "to discuss the implementations of the commission's report" and, specifically, how to deal with Sharon's refusal to follow the recommendation that he resign. Finally, dramatically, in February the cabinet resolved—sixteen in favor, with only one member (Sharon) voting against—to remove Ariel Sharon from the Defense Ministry; he officially vacated that office three days later.

11

The Consensus That Disappeared

THE war in Lebanon was the first of the six wars waged by Israel in its thirty-four years of independence that did not enjoy the support of an overwhelming majority of the population. This was also the first war that was not forced on Israel directly; Israel was not under any immediate threat but initiated the war. The first departure clearly stems from the second.

In 1948, forces from the five neighboring Arab states (including Iraq), augmented by troops from more distant countries, invaded Israel even before independence was formally declared; Israel's survival depended on winning the war. In 1956, the Arabs openly declared that the Fedayin raids from the Egyptian-held Gaza Strip—raids that terrorized towns and villages in southern Israel—were the prelude to the "liberation of Arab Palestine." The Six Day War in 1967 was forced upon Israel when Egypt expelled the United Nations troops from Sinai, blockaded the Straits of Tiran, and massed a huge army in Sinai, poised for attack at any moment. The 1969–1970 war of attrition, initiated from across the Suez Canal, was for a long period purely defensive—before Israel went on the offensive against Egypt. In the Yom Kippur War, launched by Egypt and Syria on the most sacred of Jewish holy days, every Israeli knew that the very existence of the nation was at stake.

The atmosphere was different in the 1982 war in Lebanon. The immediate threat of hostilities came in the summer of 1981, when PLO artillery and Katyusha rocket attacks on Kiryat Shmona, Nahariya, and several other border settlements and kibbutzim brought Israel close to launching a big retaliatory operation. The intervention of U.S. Special Ambassador Philip Habib defused the immediate threat of a clash and the PLO abstained from further attacks on towns and settlements in northern Israel. It was, however, clear to all that Defense Minister Sharon and Chief of Staff Eitan believed that the PLO menace in southern Lebanon required "fundamental treatment" and were pressing the cabinet to approve an attack to eliminate their presence. The Israeli press and several Labor party leaders repeatedly warned the government against initiating the war, and the cabinet several times actually voted down both Sharon's "big" and "small" campaign plans. The strength and extent of the objections to Sharon's war plans, which were public knowledge by then, left little doubt that the Israeli public was, for the first time, split almost down the middle on this issue.

On June 4, 1982, Israel bombed PLO targets in Lebanon in retaliation for the shooting of Israel's ambassador to Britain the day before. When the PLO responded with a broad artillery and rocket barrage on towns and settlements in western and northern Galilee, the cabinet finally gave the green light to Sharon to start his "small" campaign. Prime Minister Menachem Begin announced that the purpose of the operation was limited to a 40-kilometer-wide stretch north of Israel's border with Lebanon, so as to push the PLO to a distance from which even long-range guns could not hit Israeli targets. When the Israeli tanks were already on their way, Begin called in the leaders of the Opposition and told them of the operation. At that time, they gave their support and, under the impact of the preceding PLO bombardment, there was also near-unanimous approval on the part of the public.

In a speech delivered in August 1982, the prime minister expounded on the philosophy behind the war in Lebanon to officers at the Staff and Command College of the Israel Defense Forces. Stating that World War II and its 30 to 40 million victims could have been prevented had France and Russia not waited until it became a "war of no choice," Begin drew analogies for Israel. Of the six wars

Israel had to fight in its thirty-four years of renewed independence, three were forced upon it: the 1948 War of Liberation, the 1970 war of attrition (along the Suez Canal), and the 1973 Yom Kippur War. These, Begin asserted, cost the highest casualties. In the 1956 Suez campaign and the 1967 Six Day War, Israel had the choice of avoiding the war but risking the continuation of Fedayin attacks or the closure of the Gulf of Aqaba. "Similarly," he said, "Operation Peace for Galilee does not belong to the group of unavoidable wars. We could have continued to watch our citizens hit in Metullah, Kiryat Shmona, and Nahariya ... [and] see explosives placed in bus stations and supermarkets. . . . [To do so] one would have had to accept the continued killing of our citizens. . . ."

Begin went on to state that "there is no obligation to wage war only when there is no choice. There is no moral commandment which says that a people must or may fight only when their back is to the sea or at the brink of a precipice. Such war can lead to disaster, if not to a holocaust." He continued: "A free, sovereign, peace-loving nation which hates war and cares about security must create conditions in which war, if it becomes necessary, should not be a 'war of no alternative.' The conditions must be such—and their creation depends on human wisdom and action—that one should emerge from war to victory with the least possible casualties."

Despite the ringing words, in 1982 there was no national consensus on such a philosophy or policy. And whether purposely or not, it seems in retrospect that both Begin and his defense minister, Ariel Sharon, misled both their own cabinet and the Israeli public as well as Israel's friends, including the United States. Chief of Staff Rafael Eitan later declared several times that he and the army never received any instructions to limit their advance to 40 or 45 kilometers (25-28 miles). Later, it became evident that Sharon had, in fact, never briefed his cabinet colleagues about the targets he had in mind nor on the nature and extent of the operations that they were, at times retroactively, approving. On the fundamental issues of the war Begin usually shared Sharon's aims and intentions clearly, even if it was convenient for him to leave the burden of responsibility on Sharon's shoulders. On several occasions, as he admitted in public, Begin himself learned of Sharon's decisions after they had been put into effect.

165

The purpose of the repeated deceptions seems to have been to obtain cabinet endorsement for the operation and to minimize domestic and foreign opposition or criticism. It soon had quite the opposite effect. As long as the troops operated within the 45-kilometer zone, the domestic consensus in support of the operation held fairly firm and the reaction of Western governments and public opinion was understanding and moderate. The operation was perceived as an act of self-defense, even though perhaps somewhat excessive. When, however, the troops moved further north (which happened to coincide with the appearance of the pictures of destruction in Tyre and Sidon), there was an angry backlash. Israeli public opinion split between a dwindling majority who continued to support the government in its expansion of the war and a growing minority who opposed it firmly. In the foreign media, the discovery that the Israeli government had not told the full truth became both an instrument and a justification for increased attacks on Israel.

Initially, domestic criticism focused on the damage caused in Tyre and Sidon. Like the foreign newsmen, Israeli civilians entered southern Lebanon along with the many thousands of soldiers; many of these saw only the ruins along several main streets. Failing to realize that much of the devastation was the work of seven years of civil war, they were deeply shocked by what they saw. The impressions they brought back to Israel seemed to corroborate what most had seen on television, pictures that also focused on ruins; undamaged buildings are not news. At this stage, curious divisions appeared in Israeli public opinion. On the one hand there was a rift between supporters of the government and its opponents over the question of whether excessive firepower was being employed by the army, causing unnecessary bloodshed and damage among the civilian population. On the other hand, as reports of the exaggerated and hostile coverage in the foreign media became known, even the strongest critics of the war were pushed into defending the government against unfair attacks which more than occasionally evoked suspicions of traditional anti-Semitism.

Criticism in the country deepened as the advancing Israeli soldiers encountered the Syrian troops in eastern Lebanon. The newspapers voiced the suspicion that Defense Minister Sharon was deliberately seeking confrontation with the Syrians. His aim, critics said, was to provoke a full-scale confrontation that would provide an opportunity to effectively smash the Syrian war machine, so that they would not threaten Israel during the remainder of the 1980s. Opponents warned of the unnecessary escalation and of the threat of Soviet intervention to aid their Syrian allies, and saw in the development yet another example of Sharon's recklessness and irresponsibility.

Government partisans claimed that "clipping the wings of Damascus" was the most important part of the war and that it would also benefit the West politically and militarily. It would hurt Soviet prestige and enable the testing of Western weapons against Soviet ones—and the rewards for Israel from a grateful West should not be far behind. When, instead, Western and even American criticism mounted, there was surprise and dismay. Sharon and some Likud proponents tried to deflect it by creating sentiment that some would call anti-American. That became another element in the vocal domestic debate. As the war continued and the area under Israeli occupation expanded, the division between segments of the Israeli public deepened.

By this time only a trace remained of the initial public agreement about the war. When advancing Israeli forces cut the Beirut-Damascus highway, professional military criticism joined that of the press and the Opposition, saying that the isolation of West Beirut was a mistake because it closed the Syrian and PLO option for a discreet, quiet withdrawal.

Public airing of this issue, in the midst of the war, was typical of the way military questions were freely debated by the Israeli press and public. It recharged the passionate arguments over the political and moral implications and consequences of this war. Israeli television, although run by a government-appointed director general of broadcasting services and controlled by a government-appointed board, played a major role in the free discussion. Again and again, prime-time audiences witnessed vigorous debates among soldiers on the front, sitting in the shadow of their tanks and arguing about the purposes and conduct of the war.

These televised minidebates, and their parallel among the public back home, climaxed over the case of Colonel Eli Geva. Geva, at

167

thirty-two the youngest officer to command a brigade in the Israeli Defense Forces, was the son of a retired general who served on the General Staff of the IDF, as well as the brother of a highly decorated tank officer who was severely wounded during the Yom Kippur War. He headed the brigade that was blockading the PLO forces in West Beirut from the south. After six weeks at the front, Colonel Geva asked the chief of staff to relieve him of his duties, explaining that, if the order came to lead his tanks into West Beirut, he would not be able to do so in good conscience. He believed that his own troops and the city's civilian population probably would suffer very heavy casualties and he did not believe that such an offensive would help defeat the PLO. To prove that he was not shirking his duty and because he hated the idea of abandoning his comrades and men on the eve of possible battle, he asked to serve as a tank commander in one of his battalions. First the chief of staff and ultimately Prime Minister Begin himself tried to dissuade Geva, but the young officer refused to change his mind. At that point, an angry Begin ordered that Geva's alternative request, to quit the army altogether, be granted.

Few questioned Eli Geva's personal courage. He was an impressive officer whose performance in the initial stages of the fighting had been outstanding—and he did not oppose the Lebanese war as a whole. He had a promising military career ahead of him, with the way open to the highest rank. He gave it up for his convictions and was respected for it by some Israelis, but not all. Many on the left praised Geva's position but others were critical. As former chief of staff (and present secretary general of the Opposition Labor party) retired general Haim Bar Lev put it, it is inconceivable that an individual officer should have the privilege of choosing which mission to undertake and which to be excused from—especially in a democratic country ruled by a freely elected government. This, essentially, was the view shared by the majority of Israelis, including soldiers and officers.

The Geva case generated a major national debate which, the merits of the arguments aside, says much about the health of Israel's democracy. It is hard to think of any other country where the prime minister and the chief of staff would spend hours with a young colonel, trying to persuade him of the moral and political correctness of government policy. Nor is there any other country which, in wartime, would publicize such a confrontation and the failure of top leaders to convince their subordinate. Most of all, in no other country would the army organize open talks among soldiers to debate whether a recalcitrant colonel was right or wrong—and let the television broadcast some of the give-and-take to the whole nation. In the controversial atmosphere of mid-1982, this was an important reminder that, after all, even among democratic nations, Israel remains a very special society, with a very different army.

Israel remains a "people's army," composed in wartime mostly of reservists. The debates on the front line echo those at home and vice versa. Thus, when the siege of West Beirut began in earnest, with hundreds of bombs and shells falling on PLO strongholds scattered among the civilian buildings, the controversy inside Israel deepened. Even though Israeli television did not show the full extent of the devastation and the horror (for example, the consequences of the use of phosphorous bombs), the debate sharpened and frequently focused on the crux of the moral issue: Was the suffering of the civilians justifiable by the fact that the PLO used them as captives and hostages, human shields for their mortars, guns, tanks and antiaircraft betteries? Should bombing be avoided—even though, without this "softening up," Israeli troops would sustain much heavier casualties storming West Beirut?

The Geva case, while it attracted the most attention, was not the only example of soul-searching in unexpected places. Another of the young critics was Avraham Burg, son of Minister of the Interior and Police Joseph Burg. The father is a senior political leader and Begin's trusted spokesman in the deadlocked Palestine autonomy talks. Avraham Burg has become one of the top leaders of the reserve soldiers' protest movement against the war in Lebanon and was one of those wounded in February 1983 in a hand-grenade attack on anti-Sharon demonstrators. The twenty-eight-year-old Burg wears a knitted skullcap, the hallmark of the religious Zionist intelligentsia, generally considered to be one of the mainstays of the nationalist movement. Brought about by the war in Lebanon, the ferment created among the cream of religious Zionist youth is one of the more interesting and significant of domestic developments. Most of them do their army service together, in units where military training is, in peacetime, combined with Talmud study. It happened that there were a large number of such young men in the tank units that suffered a disproportionately high share of casualties. What they saw in Lebanon, among their own and among the refugees, suddenly gave a direct, personal, and different meaning to such tenets as keeping the West Bank at any cost. The quiet ferment among numbers of the young generation reinforced the growing suspicions of some of the doves among their elders in the National Religious party that participation in Begin's coalition was not only ideologically wrong but also a political mistake.

Opposition to the Government's Lebanon policies acquired entirely new dimensions after the Phalangist killing of Palestinians in the Sabra and Shatilla camps. President Yitzhak Navon, whose constitutional role is strictly representative, went on national television and demanded the appointment of an inquiry commission, to look into the massacre. And as we have already seen, nearly 400,000 people, the largest number ever assembled in Israel, joined a rally in Tel Aviv to protest Prime Minister Begin's refusal to appoint the commission.

For the first time, senior officers of the Defense Forces stood up against their defense minister. The first to speak out was Brigadier Amram Mitzna, commander of the National Staff and Command College, who met Sharon and after claiming that the minister had lost the confidence of the military, requested leave for the duration of the war. He was followed by a colonel commanding one of the finest army brigades fighting in Lebanon, who demanded that Sharon resign outright. Next, a large group consisting of the majority of officers of general rank met with Chief of Staff Eitan to voice sharp criticism of Sharon. The officers stated that Sharon, in his public appearances and on camera, was trying to push the blame of his own political mistakes onto the military and that they refused to accept it. When the minister heard of the meeting, he asked them to convene for a second time, in his presence. Sharon arrived in the company of Major General Yisrael Tal, one of the most respected senior officers, and told the generals that Israel was not a Latin American banana republic where generals tell the government what to do and whom to appoint or dismiss as defense minister. If they wanted to engage in politics, they should take off their uniforms and run for office, as he had done several years before. None of the officers resigned and the open "revolt" died down, but the defense minister had been given to understand that there were definite limits beyond which he could not be sure that the military would carry out his instructions. His authority was clearly impaired, and his influence gradually declined from then until his removal in February 1983.

Ariel Sharon was forced to quit the Ministry of Defense, where he had been the moving force in planning, initiating, and, finally, mishandling the war in Lebanon. He remained a member of the cabinet, a minister without portfolio, but with hopes of soon being able to influence Begin and his colleagues as he had done before. Politicians were betting that ultimately Sharon would be forced to quit the cabinet altogether, once he was bereft of the prestige of heading the Defense Ministry. Certainly his colleagues were unhappy with his abrasive behavior. One example of his roughshod manner was his statement that he had "succeeded in staying in the cabinet" in order "to protect the West Bank"; but there was a danger, he said, that, after the Inquiry Commission's report and after his ouster from the Defense Ministry, the Israeli government would not dare take "preventive steps" if the Egyptians sent forces to Sinai or if an Arab country attained nuclear capability. The implication was that, without him, the prime minister and the rest of the cabinet were too weak and indecisive—charges that neither Begin nor his colleagues took kindly.

By the removal of Sharon from the Ministry of Defense, the Government managed to limit the domestic damage of the report of the Kahan commission of inquiry. Opposition hopes that the events following the commission's report would actually undermine the government's standing were dashed by the public opinion polls and by the growing hostility of the marketplace toward the inquiry commission and its recommendations.

Yet even many Likud followers felt that Ariel Sharon's days as a member of the cabinet, even without portfolio, were numbered. With time, many of the public would conclude that Sharon had made crucial mistakes, not only on Sabra and Shatilla but on Lebanon as a whole, and that he had led the country into a war with

171

aims Israel could not attain. In early 1983 the deterioration of relations between Israel and President Amin Gemayel and between the Israeli forces in Lebanon and the Phalangists was a direct consequence of some of the apparent misconceptions embodied in Sharon's strategy. Besides the notion that the Palestine problem could be solved by destroying the PLO in Lebanon, some of his basic assumptions had been proved false: in the chronically divisive Lebanese society, there were no permanent interests or enemies and, therefore, no permanent allies, either. To build Israel's entire Lebanon policy on alliance with the Gemayels obviously was a serious mistake.

Equally mistaken was the hope that by massive employment of superior mechanized power Israel would be able to eliminate all PLO presence in southern Lebanon. Less than six months after Arafat was expelled from Beirut, Israeli troops, exposed to ambushes, had to move in heavily guarded patrols and convoys on the main roads of Lebanon, even in the daytime.

Like the Syrians who entered Lebanon six years earlier, the Israelis were getting bogged down in the snow, mud, and maze of Lebanon. They were approaching the unpleasant choice between getting out and cutting some of their losses or sinking deeper into the morass. At the negotiating table they were engaged in a race to extract some benefit from the affair before they would have to write off most of the blood, pain, money, and goodwill they had invested in the war that was supposed to be won in forty-eight hours.

Still, until the Sabra and Shatilla tragedy, the intensity of domestic reaction to the expansion of the war lagged behind that voiced abroad. The Opposition seemed to be of two minds, even after the breakdown of the consensus over the first (45-kilometer) phase of the operation. The notable change came after the massacres when the public outcry and soul-searching in Israel exceeded the outcry in most Western countries and certainly that in Lebanon itself. Yet it is important to realize that the shifts and changes were not only— and perhaps not even primarily—between coalition and Opposition but within each of the two camps. Though, by and large, the coalition led by the Likud is hawkish while the Opposition, led by the Labor alignment, is less so, both have components of the opposite feather.

The more moderate Liberal party component of the Likud defers almost unquestioningly to the hawkish Herut component and to Prime Minister Begin in particular. On the left the dovish elements such as Mapam, the Civil Rights movement, and the left wing of the Labor party do not dominate the Labor alignment. The radical Ahdut ha-Avodah, the cooperative farmers' movement, and some of the Rafi elements in Labor by and large balance the dovish factions. This keeps the entire alignment somewhat to the left of center.

Reports of the killings in the refugee camps reinforced certain feeble, moderate voices of the Liberals. More important, doves and hawks in the alignment, backed by the soul-searching among the National Religious party coalition members, found common ground in demanding the establishment of a commission of inquiry. Their unanimity contributed greatly to the enormous success of the huge Labor-initiated rally held in Tel Aviv which finally convinced the prime minister to appoint the commission.

The embittered enmity of former prime minister Yitzhak Rabin toward the head of the Labor party, Shimon Peres, was not suspended even during the war in Lebanon. Rabin, obliquely courted by Begin, from time to time showed understanding for the prime minister's policies. This obliged Peres, so as to satisfy the rightist elements in his party, to adopt more hawkish positions than his own inclination might have dictated. The ideological division and the personal infighting of the Labor alignment were probably the major reasons for the Knesset's not becoming the main platform for the debate on Lebanon (or on the other central political issue, concerning the ultimate fate of the occupied territories). There was only one thing over which the entire alignment could be mobilized without internal dispute: an attempt to cause the downfall of the Begin government by some parliamentary maneuver that would provide an *ad hoc* majority in a vote of no confidence. Although there were several such attempts, these were not related to either of the main issues; a motion clearly relating to the fighting in Lebanon or the future of the West Bank had no chance of gaining an antigovernment majority.

Sharon's behavior was soon overshadowed by other events. For a short time, Knesset members from both the Likud and the Labor alignment were trying again to bring about a meeting between

Prime Minister Begin and Shimon Peres to discuss the possibility of a national unity government. It was agreed that the chances were slim but the effort reflected the widespread concern over more pronounced political and ethnic rifts in the Israeli public. Labor still had many supporters from among the Middle Eastern and North African communities and many Ashkenazi Jews from Europe and America were members and supporters of the Likud. But the most vocal and violent of the Likud faithful appeared to come from the less-educated segments of the "Oriental" communities, while Peace Now and the left-of-center segments of the Labor alignment seemed to consist almost entirely of "elitist" college-graduate Ashkenazim.

The division was clearly evident when, on Thursday, February 10, two days after the report was published, a large group of demonstrators, calling for immediate cabinet adoption of the Inquiry Commission's report and for the dismissal of Sharon, walked through the center of Jerusalem to the prime minister's office. The marchers were almost exclusively Ashkenazi, while the bystanders who taunted the demonstrators, and threw an occasional stone, were almost exclusively "Oriental." The demonstration reached its tragic climax just when the marchers were about to disperse peacefully and one of them, Emil Grunzweig, a young ex-kibbutz member, was killed by a hand grenade tossed at the group. Next day in Haifa, during his burial, references to Auschwitz and gas chambers in the curses yelled at the marchers dramatically underscored the ethnic content of the split between the extreme right and much of the left. It shocked both Begin and Peres enough to cause both men to express willingness to meet and discuss efforts to moderate the passions burning in both camps and, possibly, even think of the formation of a national unity government. However, as in previous suggestions to bring Labor and Herut together, these efforts came to naught.

Israel's much discussed "ethnic division" does not run entirely along the line between doves and hawks. Among the moderates there was a significantly higher proportion of Ashkenazim, or Jews of European origin, while among the militants could be found a considerably higher proportion of Sephardim, or "Orientals." Yet Defense Minister Sharon, Foreign Minister Shamir, and Chief of

174

Staff Eitan, the leading hawks in Mr. Begin's administration, are all of East European origin, while among the relative doves in the government, trying to restrain Sharon during the Lebanon war, were Deputy Prime Minister David Levi and Social Welfare Minister Aharon Uzzan, both leaders of the North African (Sephardi) Jewish community in Israel. Since tensions between Ashkenazi and Sephardi communities appear to have become a major theme of Israel's political life in the early 1980s, and in view of the strong identification of the majority of the Sephardim with Mr. Begin, the inner balance between hawks and doves in the ethnic groups is of considerable significance in assessing future trends in Israeli politics.

In the more immediate future, other developments are likely to influence the extent and direction of political consensus in the country. One is the possibility that the now retired President Navon will eventually reenter politics at the head of the Labor list. Navon is a moderate Sephardi and his entry into politics may improve the chances of Labor and help diminish the tendency toward ethnic polarization, now to some extent influencing political divisions.

More important may be the economic developments. Should there be a major recession, a significant drop in American economic aid, or a serious collapse of the highly inflated Israeli stock market, unemployment and inflation are likely to become the main political issues. The Middle East is a volatile area where new, unanticipated factors come into play daily and change the public climate.

By the summer of 1983, the economy had become one of the two major issues in Israel's deepening domestic crisis. As the damage caused by Finance Minister Yoram Aridor's populist principles to the country's exports and foreign currency reserves became apparent, cabinet members began to call publicly for either a complete change in policy or his resignation. The Prime Minister vacillated between backing his finance minister and ordering him to change course, feeding, by his indecisiveness, rumors of his ill health. When, on July 19, Begin cited "personal reasons" for his abrupt cancellation of long-laid plans to visit Washington the following week, his physical and mental condition after the death of his wife and the Lebanon morass became the second, possibly dominant, issue in the looming domestic crisis. Six weeks later, visibly exhausted, he announced in Cabinet "he could not continue," and on September 15 officially tendered his resignation.

Yet, it is too early to predict whether the huge floating vote of the middle class and of workers who have supported Begin and the militant policy of the Likud will stay where it is; it may shift to the Opposition. The advent of a post-Begin Likud era or an economic recession or depression may make those voters begin to question the economic and social costs of the war in Lebanon and, possibly, the intensive West Bank settlement program. The Likud could stay in power throughout the 1980s but changing events might influence many of their supporters to desert the government in droves.

The PLO and the Palestinians

DURING the fortnight when the PLO fighters left the besieged city of Beirut—12,500 by sea, another 2,500 overland with units of the Syrian army—their leaders seemed to be conducting a fantasy come true: a victory parade. Shooting bullets into the air, settling accounts, killing a few opponents, kissing families and babies goodbye for the benefit of the media photographers, they climbed onto the trucks and boarded the ships, making the victory sign as they left. It looked more like a triumphal march than the expulsion of a defeated paramilitary organization which had just lost its fighting base and was off into the wilderness.

Led by Yasser Arafat, chieftains of the various PLO factions seemed to bask in the sympathy extended to them by the West. They appeared delighted that the standing of Israel, their mortal enemy, had declined to unexpected depths; they were proud of having held out "longer than any other Arab army against the Israeli agressors." Admitting that, finally, the "American-supported" Israeli force had succeeded in overwhelming them, they promised that the fight nevertheless would go on from wherever they were temporarily based—Tunisia, South Yemen, Libya, the Sudan, Syria, Jordan, or elsewhere.

People who met with Arafat received the impression that he had expected the Israeli attack before others realized that it was inevitable, but that he did not imagine his defeat would be as immense as it turned out to be. In his mind, he had apparently developed a scenario according to which his enemy would attempt to move up to the Zahrani River or, at worst, to Sidon, some 3 miles farther north. But he never dreamed that Sharon would insist on reaching and occupying Beirut.

The PLO leader realized that his organization would suffer heavy losses but must have hoped they would be able to slow down the Israeli advance so that it would take them as long as ten days to reach the Zahrani-Sidon line. As he must have seen it, slowing down the Israelis would add to the prestige of his organization and strengthen the morale of his men. By the end of a week's fighting, the United Nations or the Great Powers would intervene and force Israel to retreat to the international border. With hindsight it is clear that, militarily, Yasser Arafat made a fatal mistake.

The hard facts that the PLO faced on the morning after contrasted sharply with the apparent euphoria in which they left Beirut. Ending their organized presence in Beirut and in southern Lebanon meant the loss of their power base, their *de facto* independent state, in which their fighters had trained and prepared for battle and where a generation of Palestinian children had been educated and forced to join the PLO ranks; where arms depots had been built up and international terror groups hosted, providing funds, respect, and influence far greater than any other nihilist establishment or liberation movement of modern times ever obtained.

Now they were to be dispersed among eight countries. However courteous the Oriental hospitality, from now on PLO movements would be monitored by and subject to the interests of their hosts. Their leaders might be received with honor but everybody would know that they were exiles.

Not least important was the fact that they would no longer be able to protect the Palestinians left behind in southern Lebanon from their Lebanese enemies. For nearly a decade, as the PLO ruled over the area of Tyre, Nabatieh, and Sidon and as far as West Beirut, the indigenous Lebanese population had been treated like second-class citizens, whose fate was in the hands of the PLO. Many of the natives had been robbed, tortured, or killed by Palestinians protected by the *de facto* PLO government. With their departure, the Lebanese had been liberated but the fate of the Palestinians left behind appeared gloomier than it had before the PLO took over.

In the following fall and winter, before it could establish its new strategy, the PLO underwent a crisis of tactics and leadership which it had hardly anticipated six months before. As Abu Iyad, Fatah's number three leader acknowledged, "We have undoubtedly lost an important position in Lebanon, a position close to Israel. . . . The opportunity to operate out of Lebanon no longer exists." In the countries to which they had been exiled, the discipline of the disarmed PLO troops was crumbling into anarchy. Many, frustrated at being behind barbed wire and apparently forgotten, deserted to Syria and even back to Beirut. Apart from small groups of guerrillas hiding out in the hills and near the coast of southern Lebanon, periodically sniping at small Israeli convoys, and a few thousand fighters protected by the Syrian army in the Al-Bika'a Valley and the area around Tripoli in northern Lebanon, the PLO's military arm had apparently ceased to exist.

The PLO leadership faced a dilemma. Should they, could they, regroup and try to start all over again? And if so, where? Or should they seek the long-detested political solution? There was much unrest at the headquarters of various PLO organizations; the leaders were almost constantly engaged in travel, conferring with the monarchs and presidents of the Arab countries, comparing notes, assessing commitments, evaluating the chances and options, and meeting officials of foreign nations of both East and West. Should they negotiate, should they fight, or should they promise one and do the other?

It all focused, for a while, on the plan for solving the Palestine problem put forward by Ronald Reagan in September 1982. Two months later the PLO Central Council rejected the American president's peace proposals, which stipulated Arab-Israeli negotiations. After a heated debate in Damascus the Central Council reiterated its refusal to recognize Israel in any form. It reasserted its claim to all the land west of the Jordan River, as Palestine to be governed by the PLO alone. Many outside observers suggested that this was an interim statement, that Arafat's followers were now ready to recognize Israel in its pre-1967 borders, if Israel would accept the PLO's right to establish a sovereign state in the West Bank and Gaza Strip. For their own regional audience, however, the PLO leaders had an entirely different message. In the fall of 1982, they reiterated that "the struggle between us and Zionism is a fight to the finish"[1] and that "the Palestinian people, under the leadership of the PLO, will continue the armed struggle."[2] Similarly,

> Recognition [by the United States] of the PLO means recognition of the Palestinian people and its rights in toto. It means recognition of its right to self-determination, beginning with an independent national state which, in the future, will demand . . . the return of Palestinian lands beyond the West Bank and the Gaza Strip—in Galilee, the coastal area, and the Negev. It means a speedy effort to regain all our rights, not just some of them.[3]

There was evidence, however, that this all-or-nothing attitude was becoming increasingly dangerous as Jordan's King Hussein and Yasser Arafat watched the pace of Israeli settlement on the West Bank. By mid-1983 there were across the "green line" 126 Jewish villages and dormitory towns, compared to 400 Arab towns and villages. True, the number of Jewish settlers was still small, but it was no longer insignificant. And PLO leaders were warned by their relatives in the West Bank that tens of thousands of Jews could be expected to move in within a couple of years unless some way was found, almost immediately, to stop them. Only the United States appeared capable of turning the tide. But the Americans had stipulated conditions, including recognition of Israel and a peaceful solution of the dispute. Could the PLO trust the Americans? Would they deliver? For the PLO it was a momentous decision that they undertook to discuss when they met in February 1983.

The plight of the PLO was more difficult than the West generally realized. To the West, the PLO usually appears as a more or less united front. Thus, after the Arab summit conference held in Fez, Morocco, in September 1982 to discuss the Reagan peace proposals, a delegation headed by the kings of Morocco and Jordan traveled to the United States and other countries to present the "Arab position on the PLO." The jittery British were "punished" by Saudi Arabia and some of its peninsular neighbors for a snub administered by Prime Minister Margaret Thatcher to the PLO representative in the delegation.

Within the Arab world, however, the position of Arafat and his colleagues had substantially weakened. In losing their state within a state, the PLO lost more than just a huge base for military operations. They lost a whole infrastructure, including a launching pad for terrorists from all over the world: Latin America, Western Europe, and the Far East. No longer did the PLO have direct, ongoing access to the communications media of the world which had enabled them to address Arab and international opinion at will. Whether in Syria or Saudi Arabia, Jordan or Tunisia, the state authorities were now free to obscure, censor, and possibly draw the sting out of PLO representations.

In the West, the PLO seemed to continue to be the heroes of the day, especially to many young people and liberals, who admired their tenacity in the face of the huge Israeli war machine. In Europe, the terrorists were romantically feted as combatants against the forces of reaction and brutality. But the Arab countries reacted differently and, indeed, were not unduly worried by the collapse of the PLO power base. In the Arab world, their mischief was more clearly remembered, their history of troublemaking and terror more closely felt. Many Arabs were privately delighted that the PLO had received a drubbing from the Israelis.

The PLO leaders were disappointed by the lack of active Arab support for their war against Israel. They felt that Syria had let them down by agreeing to a cease-fire while the PLO was still fighting; they were angered because not even the rejectionists used the oil weapon to aid them and shocked by the unenthusiastic reception encountered in their new countries of exile.

Within days, the disenchantment became mutual. Instead of international Beirut, which even during the most intense fighting remained a cosmopolitan center where West met East in bars and nightclubs, they found themselves inside paramilitary compounds, surrounded by barbed wire and miles away from the provincial Arab capital of their new host country.

Surely it was now clear to the PLO leadership that not only had their infrastructure been crushed but, in the aftermath, their organization was in danger of disintegrating. As a military power they had suffered a thorough defeat and, after warnings from East and West, they showed little enthusiasm for reverting to international terror.

Many of the veteran PLO men, now in their forties and fifties, had been fighting the Israelis for a generation, yet, except for increasing Western sympathy, had little to show for their pains. Many of their colleagues had been killed. The survivors had aged rapidly, and the experiences of attrition were evident in their faces. They were tired and depressed, close to despair. From their perspective Israel was stronger than ever, more determined, rapidly settling the West Bank. It showed no signs of going under or disintegrating. Some of the more moderate among the PLO leaders were reported to be pressing for political maneuvering rather than the use of force. The Western press repeated rumors that some even dared consider a possible compromise solution with the Israelis or, at least, with the Americans. Nobody acknowledged it publicly. Still, when speaking to Western audiences or in private conversation with their own "liberals," PLO leaders sounded more accommodating than before. Certainly the decisions taken in Fez in the early fall of 1982 stopped short of any mention of recognition. The gap between the resolutions adopted in Fez and the Reagan Middle East peace plan is considerable.

The winds of change seemed to have reached Yasser Arafat. In his luxury hotel in Tunis, where he set up headquarters after expulsion from Beirut, he met with leaders of the Israeli-Palestine peace movement, including Sheli Party leader Uri Avnery, retired general Matti Peled, and former Finance Ministry director general Dr. Yaakov Arnon. Flanked by three members of the PLO Executive Committee, this was the first time that Arafat had publicly received Israelis whom one could even remotely call "establishment" figures —as opposed to Israeli Communists and the like. Arafat showed some evidence that he had begun to believe, after the war in Lebanon, that there seemed to be no military option, only a political one.

If anybody could test the intentions of the PLO and show up the considerable differences between the U.S. President's plan and the resolutions adopted by the Arab leaders, it was the Israeli government. But the intransigence with which Israel rejected any form of direct negotiation made it difficult to call the PLO bluff. As it turned out, however, there was no need for that—yet.

After ostensibly flirting with a "peaceful solution" of the Palestine problem, the PLO had rejected President Reagan's peace plan and refused to recognize Israel. And when the Palestine National Council met in Algiers on February 14, 1983, they, in essence, confirmed this position once again. For a short time the PLO proved successful in its attempt to present its various factions as a united front but at the price of adopting a set of resolutions with a very general common denominator of minimal progress toward any sort of solution, military or peaceful. Thus, while the council did not reject the Reagan peace plan outright, they labeled it "insufficient," claiming that it failed to provide "a sound basis for a just and lasting solution to the Palestinian cause." They accepted the Fez plan, adopted by the Arab League in September, despite a clause which implicitly, without actually mentioning Israel by name, recognizes its existence. They also stressed their "appreciation and support" for the Brezhnev plan, which affirmed "the inalienable rights of the Palestinians to self-determination and to the establishment of their own independent state under the PLO, the sole legitimate representative of the Palestinian people." They recommended that after full Palestinian statehood was achieved, the principle of confederation with Jordan should be studied, clearly refusing King Hussein a public mandate to negotiate with Israel.

His earlier seeming attraction to a political solution notwithstanding, Arafat's public statement that the political and *military* struggle against Israel would continue until a just peace has been achieved and the Palestinian flag is hoisted over the mosques and churches of Jerusalem would hardly entice the Israelis. "The Jerusalem to which Mr. Arafat seems to aspire is a Jerusalem without Jews," commented one seasoned observer.[4]

The Palestine National Council, by now a mature assembly, was not only slow to establish a new strategy, it failed to assess the rumblings of the PLO fighters still confronting the Israelis in the Lebanon, or the increased Syrian hostility toward them. The revolt against Arafat that erupted in the Al-Bika'a valley in June 1983 made the prospect of PLO moderation moving toward a political solution more remote than ever. The outbreak was ostensibly trig-gered because certain Fatah field officers opposed the appointment to new commands of three other PLO officers whom, they charged, had abandoned their previous assignment in the June 1982 fighting in southern Lebanon. In fact, the revolt was against Arafat's general policies and leadership. The rebels were particularly bothered by the suspicion that he was opting for a political path rather than continuing the armed struggle.

The revolt against Arafat in the PLO ranks and the fighting between his loyalists and those who support his challenger, Col. Abu Mussa, was obviously being backed and encouraged by the Syrians. Damascus radio and television spew obscene invectives against Arafat; Syria has provided several Soviet-made T-54 tanks to Col. Abu Mussa; and Syrian units have cut off supply lines to pro-Arafat PLO bases within Syrian controlled areas of north and east Lebanon. However, the revolt itself is not of Syria's making. It is a genuine act of defiance from within the ranks of the PLO. Some of the rebelling officers were Arafat's closest associates during the 1982 siege of Beirut as was Abu Mussa (who in the past was not politically active). Abu Mussa, a British-trained officer and a battal-ion commander in King Hussein's forces, deserted the army in September, 1970, when the Hashemite monarch ruthlessly and effectively set out to remove all PLO presence from his kingdom. His mother has lived all her life in East Jerusalem and now, in her old age, receives her social security payments through the Israeli authorities. Abu Mussa and his colleagues can by no means be suspected of acting as Syrian stooges. The mutiny is, by all indica-tions, a "natural" if somewhat delayed consequence of the smash-ing defeat of the PLO in Lebanon last year.

Dissent against the leader after a lost war is, of course, a common phenomenon. The rebels, however, question not only Arafat's mil-itary leadership but also his political leadership. Outwardly, they oppose what they claim is Arafat's willingness to negotiate with Israel via King Hussein of Jordan. (In fact, Arafat refused Hussein's and most Arab countries' suggestion that the Jordanian ruler should enter into negotiations about the Reagan plan.) What in fact the rebels reject is Arafat's belief that the chances of wrestling concessions from Israel by military means are practically zero; he appears to them to believe that gaining further political and public opinion support in the West by presenting an image of moderation and compromise is a much better way to put effective pressure on Israel.

The Palestinian community was clearly aware of the PLO losses and the ensuing political crisis. Arafat was never loved or even much respected by the Palestinians but, in his way, he had become a symbol of their more realistic aspirations. If he and his allies were crushed, so would his and their dreams be finished.

Just how fatigued the PLO had become was most noticeable when, at its urging, the United Nations held an expensive international conference on the question of Palestine in Geneva, at the end of August, 1983, after much costly and time-consuming preparation. Most of the 157 delegations and observers paid their respects to Chairman Yasser Arafat, who had, in the past year, lost so much of his authority over his following and failed to offer a path out of the Middle East muddle and on to peace. It was clear to many that his rhetoric and generalities had failed the cause of the Palestinians.

Much has been said in the Western press about the massacres in Sabra and Shatilla on September 15 and 16. One of the lessons learned is that hatred of the now defenseless Palestinians living south of Beirut—in the camps around Sidon, Tyre, and Nabatieh— and the ensuing danger, is such that the Israeli army has had to post many troops to protect the refugee camps from attack by the native inhabitants, Christians, and Moslem Shiites alike. But it was not only in Lebanon that the Palestinians were at a loss. If, early in 1983, Arafat succeeded in avoiding schism in the movement by a set of fuzzy, evasive council resolutions, the Syrians in the summer appeared intent on splitting it wide open. Hence the desperation on the West Bank.

Where does this leave the Palestinians living under Israeli administration? The defeat of the PLO and the destruction of its bases in Lebanon constitute one more bitter disappointment. Having lived close to the centers of Israeli power for sixteen years, they do not really believe that it will be through military force that the PLO will "liberate" them. Yet they had been proud of the political headway the PLO made over the preceding decade and this, too, seems sadly compromised.

Most West Bank Palestinians have little regard for King Hussein.

The older generation remembers his tough, often cruel treatment of the West Bank before 1967. The younger ones cannot forgive him for the slaughter of the PLO in September 1970. Though dependent on Jordan for the preservation of their fragile social and economic links with the Arab world, few wish to return to the rule of King Hussein.

Palestinians in Israeli-controlled territories find it frustrating to have to deal with the Likud government. They have had to respect its hard-line stance. They are overawed by the speed with which settlements are being built and roads laid on the West Bank. The dismissal or expulsion by the Israelis of the more outspoken Arab mayors clearly indicates to the indigenous population that the government views with disfavor the budding of any pro-PLO local leaders.

Yet the Israelis in 1983 are very different from the demons they expected when they first encountered them after the Six Day War. Certain elements in the Palestinian population, the proletariat and to a large extent the farmers and the merchants, have visibly improved their standard of living in the sixteen years of Israeli administration. Yet most have been, on some occasion or other, humiliated by the Jewish rulers. When matters become political, as they invariably do at the West Bank colleges in Nablus, Bir Zeit, Bethlehem, and Hebron, the atmosphere turns unpleasant and demonstrators experience what they consider to be the brutal side of the Israeli administration. The pressures on the indigenous population of Hebron, where extremist Jewish zealots were pushing to resettle the buildings in which a lively Jewish community had lived for centuries right in their midst, until the Arabs massacred some sixty-nine of them and scattered the survivors in a pogrom of 1929, remained explosive. But to Palestinians who grew up in the midst of cruelty and abuse of power, the determined crushing of riots is less shocking than to Westerners whose double standard expects more forebearance from the "People of the Book" than from other "occupiers." The radical Palestinians spread rumors that the minister of defense, Ariel Sharon, planned to expel all or most Palestinians. But the majority obviously knew that, unless matters became substantially worse, they would survive where they were. The more sophisticated Palestinians had become very cynical about the Israeli military government. "The Israelis complain of the standards by which the West judges them. Are they not aware of the extreme differences with which Jew and Arab are treated on the West Bank?" they complain and go on to enumerate a seemingly endless string of cases in which civil rights are interpreted to benefit the Israelis at the expense of their Palestinian neighbors.

The Palestinians, finding themselves once again the victims of the folly of their brethren, are in a dilemma. Few believe that they can still rely on Arab aid; fewer have any expectations from the Israelis. They distrust the policies of the Israeli military government and will not collaborate openly with their new, expanding Jewish neighbors. A young practicing lawyer and author, Rajah Shehadeh of Ramallah, has written that "between mute submission and blind hate—I choose the third way. I am *Sàmid*"—meaning the steadfast or the persevering who, in dignity, intends to stay put.[5]

But many are resigned. There are indications that they are tired of fighting and there is less reaction to the new Israeli settlements. After all, most of the settlers mind their own business and seem peaceful enough. When asked, an increasing number of Palestinians express interest in the possibility of Israel annexing the West Bank and the Gaza Strip. True, such an event would change the status quo. But then, as the Israelis in any case treat these territories as their own, annexation will give the Arabs the hope that more human rights and, possibly, civil liberties will be granted them, with, ultimately, a voice in the Knesset. Could they dare come up with a demand of "no annexation without representation"? The Jews cannot afford a sizable, completely disenfranchised minority in their country. Even the rightist Kach party of Meir Kahane recognizes part of that thesis and says that Arabs who will not agree to remain without the vote or become disenfranchised must leave the country or be expelled. And though the prospect of annexation may sound ignominious to many liberals, ironically it might ultimately lead, with Arab enfranchisement, to a binational secular democracy, possibly in cantonlike form and with a presumed perpetual Jewish majority. In a way, this would be something close to the solution demanded by Yasser Arafat.

13

The New Lebanon

E ARLY in 1983, the Lebanese government was seeking ways to reassert its authority over the country, which appeared as divided as ever. The challenges it was facing would have tested the leadership of more cohesive societies: how to convince the PLO, the Syrians, and the Israelis that Lebanon could look after itself and also protect the vital interests of its neighbors to the south and to the east and that, therefore, their troops should leave Lebanese soil; how to bring the Kataeb militias into the Lebanese army; and how, somehow, to stop the hostilities between the Druse and the Christians in the Al-Shouf mountains.

There were factors in favor of normalization. The pace of reconstruction of Beirut and the towns and cities on the coastal road to the south was impressive; the support of the Shiite politicians for the government was encouraging. Some of the impatient Israelis, who over the years have grown to see Lebanon through Phalange eyes, failed to realize that the Lebanese are a pluralistic society and that political compromise is essential if the republic is to survive. Successfully attaining such an understanding, taking into account the needs not only of the minorities and local chieftains but of Lebanon's two overpowering neighbors, was the task the leaders of Lebanon were called on to achieve. By autumn 1983 it was still doubtful whether they would succeed.

On Monday, August 23, 1982, thirty-four-year-old Bashir Gemayel was elected by the Lebanese parliament to be the next president, to assume office a month later. To achieve constitutional legitimacy, the first requirement was to have a quorum of two-thirds (sixty-two members) of the parliament present for the vote. Once this was achieved, Bashir's chances to obtain, on the second vote, the required simple majority of those present looked good. And he succeeded. Although many of the Moslem leaders and some of the Christians—notably Walid Junblatt, the Druse leader; Rashid Karameh, the Moslem from Tripoli; and ex-president Suleiman Franjieh, Bashir's mortal enemy; as well as some pro-Syrian parliamentarians—boycotted the assembly, Gemayel received the support of fifty-seven out of the sixty-two voting on the second ballot.

The anti-Gemayel faction alleged that Bashir had been elected "on the bayonets of the Israelis," but his supporters claimed that the voting had not been more irregular than six years earlier when the retiring president, Elias Sarkis, was elected with Syrian support, or twelve years earlier when Franjieh was chosen. Parliament itself had been elected ten years earlier, in 1972, and seven of the original ninety-nine members had since died, without being replaced. With the civil war and the many changes in the country during the decade, it could be argued that the parliament was no longer quite representative. Yet, though the atmosphere was still warlike when the body convened, the election was recognized as a legal and democratic procedure and respected by foreign countries. On the day before, it was decided to change the place of assembly from the parliament building in the western part of Beirut, near the dividing line; it was felt that there were still too many PLO, Syrian, and Israeli troops around for safety, certainly too many for comfort. The alternative chosen was the camp of Fiyadiah, to the southeast on the highway to Damascus, not far from the president's mansion in Ba'abdeh.

Bashir Gemayel's success was greeted with genuine satisfaction and hopes for peace and stability, not only in East Beirut but also in other parts of Lebanon. People noted with pride that, in spite of the long period of wars and fratricide, destruction, and chaos, the symbols of government and democracy had survived.

190

Foreigners, cynical about the Lebanese way of life, sometimes say that "the Lebanon is not a country, it is a business." There may be some truth in the cliché, but there is also in Lebanon great respect for the constitution. One president replaces another in accordance with the constitution, and the reins of power, however feeble at times, are transferred in an orderly fashion. None of the parties represented in the parliament—many with strong motivation and quite a lot of force behind them—had ever attempted to usurp authority or carry out a coup or a revolution. The Lebanese may lack the power to prevent foreign invasions, PLO occupation, feuding, killings, and atrocities, but they obviously prefer their weak, fragile democracy to any alternative. In electing young Bashir Gemayel, they had voted for the survival of Lebanon and, they hoped, for its revival.

Many observers of his career in recent years thought they could discern a cruel edge to Bashir's determined ambition, but they felt that the situation of Lebanon was so desperate that he might just prove to be its savior. Bashir had set out to become president months, if not years, earlier and, to that end, throughout the summer he had had to evade public recognition from the Israelis. As an Arab statesman, he avoided antagonizing the Moslems too much, either in his own country or in other Arab countries. He was concerned mainly with the rebuilding of Lebanon, to commence as soon as the alien forces—Syrian, PLO, and Israeli—had left.

It was late summer 1982, and Prime Minister Begin was spending a brief vacation in Nahariya, the seaside town that earlier in the year had come under PLO shelling from Lebanon, six miles to the north. At that time Begin had assured Nahariya inhabitants, many of whom make their living from the tourist industry, that he would come here for his next annual vacation. And early in September he did indeed return to Nahariya, by now secure and peaceful.

On Wednesday night, September 8, Begin left his hotel for a secret meeting with the Lebanese president-elect. He had asked his defense and foreign ministers to join him, along with a team of senior army officers and civil servants. Gemayel, too, was accompanied by an entourage of allies and colleagues of seven years and more. He was looking forward to the encounter. He had met the

191

prime minister several times and appreciated that Begin was cast in a mold different from that of the other elderly gentlemen he knew. And he was invariably impressed by Begin's warmth and largesse. He respected Begin's judgment and was grateful for the aid he had received the past months, which had led to the expulsion of the PLO and had abetted his own election. He felt that there were further opportunities for imaginative joint ventures with Israel and was looking forward to more of the sensible cooperation of recent years.

When the smiling president-elect arrived in the secluded lounge, the prime minister stood up grimly. Bashir came over and, as is the Oriental custom, smiling warmly he hugged Begin again and again. Begin stood erect, unmoving, hardly reacting. What Bashir did not know was that the prime minister's mood had changed since the two had last met. In Israel there was growing criticism of the extension of the war in time and territory. The initial glow of the removal of the PLO was fading and America's hopes for quick withdrawal of Israeli (and Syrian) troops was turning into impatience. Begin was under pressure to deliver the fruits of victory. He was brusque, short-tempered, indeed rude.

The rest of the evening turned out to be a minor Middle East disaster. The prime minister started out by demanding that the first thing the president-elect must do, upon taking office, was to sign a peace treaty with Israel. That, answered Bashir Gemayel, was quite impossible. It would be unacceptable to the Moslem citizens of his country; he would be ostracized by important elements of the Arab world, including Saudi Arabia, on which his country's rehabilitation depended. In short, it would be the wrong political move and could be counterproductive for everybody. He advocated patience and assured Begin that such a treaty could be negotiated within six months to a year. Gemayel did promise to maintain, meanwhile, the special relationship that had developed between Israel and his country, to keep the borders open, and to encourage trade.

Begin would have none of it. The atmosphere dropped to nearly freezing point as he tried to bully the Lebanese. Bashir held out his wrists and exclaimed that Mr. Begin could have him handcuffed and arrested but could not force the treaty on him.

As the Lebanese contingent was leaving, Bashir was furious.

192

"Never have I been so insulted," he exclaimed. "I don't want ever to see Begin again!"

In retrospect, some of those present believe that both men would have met again and tried to mend the breach. Others suspect that the drama of that Wednesday night was not an accident of bad mood or impatience but an expression of the inevitable parting of the briefly complementary interests of the Maronites of Lebanon and the Gemayel family, on the one hand, and those of Israel and the Begin government, on the other.

Nobody will ever be able to know for certain. Less than a week later, on Tuesday afternoon, September 14, a bomb exploded in the headquarters of the Kataeb in Beirut. Bashir Gemayel and more than twenty of his followers were killed inside the building. For the Gemayel family and its followers, the death of Bashir was a stunning setback; their leader, their dreams, the carefully drawn plans—all appeared suddenly struck down and gone.

Here, however, a typical Lebanese development took place quickly. Even before the body of the slain president-elect was laid to rest, the Gemayel family decided not to give up the prize of the presidency but to claim it for Amin, the older brother of Bashir. And Moslem leaders in West Beirut, just as quickly, realized that this presented an opportunity to close the chapter of direct confrontation with the Maronites, and the Gemayels in particular, and accumulate some political assets for the era of Amin's presidency. They understood that Amin needed them more than Bashir had and would therefore be more pliable than his brother would have been. They rushed to join the mourners of their assassinated opponent and voiced support for Amin; some tried to accuse Israel of responsibility for his brother's murder.

Then came the Kataeb massacre of Palestinians in the Sabra and Shatilla camps and, with it, the further opportunity for the Moslems to try to create a joint front with the Christians, to deflect the blame onto the Israelis.

Those acquainted with the customs and mentality of the Middle East in general and the Kataeb in particular, who witnessed the shock and pain of the Beirut Christian community and the Gemayel family at Bashir's assassination, were not surprised by their revenge in Sabra and Shatilla. When world opinion immediately united to condemn the Israelis, the Lebanese, accustomed to periodic massacres, did not quite comprehend what all the fuss was about. Later, when it became clear that Lebanese had perpetrated the murders, they made some faint attempts to deny the allegations, then appointed the prosecutor general of their army—a Christian—to conduct a perfunctory investigation. Eyewitness reports stated that the commander of the Christian troops during the killings was Eli Hobeika, the Phalangist chief of Intelligence, one of Bashir's closest lieutenants. Later, in fact, this was informally acknowledged by Hobeika himself. Still, although outsiders also clearly identified individuals who were the Kataeb officers heading the troops under Hobeika in Sabra and Shatilla, not one of the commanders of the Lebanese forces was asked what he was doing at the time of the massacre.

There seemed to be no curiosity among any of the Lebanese—Christian, Druse, or Moslem—about the full sordid details of their involvement. Rather, emphasizing the need to preserve national unity, they seemed to wish to gloss over events. It was a full nine months after the massacre before the prosecutor general published his findings: evading all questions of Phalangist responsibility, he charged that since Israel was the occupying power at the time, she was responsible, under international law, for whatever happened in areas under her control.

A week after the murder of Bashir, when parliament reassembled, Amin was elected president of Lebanon by the votes of all sixty-two members present. Two days later, on Thursday, September 23, he was sworn in, took office, and moved into the president's mansion in Ba'abdeh.

Amin was considered to be more cautious and moderate than his younger brother and was better accepted by the older generation of Lebanese and by the Moslem element, not least because, in a traditional Lebanese family exercise, while Bashir was maintaining contact with Israel, Amin kept the lines open to the Moslems—and the Syrians. He faced as difficult a challenge as his brother would have but without the gift of charismatic leadership. He had to reestablish a working central government, enforce law and order, and put an end to hostilities in Beirut, in the Al-Shouf mountains, and the north, and especially in and around Tripoli. To do that he needed the cooperation of the power brokers of the land and they, in turn, would only expose themselves and back him if they believed he would survive. Indeed, some of his Christian backers feared that, as his older predecessors from Shamoun to Sarkis before him, Amin Gemayel also would go too far to pacify the Moslem radicals. His request of Shafik al-Wazzan to stay on as prime minister only reinforced these suspicions.

For many Lebanese politicians, including Amin Gemayel, the most important lesson from the aftermath of Bashir's assassination, and from the readiness of the West to blame Israel for the Sabra and Shatilla massacre, seemed to be that Israel (and the Kataeb) had ceased to be the winner with whom a deal should be made about Lebanon's future. Paradoxically, this change of attitude in Beirut was taking place just when the Christians, thanks to Israel and the Kataeb, were regaining the upper hand in major parts of the country.

Until the summer of 1982, the Syrians, the PLO, and their Moslem allies controlled more than four-fifths of Lebanon. After the PLO were destroyed in the south and expelled from Beirut and the Syrians had retreated to the northern Al-Beika'a, this was no longer so. In the aftermath of the Israeli invasion, the Kataeb became the dominant paramilitary force in many parts of Lebanon, and including, they believed, in the south.

Although the Kataeb were the totally committed, faithful followers of Bashir Gemayel, their relations with his brother Amin remained just as ambiguous after he assumed the presidency as they had been when his younger brother was alive. They did not regard him as their commander in chief and, accordingly, Amin treated them with caution. In the early fall of 1982, the official Lebanese army was able to assert itself and take over control of West Beirut for the first time in years, but they were very cautious about the eastern part of the city; there the dominance of the Kataeb was unquestioned and it was not until early 1983 that the army was able to replace them. The Kataeb continued to pay lip service to the president and to the need to disband and merge into the Lebanese army, yet no one in contact with them believed that that would be easy to achieve.

Their new leader, Fady Frem, handpicked by Bashir Gemayel to be the commander in chief just two days before the former was murdered, assumed the responsibilities of his martyred leader and established close contact with the family's patriarch, Sheikh Pierre Gemayel.

Shocked and at first dazed by the death of their leader, the Kataeb commanders regained control of themselves and their forces, hoping, as victors in the seven-year war, to control the state. They rejected the policy of compromise favored by the Christian leaders of the previous generation, which they claim was ultimately the cause of the rape of their country. They were confident that if they showed sufficient determination they would be able to influence radically the policies of their government. Fady Frem reinterated this commitment in October in a tribute he paid to the assassinated president-elect. Regarding Amin as an equal, he said:

> The Lebanese Forces will not allow this victory to be interfered with, nor will they allow its benefits to be lost in the sort of compromises that were practiced in the past and in formulas that have proved themselves failures.[1]

When the negotiations with Israel commenced on December 27, in Halde outside Beirut, more than three months after Amin had assumed the presidency, it was still unclear who in Lebanon had the upper hand: was it Fady Frem, Amin Gemayel, or Shafik al-Wazzan? The answer could be crucial to the very survival of the country. The route charted by al-Wazzan or, rather, by Saib Slaam, the Moslem leader of West Beirut, dictated adherence to the Arab world, distance from Israel, compromise with the Syrians, and accommodation with the radical Arabs, even at the price of blurring the Lebanese identity. The Gemayel path, supported by the Christian forces and some Moslems, mainly Shiites, called upon a determined Lebanon to reassert itself, insist on withdrawal of all foreign armies, and establish full independence and an identity distinct from its Arab neighbors or Israel.

During his early tenure in office Amin Gemayel had only a limited following among the Kataeb militias. As fall moved into winter they were worried that he had made too many concessions to his anti-Israel, pro-Syrian allies. They were even more bothered by his pledge, which would almost inevitably be tested, to disband the Lebanese Forces, along with all other private armies.

Meanwhile, bitter fighting erupted in the Al-Shouf Mountains and in the Tripoli region, to a degree reminiscent of the fratricide of the mid-1970s. The Al-Shouf, southeast of Beirut is the power base of the Druse Moslems. Christians are a minority here, forming 20 to 25 percent of the population. There are Druse towns and villages and there are Christian ones; some are mixed. Soon after their radical leader, Kemal Junblatt, was assassinated early in 1977 (probably by the Syrians, though that was never conclusively proved), the old intercommunity hostilities erupted again as the Druse set out on a vendetta against the Christians, mainly those in the mixed towns and villages. Many were murdered, others fled. When the Israelis arrived in the summer of 1982 and made contact with the Lebanese Forces in the Matten Mountains to the north, some of the Christian survivors decided to return to their homes, only to find that these were now occupied by their Druse neighbors.

The Christian forces, both the Kataeb and the Shamoun followers, have long dreamt of extending their territorial sphere of influence south, through the Al-Shouf Mountains, to make contact with their brothers in the Al-Bika'a Valley and southern Lebanon. The Druse presence was a clear obstacle. Thus, when the Christian refugees tried to return to the Al-Shouf they were resisted, but they found ready support from their militias. Shooting erupted again and the Israeli forces, trying to maintain neutrality, once again found themselves embarrassingly involved in the middle.

No Israelis, though, were even indirectly involved in the fighting that broke out in the north, in and around Tripoli. There the expanding Alawites, supported by the Syrians, directed telling artillery fire at the indigenous PLO-aided Sunni population. It was clear that both in the Al-Shouf and in Tripoli the new Lebanese administration lacked the power to intervene and establish law and order.

For most Beirutis, certainly for the more affluent, the massacre at Sabra and Shatilla, the shelling in Tripoli, and even the fighting in

197

the Al-Shouf Mountains were, at first, nonevents. The city had at last been freed of the Syrians and the PLO and, as a Christian merchant said, it was rapidly "dusting itself off from the war." Even at the height of the siege it was clear that the businessmen were looking optimistically forward, planning for the reemergence of their city as a financial center. Early in 1983, trade and real estate prices were booming and the Lebanese currency was more in demand than ever. In relation to the U.S. dollar and other hard currencies it rose by more than 40 percent in the second half of 1982.

Outside Beirut, the city of business, the threats, murder, and fighting continued while foreign powers tried to resolve the problems of Lebanon. The U.S. marines were flexing their muscles near Beirut International Airport, French and Italian soldiers drove around the city and harbor; the Israeli tanks were in Aley, the Syrians a bit farther off. The Druse and Christians were shooting it out in the hills. But in Beirut, for close to nine months, these events seemed far away. Until the late spring of 1983, when the ominous sound of explosions became more frequent and closer, Beirut seemed to be returning to its old self.

In spite of the maddeningly slow negotiations between the Lebanese government and Israel, social and, especially, economic ties between the two countries were growing stronger. Trade that commenced right behind the advancing Israel troops was doubling every second month. Exports from Israel reached $20 million by the end of 1982, an estimated 10 percent of total Lebanese imports. Some of the commodities had later been reexported to other parts of the Arab world.*

As many Lebanese came to spend their Christmas vacations in the Holy Land, this *de facto* normalization enhanced the desire for peace with Israel. Wrote one Beirut editor:

> There is also a readiness, on the part of the Lebanese people themselves, to be at least on friendly terms with the Jewish state. The

---

*A news item late in January 1983 mentioned that many of the Iraqi soldiers on the Iranian front were munching Israeli biscuits. In March 1983, however, Saudi Arabia and Jordan imposed a "certificate of origin" requirement on imports from Lebanon to prevent the entry of Israel-made goods.

advantage the Lebanese have gained from Israel's intervention has surpassed by far the "support" they received from the Arab countries during their time of need.[2]

But matters were more complicated than that. Shafik al-Wazzan, the Lebanese prime minister, warned his people that anyone dealing in Israeli products would be stripped of his nationality. "I asked my *qadi* (Moslem judge) and he said I could go on trading as long as the name 'Israel' was not written on the boxes" was the reaction of one merchant to the prime minister's official statement.

In many ways that, too, was the approach of the Lebanese delegation chosen to solve problems of mutual interest in talks with Israel, early in 1983. The Israel-Lebanon negotiations were bound to be complicated for every side, including the Americans. No party came up with a clear idea of what it intended to achieve. The contacts began through several separate channels, some months before the formal talks started publicly in December. The Americans, headed by Ambassador Philip Habib and his aide, Ambassador Morris Draper, were impatiently commuting between Beirut, Jerusalem, and Washington and strongly urging the sides to start official talks but were making little headway. To judge from later claims by Ariel Sharon, the Israelis had succeeded in establishing discreet contacts with persons in the immediate entourage of President Amin Gemayel. Gradually, in a series of meetings, the basic tenets of an understanding between the two countries seemed to emerge. When the parties appeared close to final agreement, Defense Minister Sharon took over, to conclude the arrangements. After he had made a final visit to Beirut early in December his associates, intent on bolstering Sharon's sagging public image, quickly leaked to the press that the minister had reported a major "breakthrough" to the cabinet: in negotiations with Amin Gemayel, agreement had been reached on all substantive issues of a settlement between the two countries.

Sharon, they claimed, had read aloud to the rest of the cabinet from the "written agreement" about "normalization of relations" including open frontiers, trade and tourism, and the stationing of official representatives in the other country's capital, as well as about "special security arrangements" in southern Lebanon including demilitarization and a special status for Major Saad Haddad's Israeli-trained Free Lebanese forces.

While government officials were still talking about how Sharon had upstaged the Americans who were obstructing Israeli efforts to reach full peace with Lebanon, many Israeli newspapers irreverently pointed out that this seemed to be another of Sharon's bluffs. As they had done during the critical weeks of the war in Lebanon, so now, too, the cabinet eagerly and unquestioningly swallowed the defense minister's statements without checking them. This time what Sharon claimed was an "agreement" with the Lebanese was actually an unsigned draft for the agenda of the talks. When Israeli, Lebanese, and American representatives finally met for their first official session, the Lebanese delegates promptly disassociated themselves from the document presented by Sharon to the Israeli cabinet. By prematurely and expansively publicizing the meetings, he set back what could have been a promising start. It was clear that if progress were to be made and publicized, it would have to be more modest and step-by-step.

It took several weeks of haggling even to agree on the agenda. In the meetings it became evident that the unnamed Lebanese with whom Sharon had reached the unsigned agreement might have, at best, agreed that the issues listed by Sharon should be discussed, but had not agreed to their substance.

Sharon's exaggerations aside, there also seemed to be a substantial Lebanese retreat from the limited progress toward the normalization they had appeared to be willing to agree to earlier. President Gemayel was under twofold pressure—from the Syrians and from his own, Moslem, pro-PLO prime minister Shafik al-Wazzan—not to give in to the Israeli demands. The proclaimed American eagerness to get the Syrian and Israeli troops out of Lebanon raised Gemayel's hopes that Washington would make it easier for him to resist the Israeli demands to make peace than the Syrian demands *not* to make peace.

Not all agreed. Said Fady Frem, commander of the Lebanese Forces, in a news program interview, "We are for normal relations [with Israel] because Lebanon has until now been under the psychological and political domination of Syria. If we can have normal relations with all our neighbors," he explained, "Syria will not be able to pose such threats as closing the borders or stopping our transit trade any more." He added that the snail's pace of the Lebanese-Israeli talks was partly caused by Lebanon's desire "to reach agreement with Israel with the least possible negative consequences from the Arab world. We are maneuvering not to get the Arabs on our backs."[3]

An official normalization agreement, Lebanese negotiators warned, would be used by the PLO and the Syrians as an excuse to keep their forces in Lebanon, which in turn would hold up the Israeli withdrawal. Then Lebanon would have the worst of both worlds: normalization with Israel without withdrawal of foreign troops.

In the meetings with Israel, held at least twice a week, mostly in Khalde at the southern approaches to Beirut or in Kiryat Shmona in the Upper Galilee, the approach of the Lebanese was candid: Lebanon could not accept an open peace treaty, with an exchange of ambassadors and the other public forms of full political recognition. Pressure for such a formal agreement would result in complete breakdown of the talks. But it could accept, live with, and encourage pragmatic, informal understandings and arrangements that would lead in stages to normalization.

One of the more difficult problems to be discussed on the road to peaceful coexistence was the fate of Major Saad Haddad, who had been posted by the Lebanese president in the mid-1970s to southern Lebanon and ordered to make contact with the Israelis and became their ally. Later, when he refused to sever relations with his southern neighbors, he was courtmartialed in absentia and discharged from the army. His militia had worked with the Israelis against the PLO during the difficult years and the Israelis were committed to having him honorably returned to the Lebanese army. There was considerable Lebanese resistance to this request.

Some of the Israeli leaders, such as Ariel Sharon, insisted on full, open declarations of Lebanese friendship. Other ministers felt that the more discreet approach, on which the Lebanese were willing to compromise, could prove to be quite satisfactory. It would provide relations with Beirut similar to those Israel had with Iran in the last two decades of Shah Mohammad Reza Pahlavi's reign. Until early 1979 the Israelis maintained an informal legation, with a military mission, in Teheran; the Iranians did the same in Tel Aviv. Israel's El Al airline flew to the Pahlavi International Airport on scheduled flights several times a week, and trade and investment between both countries thrived. The Israeli minimalists and many of the Lebanese believed that, if the more radical elements of both countries did not upset it, a similar relationship could be established between Israel and Lebanon. The Lebanese politicians, however, were insecure, suspicious of one another, and continuously worried lest other Arab countries prod Lebanon's various minorities into renewed hostilities.

There were indications that the majority of the Moslem leaders would accept an informal settlement: an Israeli mission, with no official address, situated discreetly in some Beirut suburb, partnered by a similar Lebanese mission in Israel, with little public mention of the ongoing trade between the two countries. But they would not come out into the open with their support; they preferred to have it "forced" upon them by the Christian president. Amin Gemayel, though amenable to the substance of the solution, would have none of the Moslem leaders' tactics. Instead, he instructed his delegation to procrastinate in the deliberations until the Moslems were willing to collaborate openly.

Although, as prime minister, Shafik al-Wazzan was a clear and obstructive remnant of the previous regime, there were changes in the Gemayel administration and it had a new look. This was most noticeable among those in the entourage of the president dealing with international matters. Foreign Minister Elie Salem, fluent in English and married to an American, was probably the first man to hold this office without being able to speak any French. Like the others close to Amin Gemayel—such as Ghassan Tuèni, exambassador to the United States, and Wadid Haddad, who headed a small advisory bureau at the president's mansion—Salem had spent years in America and was a committed pro-American. Indeed, it was in the aftermath of the Israeli invasion that the United States, for the first time, gained a position of considerable influence in Beirut.

Much of the Lebanese dilemma was evident from the behavior of the members of their delegation in the early part of their long-drawn-out meetings with the Israelis. Composed of Christians (including one Maronite, one Greek Orthodox, one Protestant, and one Chaldean), as well as Moslems (both Shiite and Sunni), well connected to the Lebanese elder leadership, they breathed down each other's necks; everyone was careful to maintain the posture Beirut expected of him.

Eager for an outside power to solve their difficulties, the Lebanese still wished to complete the negotiations, knowing well that a breakdown would enable all the foreign troops to remain in their country. They were encouraged by the Americans, who assured the Lebanese that they were right to adopt a careful stance and who promised that the United States would do all it could to press upon the Israelis a quick retreat from their country.

The tension between the Israeli and American sides in Khalde was worsened by mutual personal dislikes on the part of some of the senior political leaders on either side. Also playing a part was the influence of the officers—civilian and military—on the spot. The Israelis had for many years suspected the American embassy staff in Lebanon of troublemaking. For years, the Beirut embassy had been headed by ambassadors who maintained informal contacts with the PLO while clearly avoiding the Christian Phalange. The U.S. ambassador, Robert Dillon, appointed shortly before the war, seemed to realize that times were changing but appeared to some Israelis to believe that he could apply to the Middle East the prejudices with which he had grown up in the American midwest; he was considered an obstacle to Lebanese-Israeli understanding. Less effective than many of his peers, his term of office was prematurely cut short in the second half of 1983. In his place the American administration nominated Reginald Bartholomew. Dillon had succeeded John Gunter Dean, born a Jew in Germany, who, prior to his transfer to Thailand and while in Beirut, had been openly critical of virtually everything Israeli and reportedly kept ongoing, if informal, contacts with the PLO.

Washington, too, was impatient to show results in Lebanon. America wanted a quick withdrawal of all foreign troops and was very sensitive to the hesitations of the Lebanese to make concessions toward normalization. As the American contribution to the negotiations diminished, the Israeli negotiators were especially disappointed with Philip Habib who, they felt, was deterring the Lebanese government from settling on the compromise that both the Moslem and Christian communities were willing to make.

Yet the Israelis refused to give up; they had their eyes on a peaceful settlement with Lebanon, which they believed to be within reach. They wanted to do their best to convert this blood-purchased breakthrough into solid diplomatic gain. They felt certain that, by remaining in their positions on the Damascus Road and in the Al-Shouf Mountains, their claims would be taken into account. The Kataeb forces, who feared that a premature Israeli retreat would expose and endanger their men facing the Druse in the Al-Shouf, supported the Israeli stand and made their opinion clear to President Gemayel.

Undoubtedly, the personal ability of George Shultz as a negotiator, as well as his prestige as the senior member of President Reagan's cabinet, played a major role in his success in finally securing, in May, an agreement between the divided Lebanese and the Israelis. But more important was the fact that Prime Minister Begin hoped, soon after, as much as anybody, to get the Israeli troops out of Lebanon as quickly as possible. Now that Ariel Sharon, the principal force in pushing Israel into the war in Lebanon, was ousted from the defense ministry and replaced by Moshe Ahrens, a former ambassador to Washington, the pressure on the Israeli cabinet to keep troops in Lebanon had diminished considerably. Sharon apparently felt that the government "must assure the political fruits of the military victory" in order to justify the war to the Israeli public. Ahrens, on the other hand, apparently shared the feeling of the majority of the cabinet that staying on in Lebanon was bringing diminishing returns and hurting Israeli-American relations, especially because President Reagan has put his personal prestige behind the effort to present some major foreign policy achievement in the Middle East.

The agreement hammered out by Secretary Shultz and approved by the Lebanese and the Israeli governments put a legal end to the state of war that has formally existed between the two countries since the day Israel was reborn in 1948. Lebanon thus became the second Arab country, after Egypt, to renounce the state of belligerency with Israel. The agreement also provides for a 45 kilometer-wide security zone in South Lebanon, where joint Lebanese-Israeli inspection teams will try to prevent the reestablishment of terrorist positions; a 15 kilometer-wide strip, along the Israel border, will be under the control of a special brigade composed of Maj. Haddad's Free Lebanon Forces, which will be reintegrated into the regular Lebanese Army with Maj. Haddad as deputy commander in-charge of anti-terrorist operations. Israel will continue to operate a liaison office in Beirut, which will have diplomatic status. The borders between the two countries will be opened for movement of people and goods six months after the signing of the agreement.

During the winter, Lebanese hopes had been raised toward regaining full independence in the post-PLO and post-Syria era. As time passed and the summer of 1983 drew to a close, the prospect of a united Lebanon that many of its citizens had believed they foresaw just fifteen months earlier, all but evaporated. The fratricide between the Shouf Druse and the Maronites in their midst and to their north resumed with passionate intensity. Women and children were massacred in many villages. The Kataeb, more arrogant and greedy following their successes in the preceding year, failed to mobilize a force to offset the more determined Druse fighters. These were logistically aided by the Syrians and mounted a ferocious attack, threatening not only a vendetta against the Christians but also posing a danger to Beirut, only a few miles away. Those who maintained that the main Lebanese tribes and their chieftains were more anxious to destroy each other than to overcome the discord among them and to get together in an atmosphere of goodwill, to collaborate in establishing or re-establishing a national Lebanese entity, found new support for their opinion. As the slaughtering in Lebanon was resumed in all its cruelty and the government once more lost nearly all control, talk of de facto partition was heard again. In Beirut, pessimism was greater than it had been for a long while.

As so often before, the mood of the Lebanese vacillated between hope and despair. Thomas I. Friedman, writing in the *International Herald Tribune* in late July 1983, pointed out the tragic irony: "The problem of the Lebanon . . . is that its disease and its cure are one and the same. The individual there has always derived social identity and psychological support from the family, neighborhood, or religious community but never from the nation as a whole. The war years have reinforced this tendency, drawing people together as a community—pulling them apart as a nation."[4]

These bonds, that enable them to cope with the violence around them, explain "their ingenious survival self-sufficiency" that "also prevents a strong government and national identity from emerging."[5]

14

Israel's Economic Needs and Independence

ISRAEL was affected far beyond the imaginings of its politicians and economists by the turbulences following the Yom Kippur War, the revolution in oil prices, and the accumulation of petropower in the Arabian Peninsula. By the end of the 1970s the price of oil was more than twenty times higher than it had been at the beginning of that decade, and yet it was not immediately realized how far-reaching the new realities would be and how deep an influence they would exert on the balance of power and on political relations in the Middle East.

Saudi Arabia, Kuwait, and some of the United Arab Emirates were now among the richest lands on earth. Wealth seemed to promise influence; whether real or imaginary remained to be tested. The whole world, including the superpowers, paid homage to the potentates. Although the Arab rulers set out on well-publicized programs of rapid economic development to bring their countries into the twentieth century, the results often seemed more for show than for future endogenous growth, and relatively small amounts trickled down to the Bedouin in their far-flung tents. Most of the surpluses derived from the export of oil remained unspent, concentrated in the hands of the Arab sheikhs, their close relatives, and a limited number of rich merchants. The rest was usually deposited with Western financial institutions.

America and the Western European countries were well aware of the mammon in their vaults and were worried by the danger of loss of balance in the banking system. They sought ways to recycle the newly deposited funds and often developed ingenious ideas for redirecting them into their economy. Selling arms to the Arabs, with their insatiable appetite for weapons, was one important way.

As the United States and the West sold more of the more sophisticated armaments to the Arab world, Israel, to maintain its deterrent power, felt impelled to increase its defensive arsenal. To do so, it had to increase its military budget, both for local production and for the import of weapons, spare parts, and other equipment that could be bought only with foreign currency. In the past decade, Israel has depended in this respect on the goodwill of the United States.*

The defense budget weighs heavily on Israel's economy. Soon, for its own good, the country must reduce the military portion of its gross national product. None of Ariel Sharon's predecessors in the Ministry of Defense accepted this. Among the main reasons for the hostility between Yitzhak Rabin and Shimon Peres, when the first was prime minister and the second the minister of defense, was the pressure to reduce the defense budget. Later Ezer Weizman, who succeeded Peres as defense minister when Menachem Begin became prime minister, resigned in 1980 when the cabinet insisted on reducing military expenditures.

Peres, Weizman, and Begin (who held the Defense Ministry portfolio as an extra duty for a year after Weizman resigned) each had his own defense policies and concepts but little interest in or patience with technical detail. All three disliked dealing with economic and financial questions and left them to subordinates who knew better than to bother their chiefs with such mundane questions as the cost-effectiveness of any proposed acquisition.

Sharon, campaigning for Weizman's job, appeared to understand the problem, at least in part. Soon after he assumed office, he announced that Israel would not continue to compete with the Arab

---

*It is of some interest to note that the total amount of U.S. aid to Israel in this period was considerably smaller than the profit American industry derived from the sale of arms to Israel's Arab opponents.

world to maintain the 1:3 deterrent balance* and that henceforth his ministry would cooperate in reducing the military budget. The outbreak of the war in Lebanon kept this promise from being put to the test.

The Lebanon war, however, appears to have imposed a relatively lighter financial burden on Israel than previous wars. Officially, the estimate is that the cost of the first six months of the fighting and occupation, to the end of 1982, has amounted to nearly $1.5 billion. Some people believe that the total will be closer to $2 billion.

The final cost of modern wars is the sum of three categories of expenses:

> The direct cost—the actual cost of feeding, supplying and moving the men in uniform, the transport of war material, and the cost of arms, equipment, and ammunition used up or lost in the field.
>
> The indirect cost—the loss to the national economy of workdays spent in the army, instead of in production, as well as the long-term economic cost of the loss of life and limb.
>
> The resulting cost—occurring after each war, when there is invariably a qualitative escalation in the type of weapon that each side wants to acquire on the basis of the lessons just learned. Frequently this means the introduction of entirely new generations of armaments. This, in the long run, can be the most expensive cost of war.

In the Lebanon war, Israeli mobilization was relatively limited and the losses of heavy weapons were small, especially in such expensive categories as fighter planes, helicopters, and tanks. There was a fairly heavy expenditure of ammunition and a significant cost in casualties. But—and this seems to be the biggest differ-

---

*A concept developed in the 1950s among the Israeli military that the country could defend itself successfully as long as the opposing Arabs did not have more than three times the weapons Israel had. Based on the present backlog of hardware to be supplied and negotiations for additional arms, the adversity ratio could reach 1:6 by 1990, with worse to come.

ence between this and previous wars—there are no indications of an immediate turn in the *qualitative* spiral of the arms race, which would force Israel to purchase new, much more expensive, major weapons systems.

As has already been mentioned, in Chapter 5, one significant exception to the general tendency to stay with the type of weapons already in use revolved around the unsolved question of what would replace the armored personnel carrier. When shot at by rocket propelled grenades, these APC's turned out to be firetraps, one of the main sources of casualties among the Israeli troops. Investing in many thousands of stronger, more protective vehicles could prove expensive.

Since the Likud government assumed office, Israel's foreign currency debts have more than doubled, increasing from approximately $12.5 billion in the summer of 1977 to well over $26 billion at the end of 1982. The short-term debt had grown far more rapidly, a fact that was also cause for worry. To some, who argued that Israel had cash deposits and investments abroad amounting to well over $10 billion, this gross foreign currency debt did not seem so worrying. Others doubted whether, if that rainy day came, these assets could be used by Israel. The country's total external debt on the eve of the Yom Kippur War was just over $6 billion; after the Six Day War in 1967, it had been less than $1.8 billion.

Israel's big problem is not only the very heavy government budget but also its composition. Even if the Israeli administration succeeded in reducing defense expenditures somewhat, approximately one-third of the total budget pie is still bespoken to debt servicing. And although much of the foreign currency debt is long-term, the cost of its servicing equals the sum of the country's entire industrial exports. The necessity of speedy rearmament following military confrontations has always been a grave setback to Israel's struggle toward self-sufficiency or a positive balance of trade. Compared with 1972, when exports reached almost 62 percent of imports, they were just 47.6 percent in 1974 though gradually rising again to more than 73 percent in 1981. There were signs that the gap would increase again in 1983.

Still, defense spending remaining high at an estimated 21.3 percent of its gross national product and debt service increasingly burdensome, no wonder the U.S. administration grows concerned in recent years to the "increasing dilemma in [the need] to bolster Israel's economy and ensure support to its budget. [These could cause] Israel to intensify its requests to the United States for increased assistance."[1]

It is extraordinary, however, how vigorous the economy is in spite of the growth in foreign debt, the runaway inflation, and the frequent labor unrest in the public sector. Unemployment is generally below 3 percent and until 1982, when owing to the world recession sales slowed down, exports grew at a faster pace than did imports. Between 1976 and 1981, exports increased by 240 percent, from $4.7 billion to $11.2 billion, while imports less than doubled, from $7.9 billion to $15.6 billion. Export figures for the first half of 1983 showed an unexpected drop that, if continued, could prove serious. Most economists related it to the inevitable consequences of the populist economic policies of the minister of finance. These policies included an unrealistic rate of exchange of Israel's currency, which encouraged imports but deterred exports, worsening the already horrendous adverse balance of trade by more than one billion U.S. dollars annually. Increasing numbers hoped that the adverse figures were of a temporary nature, that these policies were soon to change and soon the trend would be corrected.

Holding its own in the export market has been a major achievement for Israel. Although an important share of exports has been along conventional lines, ranging from polished diamonds to textiles and clothing, Israel has in the past decade, taken a place in the areas of electronics, high technology, and sophisticated weaponry. A long-time citrus producer, Israel has also become a major supplier of early and out-of-season fruits and vegetables to the Common Market. But it is in military and related manufacture that Israel's pace of exports has increased most rapidly since the early 1970s.

Unlike small European countries such as Holland and Denmark, which market well over half their exports to their neighbors, well within 500 miles of their production lines, Israel's markets are much farther off; more than 90 percent of its exports are shipped by sea or air to destinations thousands of miles away.

Breaking into these highly competitive overseas markets was a challenge Israeli producers met with gusto. Often they encountered

211

political obstacles—countries that maintained no diplomatic relations with Israel or that publicly followed the dictates of the Arab boycott. Ingenious ways had to be found to circumvent these obstacles. Particularly difficult problems were posed by some foreign (usually American) suppliers of parts and semifinished products; these sources often contractually prohibited Israeli remarketing of the materials without explicit permission.

Israel's sophisticated arms industry continued to be one of the mainstays of her exports. It is the direct outgrowth of the uncertainty of the supply from abroad. Bitter experience—such as the 1967 French arms embargo imposed by President Charles de Gaulle even before Israel moved to expel the Egyptian troops blockading the Straits of Tiran—has taught Israel two hard lessons. First, arms dependence exposes the country to political pressure. Second, the rate of attrition in modern warfare can make a non-self-sufficient party a completely dependent hostage of a vital supplier. Moreover, even in peacetime, the chances of upgrading armament systems and keeping up in the arms race with potential enemies are dependent on the goodwill of the manufacturing nations. Reminders of this problem, so far on a limited scale, have occurred in 1981, after the bombing of the Iraqi nuclear plant, and twice since, when the U.S. government ordered temporary halts in the supply of F-16 fighters and cluster bombs, respectively.

When Israel decided to become as self-sufficient in weapons as possible it became essential to develop an export market to reduce the cost per unit of its arms production to a reasonable level. Thus, Israel began to look for foreign markets. However, since even local manufacture of modern weapons includes some foreign components, here again Israel encountered the problem of licensing. And this time it involved political as well as business considerations. An example is the export of sophisticated systems such as Kfir fighter aircraft produced by the Israel aviation industries. The airplane uses American engines. Wherever the United States wished to sell its own fighter planes, it was virtually impossible for the Israelis to export theirs. Usually it was only to pariah or quasi-pariah states, about which the U.S. Department of Defense feared questions from Congress and comments from the media, that permission was granted for Israel to export weapons with American components.

Thus, in the 1970s Israel exported arms to Augusto Pinochet Ugarte's Chile and to Anastasio Somoza's Nicaragua. Later, it supplied other Central American republics as well as Argentina. Similarly, although the volume may not have been great and the connections low-key, critics of Israel repeatedly charged in the foreign press and at United Nations forums, that Israel was also maintaining contacts with South Africa, Taiwan, and other countries with which the United States preferred not to trade directly.

In the immediate aftermath of the Yom Kippur War, President Richard Nixon asked the U.S. Congress to approve a $2.2 billion military aid program to Israel. It was passed by a large majority and America rapidly refilled Israel's arsenals, in certain cases temporarily drawing down its NATO reserves in West Germany. In the decade since, Israel has become far more dependent on American generosity than is widely realized. In the nine years ending December 31, 1982, for instance, Israel has received nearly $23 billion in assistance from the United States, or some 24 percent of the total $94 billion American foreign aid. Approximately $12.3 billion is in outright grants and the remaining $10.7 billion in long-term, interest-bearing loans. Altogether, U.S. assistance to Israel since establishment totals over $25 billion, of which over $16.5 billion were in military loans and grants; over $6.5 billion in economic assistance under the security assistance program, and over $2 billion in other nonsecurity assistance programs.[2] "And levels have increased significantly since 1973.... Following the 1979 Camp David accords, Israel remained the largest recipient of U.S. economic and military assistance," wrote the U.S. Comptroller General.[3]

In the previous decade, 1964 to 1973, total U.S. overseas assistance was $71.6 billion, with Israel's share some $1.6 billion or just 2 percent. In the first fifteen years of Israel's existence, American aid was some $750 million, which was less than 1 percent of all U.S. foreign aid during that period. The American contribution to Israel, however, was acknowledged to be material. i.e., "Israel documents show that U.S. assistance funded by percent of its defense budget" in 1982.[4]

In the wake of the Lebanon war, the size of American economic support for Israel became a greater political issue than before, both in the United States and in Israel. In America, the debate started in the summer of 1982, mainly among liberal Jews who were worried by Israel's bombing of Beirut and shocked by the massacre in the Sabra and Shatilla Palestinian refugee camps. Almost personally angry with the Begin administration and frustrated by their own helplessness, they decided that one thing that could be done was to punish Israel by decreasing or holding back altogether on economic support.

In recent years, the amount of money contributed to Israel by the Jewish community through the United Jewish Appeal and through sales of Israel Development Bonds has amounted to less than 20 percent of the American government's assistance. The contribution, equal to some 3 percent of Israel's import bill, has become far less significant than in the early years of statehood. Therefore, a far more potent weapon than reducing contributions from Jewish sources was the threat of cutting back on more than $2 billion of American government aid. In summer and fall 1982 some two-thirds of the letters sent to congressmen and senators—especially those sent to legislators with links to the Jewish community, the Middle East, or both—demanded that support for Israel be reduced or stopped altogether.

The criticism voiced at Israel by members of Congress who were usually counted among its staunchest friends was less expected than some of the comments coming from the administration. Then, in the midst of the dispute over the terms of the Israeli withdrawal from Lebanon, Congress decided to increase the grant portion of aid to Israel—despite strong opposition from the White House. Were different segments of official Washington working at cross purposes on the Middle East? Or was the administration's position only a stand to impress the Arabs while in fact it was rewarding Israel for having served American interests in Lebanon, as certain leftist circles allege?

There is no evidence of collusion of that kind. But neither is there reason to believe that the administration wanted to prevent more generous aid for Israel. Yet whatever was to be done could not be susceptible of interpretation as a prize for Israel; the administration did not want to again send a misleading signal to the Israeli government, as former secretary of state Alexander Haig had done before the war. American officials maintain that the more attractive terms were the result of effective lobbying by the Israeli embassy in Washington and the American-Israel Public Affairs Committee (AIPAC). By May 1982 the lobbyists had convinced a considerable number of senators and congressmen that Israel urgently needed help to relieve its debt repayment burden, and Senator Alan Cranston of California presented an amendment that would peg the size of the grants to the size of the debt-servicing requirements. The administration, mainly as a matter of principle, objected and exerted its own pressure; the Senate debt repayment amendment was then defeated in committee, nine to eight. Still, the administration made several tactical mistakes in handling the issue in Congress and the merit of its argument gradually lessened for the senators and congressmen.

The case of the grants to Israel raises a fundamental question about the limited effectiveness of aid as an instrument of Great Power foreign policy, especially when the country receiving the help is in difficult economic circumstances. Congress may not always be ready to legislate loan repayment amendments but the very risk of the recipient country's inability to service its debt burden may prevent utilization of the grantor's debt leverage when it might otherwise be most effective.

There are those in Washington who insist that the cost of financial support of Israel is not only reasonable but actually a bargain. Senator Rudy Boschwitz of Minnesota, former chairman of the Senate Foreign Relations Subcommittee on the Middle East, has compared it to the cost to the United States of protecting Europe.

On November 30, 1982, Under-Secretary for Political Affairs Lawrence Eagleburger, answering his subcommittee, estimated the American contribution to Western European defenses in actual cash outlays to be in the range of $50 billion to $80 billion a year. Professor David Calleo of Johns Hopkins University has estimated that the cost to the United States of NATO defenses in 1981 was $81 billion.[5]

Whatever the political criticism, there appeared to be, toward the end of 1982, little inclination, either in the administration or in Congress, to punish Israel by reducing the level of assistance. But the question would not simply go away. Was there now a funda-

215

mental contradiction between the purpose for which the U.S. government was providing assistance to Israel and the aim of the Israeli government in using it? Washington wanted to advance a compromise settlement in the Israel-Arab dispute and hoped to make Israel feel more disposed to compromise. The Jerusalem government has used part of the aid to establish new settlements and foster other policies which make territorial compromise unlikely. This must ultimately lead to a head-on collision. The Israeli government should realize that to continue to be the largest recipient of American government aid would require collaboration and cooperation to a degree that neither it nor its citizens are ready for. If the Middle East policy of the United States remains based on the Reagan peace proposals, which the Israeli government finds unacceptable, and if the U.S. administration intends to try actively to implement them, the continuation of American economic support for Israel should not be taken for granted.

Yet the Israeli government relies on the belief that the Jewish state is a strategic asset for the United States and that it can, therefore, depend on continued American aid under practically any circumstances. There are no signs that the Israeli government has even begun searching for alternative economic policies.

Whatever past commitments America may have had toward Israel, whatever the theoretical arguments for supporting it may be—and some are very weighty—there are pressures to reduce the level of American aid to that country. It would be prudent to assume that those pressures will be more powerful when aid programs are presented to Congress in the mid-1980s.

15

Is Israel
a Strategic
Asset?

The touchstone of our relationship with Israel is that a secure, strong Israel is in America's self-interest. Israel is a major strategic asset to America. Israel is not a client, but a very reliable friend.
—Ronald Reagan,
        speaking during the presidential campaign, 1980.

THE credibility of Israel's statements has been one of the casualties of the war in Lebanon. With it went much of Israel's image of reliability. The beginning of the erosion of both predates the war by several years and was accentuated with the change of government in 1977. Much of the world at large as well as the losing minority of the Israeli electorate suspected Menachem Begin's intentions from his first day in office. Statements that can be misinterpreted or misleading, the daily bread of governments everywhere, acquired enlarged proportions as the new policies were implemented. It took several months before the new prime minister managed to reinstate his earlier image as a man of honor whose word is his bond; that image of the Israeli leader probably was essential for Egyptian president Anwar Sadat to make his decision to visit Jerusalem.

The regained image of respectability showed its first crack after the Camp David accords. Begin's promise to freeze further Jewish settlement of the West Bank, understood by President Jimmy Carter to be valid for the duration of the negotiations, was claimed by the prime minister to be limited to three months only. Indeed, the implementation of the settlement policy continued to be the source of much of the contradiction between what the government seemed to proclaim and what it appeared to implement. The leniency toward the religious-nationalist squatters who moved into the Rafiah salient in the last months before the final evacuation of Sinai—and the tacit support given them by Defense Minister Ariel Sharon—increased suspicions in Israel and abroad that after President Sadat's assassination, Prime Minister Begin was having second thoughts about the wisdom of completing the withdrawal.

The Begin government was delighted with President Reagan's appointment in December 1980 of Alexander Haig as secretary of state—a good friend of Israel, they were told. Toward the end of the Carter era, tensions between the two governments had clearly been increasing. As Harold Saunders, Carter's assistant secretary of state for Near Eastern and South Asian affairs, noted, there was "a rising tide of resentment in this country, among officials and private citizens alike, that Israel seems to expect limitless support from the United States, regardless of what it does, without regard for the interests of the United States." The fact that many friends of Israel protested the tone of the statement could not erase its content or the suspicion that it had the backing of the White House.

The aura of reliability was seriously clouded in the summer of 1981, just before the general election, by the bombing of the Osirak nuclear reactor near Baghdad. For Begin and many Israelis there was no question about the justification of the spectacularly precise operation. Iraq, which was about to gain nuclear capability, considered itself to be at war with Israel and had issued public statements indicating that its nuclear achievements would be directed against Israel. Yet this was something that had never been done before: attacking the nuclear facility of another country for any reason, let alone for the purpose of preventing its use for weapons production. It was something shockingly different and unforeseen and introduced a new element of unpredictability into international relations while reviving the image of Begin's Israel as a wild, unreliable country. Begin had never promised immunity to Arab nuclear facilities capable of producing weapons-grade material, but the West, although aware of the inefficiency of the inspections by the International Atomic Agency, feared that Israel's decision to take the matter of "safeguards" into its own hands would create a dangerous international precedent.

Although there was much admiration in the West, the Third World, and even in the Communist countries for the accuracy with which the Israeli intelligence and air force planned the bombing of the Osirak installations, the shock caused by this unilateral action is believed to have affected many of the senior officers in both the American and the Soviet administrations. Even close friends of Israel in Washington had no indication of Israel's plans. The unilateral nature of the action infringed the implicit agreement—to keep one another abreast of major steps about to be taken—that had been believed to exist between the leadership of both countries.

When Israeli tanks crossed the border into southern Lebanon the West was still under the impact of the shooting of Ambassador Shlomo Argov in London and the broad shelling of border towns and villages by the PLO. The 45-kilometer limit of the Israeli advance, announced by Begin personally, was seen as an undertaking to stay within tolerable bounds. Criticism was relatively mild in most of the Western media. Things changed drastically, however, when Israeli troops continued beyond the announced limit. That was also where the government and the Opposition parted company. From supporting the invasion as a necessity for the defense of northern Israel, the Opposition shifted to bitter criticism of the expanded scope of the fighting and occupation. Simultaneously, foreign politicians, journalists, and much of their publics felt misled and deceived by Israel. (Unlike Israeli politicians and commentators, their foreign counterparts could not conceive that the Israeli government was letting itself be dragged step by step into the war by an adventurous minister of defense. They judged that the entire cabinet must be partners to a preconceived plan of deception.)

Had George Shultz become secretary of state in June 1981, it probably would not have prevented the war in Lebanon. But the fact that Alexander Haig remained secretary until the end of June 1982 probably did have an important influence both on American behavior toward Israel and on Israel's interpretation of and conclusions about what America's interests were. It almost certainly contributed to Israel's persistence in carrying out its more than seventy-day siege, from June to August, 1982, and the repeated bombing of West Beirut.

In the second half of June, President Reagan was assured by visiting Prime Minister Begin that Israel had no intention of entering West Beirut. But the day after Begin left Washington there was an escalation in the Israeli application of power: the Syrians were attacked on the Beirut-Damascus highway and a major Israeli bombardment of Beirut took place. It was at that time that Washington's attitude began to turn. So long as Israel's credibility was maintained and it could be argued that Israel's aim was the establishment of a 40- to 45-kilometer-wide security zone north of its border, the approach of the United States was one of understanding, interpreted by some Israelis as positive encouragement. Secretary Haig could persuade the administration not to take steps that might lead to the loss of the fruits of the operation—for Israel and for the West alike. But his influence was impaired when the Israelis arrived at the outskirts of Beirut. It deteriorated rapidly in the week after Begin's visit, as the suspicions increased that the United States—and the president personally—had been misled by the Israeli prime minister.

The pictures of the bombing of a big city, presented in closeup every night on television, had considerable influence on the decision makers in Washington. No means exist yet, so it appears, to neutralize for long the visual impact of smoke, flames, and casualties. Every television newscast showing more carnage and destruction in Beirut lowered White House tolerance for Israel's actions and brought it closer to those people in the American administration who, from the beginning, had opposed Secretary Haig's line. For weeks, President Reagan and Secretary Haig had overruled the critics, but on that crucial weekend at the end of June the president instructed the secretary to send a stiff note to Israel. Although he reportedly felt that stopping the Israelis at that point was a mistake, that the offensive was almost over, and that two or three more days of bombing would get the PLO out of Beirut, the secretary obeyed. The Israeli bombardments temporarily stopped—and then Haig resigned. It was the culmination of several policy disputes but the one over the Middle East was among the most obvious. Haig was ready to face more of the pictures on television but the president was not willing to tolerate the sight of what many in the administration perceived as a ruinous influence on America's image.

American Middle East policy, intended to be pragmatic, often appeared indeterminate, sometimes vacillatory or fickle; it probably led to more international misunderstanding than was really necessary. This can be explained, at least in part, by the relative ease with which top American officials are handling relatively minor emergencies, thus running the risk of losing their way in the Middle East maze. Yet among those assigned to implement this policy were some of the best of the State Department professional corps. Senior among them was Ambassador Philip Habib, recalled from retirement in the spring of 1981 to act as the president's personal representative on the spot—the troubleshooter. It was he who was delegated to deal with the PLO still in Beirut.

Now it appeared that Israel's hand was being restrained, and because of that Yasser Arafat understood that although the PLO eventually would have to get out, he had the leeway to bargain for a very long time for terms that would allow him to present the evacuation as a military and moral victory. The American policy was making Ambassador Habib's task more difficult. And at the same time, different evaluations of American political gain from the outcome of the war in Lebanon contributed significantly to the widening gap between the Reagan administration and the Begin government.

The Israeli government believed from the outset that American interests could and did benefit greatly from Israel's achievements in Lebanon and expected this to be reflected in Israel-U.S. relationships. But the Americans felt that whatever benefits the United States could have gained were largely dissipated when the bombardment of Beirut began. From the moment Israel assaulted a major Arab capital, any association with the operation (and any alliance with Israel) became, in Washington's view, a burden vis-à-vis the Arabs. "Guilt by association" was and remains a major cost factor of the war.

Moreover, American official circles remained skeptical about many of the benefits Israel claimed to have provided the United States. To begin with, the assumption that destroying its base in Lebanon has eliminated PLO terror worldwide has not been proved. Even less certain is the measure of the blow given to international terror in general. The capacity of Palestinian extremism was not necessarily eliminated; it may just be biding its time until it has recovered and sees which way Arafat goes. It still may be capable of a new wave of terror and hijacking, possibly or especially against American interests.

Secondly, the improvement of the American strategic position in the Middle East as a result of the war was also strongly questioned, as well as the benefits of stationing U.S. troops in Lebanon. Bringing American forces so close to Syria made many in the Pentagon quite nervous since it could make them a "lightning rod" for Syria's actions.

As an opportunity to test the effectiveness of certain Soviet weapons and as a demonstration of the superiority of American arms, the war was certainly useful. But Israeli assertions that the defeat of the Syrian-operated MiGs and SAMs changed the perceived balance between NATO and the Warsaw Pact countries in Europe was considered to be a gross exaggeration.

Finally, it was not the war in Lebanon that reduced the Soviet foothold in the Middle East. The Russians were out in 1973 and were no closer to coming back in 1981. The centrality of the United States for any peaceful settlement remained crucial—also in the eyes of the Arab world—but not more so than in 1981.

The Syrians posed another problem. Since the summer, the Americans had thought that Hafez al-Assad's regime was signalling that they would, in principle, be willing to move their troops out of Lebanon. At the United Nations, on October 18, 1982, President Gemayel called "for the immediate and unconditional withdrawal of all non-Lebanese forces from Lebanon." On November 20, at the 20th Congress of the Union of Workers, President Assad declared over Radio Damascus that "we have voiced many times our readiness to leave the Lebanon." As early as September 9 of that year Secretary Shultz had reported in hearings before the House Foreign Affairs Committee that the Syrian foreign minister had told him that "if the government of the Lebanon asks us to leave, we will leave." To which Shultz answered, "I will take you at your word."

But it was clear that there were those who were skeptical of the Syrian commitment, while others hoped for the best. Schultz, for instance, quoted Philip Habib who said that when somebody makes a statement like that "you take it and put it into your pocket, and you bring it back out again occasionally."

All in all, Americans felt that in late 1983 it was still too early to draw up the final balance of the costs and benefits to them of the war in Lebanon. It may take two to three years to do so because it may take that much time before the fundamental question of the war's effect on a peaceful settlement of the Palestine dispute can be answered. For example, if, early evidence to the contrary, the dispersal of the PLO from Beirut has indeed created an opening for Jordan to enter into the negotiations, and if this in turn has resulted in the completion of the Camp David peace process, that could constitute a major gain for America. If all foreign forces were to leave Lebanon and it were to be reestablished as an independent and sovereign country and an island of stability, and if the United States was perceived as having been instrumental in achieving this, then America could conclude that the costs were not as great as the benefits.

On September 1, 1982, under the television impact of the siege of Beirut, President Reagan put forward proposals for the solution of the Palestine problem in the form of full autonomy for the West Bank in association with Jordan. It was a comprehensive policy statement, giving cognizance to the Palestinians in the Gaza Strip and Judea and Samaria more clearly than any previous president or administration had done, and it was approved by most Westerners in general and Americans in particular as soon as they perceived the gist of the plan. Although it offered firm commitments to the security and viability of Israel, Prime Minister Begin precipitously and loudly rejected the Reagan plan. The PLO, more quietly at first but not less firmly, did the same. Jordan, which was to join the talks as senior partner in a joint delegation with non-PLO Palestinians, wanted approval from the PLO to represent it in negotiations on the Reagan plan. This did not prevent Jordan, as well as Egypt and other "pro-Western" Arab states, from declaring that they could not sit down to negotiate with Israel as long as Israeli soldiers were still in Lebanon. Washington therefore redoubled its pressure to get the Israeli (and Syrian) troops out as fast as possible, to open the way to the "central issues" of autonomy. (For this very reason, of course, Israel was in no hurry.)

The sense of a breach of confidence between Jerusalem and Washington was revived with added bitterness when Israeli troops moved into West Beirut after the assassination of President-elect Bashir Gemayel. It was contrary to assurances given and understandings reached between Israel and the United States before the marines arrived in Beirut as part of the multinational peacekeeping force. The Israeli government claimed that the unexpected turn of events necessitated an unforeseen response. The Americans felt that Israel was just waiting to make a grab for West Beirut. The argument took on a tragic dimension within two days when the massacre in the refugee camps occurred. Israel was publicly castigated for having justified the entry into West Beirut by the need to keep law and order following the assassination and then having made the massacre possible. The Israeli government's credibility was now badly shaken.

Erosion of credibility, however, was not entirely a one-way affair. Many Israelis felt that, having first shared Israeli attempts to free Lebanon from PLO and Syrian occupation and restore its full sovereignty, Washington got cold feet and joined the Arabs condemning Israel.

Israel has been stung by high-handed American policies before. The embassy of the United States, for instance, is located in Tel Aviv and the ambassador has no authority over the consul general who resides in Jerusalem.* Neither the consulate nor the embassy in Tel Aviv recognize Jerusalem as the capital of Israel. The American Fourth of July receptions in Jerusalem are usually held on July 3 and 5, with Jews invited separately from the Arab guests. American government officials visit the West Bank but make a point of not

---

*The only other American consul general with independent status is in Hong Kong.

224

landing in Jerusalem's Atarot airport, considered part of "occupied territory."

The Arabs, for their part, felt they could insult the Americans with impunity. For instance, secretaries of state and their representatives could be kept waiting for hours and sometimes days before being received by the Saudi king. In August 1983, the Kuwaiti government blocked the appointment of Brandon Grove, Jr., as the next American ambassador to their country, just because his previous position had been that of consul general in Jerusalem. They were totally uninterested in the fact that the consul was thoroughly disliked by the Israelis and were adamant in their refusal to recognize him, although the Americans went out of their way to emphasize that they had never recognized the annexation of East Jerusalem by Israel or, indeed, that Jerusalem was the capital of Israel.

Defense Secretary Caspar Weinberger has repeatedly been just as abrasive about the Israeli leadership as the Israelis are about him, and when the American marines landed in Beirut late in 1982 he prohibited them from making any formal contact or having any informal fraternization with the Israelis. Similarly, the U.S. Mediteranean fleet only rarely stops in Israeli ports and makes it a point to relay the message loud and clear to the Arab world.

There are other increasingly more difficult areas of relationships, especially the exchange of information about military equipment. This mutual aggravation and suspicion created the atmosphere in which a minor incident between American and Israeli patrols in Beirut could be turned by Secretary Weinberger into an Israeli provocation and by Defense Ministry sources in Tel Aviv into charges of drunkenness on the part of a U.S. marine captain.

The Israeli patrol was apparently within the area allotted to it in an agreement reached a week earlier between local commanders, but Washington's failure to approve that agreement heightened Israeli suspicions of ulterior American motives. Despite the comic opera quality of the announcement by Weinberger that the marine officer had singlehandedly stopped three Israeli tanks south of Beirut, the incident and its dramatization in the media showed how far Israeli-American relations had deteriorated in the aftermath of the war in Lebanon.

Israel undoubtedly shared responsibility for the turn of events.

The government's need to show progress toward the political aims of the war clashed with the more and more open efforts of President Amin Gemayel to distance himself from his party's (and his late brother Bashir's) association with Israel. The Commission of Inquiry into the Sabra and Shatilla massacres was about to present its findings, and a breakthrough in the negotiations with Lebanon could have helped the government to balance criticism in the report by showing success in attaining political goals in Lebanon. Defense Minister Sharon, who had reasons to be particularly concerned about the report, was engaged in increasingly desperate efforts to show some progress. As his announced "success" after repeated "secret" meetings in Beirut evaporated into thin air, Sharon put the blame increasingly on the Americans.

Sharon's personal vendetta with the United States—paralleled by what many in Israel felt was Defense Secretary Weinberger's personal animosity toward Israel—tended to distract attention from some of the real and important failures and mistakes of American policy in the Middle East. Washington often seemed to read the map wrongly. Whether because of faulty intelligence reports or incorrect interpretation, the United States again appeared to have set out on a path that in recent years has led it to be caught by surprise after surprise: by the visit of the Anwar Sadat to Jerusalem, by the fall of the shah of Iran, by the capture of the holy shrines of Mecca by religious Moslem fanatics, and by Saudi Arabia's refusal to support the Israel-Arab peace process.

Washington also appeared to believe that King Hussein of Jordan fervently wished to join the peace talks with Israel, that Saudi Arabia was backing the moderates in the Arab world against the hawks, that the Israeli prime minister could hardly wait to renew negotiations on autonomy for the Palestinians, and that Lebanon needed American protection against Israeli pressures. All four assumptions were in essence incorrect.

Only the most naive of observers could believe that King Hussein yearned to again become the focus of intrigues and controversy in the Israel-Arab confrontation, to get into a new fight with the Palestinians, or to pull the PLO chestnuts out of the fire. In fact, Hussein seemed to be doing his best to *postpone* the moment when he would have to decide whether to join or not. The last thing in which Hussein was interested was the first thing many Israelis (especially the compromise-minded doves) wanted him to do: take on the headache of ruling over another million restless Palestinians. And the one thing Hussein wanted most was to get back East Jerusalem—which was exactly the concession that practically no Israeli would be willing to make, even for the sake of a peace treaty. Thus, when Washington saw Hussein as the key to further progress in the Middle East peace process, it was tying the first step in that process to the very thing to which Israel was most unlikely ever to accede.

Similarly, Washington was slow to realize how misconceived was the idea of Saudi Arabia's helping the peace process. The entire Saudi foreign policy has for decades been based on the principle of never sticking its neck out. The Saudis never helped Washington to moderate the extremists in the Arab camp. The House of Saud never wanted to upset anything or anybody in the Arab world or do anything that might appear out of the ordinary. The Saudis always worked for Arab consensus—which would obviate the need for them to take a stand of their own. They disappointed those Americans who hoped that Riadh would cushion the oil crisis of 1973/74, restrain the PLO and the Syrians in the Lebanese civil war, and support the Camp David agreements in 1978. In fact, through its actions the Saudi government has shown that it worries about one single problem: how to avoid the fall of the House of Saud. To that end, the Saudis have been bribing the most extreme elements in the Arab world—including groups that openly call for their overthrow. Yet, instead of America using Saudi fears to the benefit of Western interests, the Saudis have been using Washington's fears to manipulate the Americans.

U.S. policy vis-à-vis Prime Minister Begin appeared equally ill conceived. The Americans repeated again and again that they wanted Israel to be more flexible in talks with Lebanon, in order to open the way for the resumption of discussions on the fate of the West Bank. In other words, Washington expected Begin to make concessions to President Gemayel of Lebanon and to President Hafez al-Assad of Syria, so as to be asked next to make concessions to Yasser Arafat. The Israeli government understood this, even without Washington's stressing the consequential linkage—and obviously saw it as a good reason *not* to hurry to finish the Lebanese business. Moreover, since the Syrians feared that if Jordan joined the peace process Syria would be even more isolated in the Arab world, they had a basic interest in preventing Hussein from joining the peace talks. When Washington says that withdrawal of foreign troops (Israeli and Syrian) from Lebanon is necessary before Hussein joins in, the Syrians are practically given the power to veto Hussein's decision.

As negotiations became enmeshed in the politics of the Levant, it became clear that Lebanon's chances of true independence did not lie in reducing Israeli pressure on Beirut to change the relationship between the two states. Instead, Lebanon's salvation was seen in reducing Syrian pressure to keep its own troops in Lebanon while abetting the return of previously ousted PLO units. Washington had virtually no influence on Damascus and could do little to get the Syrians out of Lebanon. What President Gemayel needed was help in resisting Syrian and PLO pressures; on this subject, Washington's help was not enough.

American tactical pragmatism was at its most flexible in 1982 and 1983. After Secretary Shultz persuaded the Lebanese and Israelis to make de facto peace in May 1983 and received their full cooperation, the Reagan West Bank proposals were quietly (and temporarily?) shelved, while the United States thrust was to convince the Israelis to delay the start of their redeployment until Syria showed a similar willingness.

But, more important for Israel, the agreement with Lebanon followed soon after the appointment of Ahrens as Minister of Defense. This was a popular choice in Washington and the two events together seemed like the start of a new page in American-Israeli relations. In the early summer of 1983, Israelis were more welcome in the American capital than they had been for some years.

One of the most controversial issues between the American administration and the Israeli government is whether Israel is indeed a strategic asset to the United States and, if so, if the fact should be appreciated and acknowledged publicly.

The idea that American global defense strategy should take the

Israeli military into account first arose in the 1960s, when Soviet penetration into the Middle East began in earnest. That was when the Russian military sales program to Egypt, Syria, and Iraq started and the presence of many thousands of Soviet military personnel in these countries became a threat, not only to Israel but to American and Western interests in the area.

It was Israel's dramatic military success in the Six Day War that induced the administrations of Lyndon Johnson and Richard Nixon to help modernize the Israel Defense Forces. Six years later, American contributions were instrumental in the extraordinary reversal of the tide in the Yom Kippur War. They helped Israel contain the Egyptian and Syrian attack and, within days, launch a counteroffensive to within artillery range of Damascus and, across the Suez Canal, to within 60 miles of Cairo. Even those critical of Israel's initial failure to interpret correctly the warning signals intercepted by intelligence, which let Israel's defense system be caught unprepared, were impressed by the capacity of its armed forces to fight their way to victory.

The American administrations thereafter undertook to supply Israel with more sophisticated weaponry and in ample quantities. The repeated assessment of American armor and air planners was that feedback received from the Israelis who handled and so creatively modified U.S.-built equipment constituted a considerable immediate dividend, and helped the Americans improve the quality of their products.

With the advent of the Begin government in early summer 1977, Israel wished to obtain public expression of the concept, never really unquestioningly accepted, of Israel as a geopolitical-military asset to the United States in the confrontation with the Soviet Union and other totalitarian forces. In his first meeting with President Carter, in July 1977, Menachem Begin tried to convince the American president to make such a statement. Whatever the private response, publicly there was a very clear lack of enthusiasm for the idea. After Ronald Reagan became president and for the eighteen months during which Alexander Haig was secretary of state (from the beginning of 1981 until the summer of 1982), the view of Israel as a strategic asset was accepted in principle. But for the Israeli premier,.

229

a great believer in explicit public statements and commitments, the absence of any formal American acknowledgment was highly disappointing.

One of the strangest episodes in pursuit of such a document occurred in November 1981 in an intensive-care unit of the Hadassah Hospital in Jerusalem. Prime Minister Begin had just undergone a thigh operation. In his sickroom a few days later, the scene was somewhat surrealistic. On one side of the room were some potted plants and an Israeli flag; in the center stood the jacked-up bed of Mr. Begin; on the other side, in a sort of semicircle, sat members of the cabinet, passing around, and seeing for the first time, the only available copy of the draft text of the Memorandum of Understanding on Strategic Cooperation between the United States and Israel. While Defense Minister Sharon elaborated on the merits of the draft (prepared by his aides) and Foreign Minister Yitzhak Shamir and Interior Minister Yosef Burg cited its discrepancies, Begin occasionally dozed off under the influence of sedatives administered to alleviate the postoperational pain. After less than one hour of discussion, at the doctors' urging, the session broke up. Sharon climbed into a waiting helicopter and rushed to Ben Gurion Airport and the plane that took him to Washington. Thus, without formal vote by the cabinet, which had not had a chance to study it thoroughly, Israel approved what the prime minister and the defense minister afterward described as one of the most important foreign relations agreements in the country's modern history. Most cabinet members attached less importance than that to the document; even the Soviet Union, against which it was unprecedentedly and specifically aimed, did not take it very seriously.

The next day, Secretary Weinberger and Minister Sharon initialled the document at a dinner held at the National Portrait Gallery in Washington. At the request of the Americans, no photographers were admitted.

Two weeks later, Begin appeared in the Knesset in a wheelchair. With no preliminary discussions, the parliament conducted a fourteen-hour shotgun debate and passed legislation extending the application of Israeli law to the Golan Heights, which had been under Israeli administration since 1967. Totally unprepared for such a gambit, most foreign states, including the United States, regarded this as tantamount to annexation of the area, which previously belonged to Syria. Declaring the move unacceptable, the U.S. government demonstrated its chagrin by postponing indefinitely any ratification of the strategic memorandum. An angry Begin accused Washington of "trying to make Israel hostage." Weinberger's subsequent willingness, in June 1983, to reinstate the memorandum would not erase Israeli memories of its earlier abrupt suspension.

In the following winter and the spring of 1982, as the invasion of southern Lebanon was being planned, scheduled, postponed, revised, and rescheduled, among the aspects discussed again and again was that of potential American support. The U.S. embassy in Tel Aviv had known since the winter that something was going to happen. In Washington, Sharon made the issue clear in his meetings with both Haig and Weinberger in May. Whatever they told him, American attitudes in the following weeks left the clear impression that Washington understood Israel's need for action and, once the operation was under way, hoped to turn it to the benefit of the West.

Yet when the Israelis reached Beirut and laid siege to it, they felt that America once again appeared unappreciative of what they had done, not only for themselves but for the good of the United States as well.

Prime Minister Begin, in June 1983 meetings with Philip Habib, pointed out that it was only through its special relationship with Israel that America had made important gains in the Middle East. Thanks to the military success of Israel in the Yom Kippur War, said Begin, the Egyptians got rid of the Soviets and set out on an American political orientation. Thanks to the peace treaty that Israel had signed with Egypt, the Americans became part of the multinational force and now have a foothold in the Sinai that could be turned into a military base of some importance. And in the wake of Israel's achievements in Lebanon and the defeat of the Syrians, there was now an opportunity to reorganize power relationships in the area, not least to the benefit of the Americans. These were all parts of a basic message: the major American achievement in the Middle East, of containing the Soviets and enhancing the U.S. position, was attained through American support of Israel for the good of both countries; therefore, America should not press too hard on Israel.

Few doubt the special relationship between the United States and Israel, one unique in the annals of history. There are many components that contribute to it and over the years it has developed dynamics of its own, although there have been and will be pressure groups from within and without that try to harm the bonds between Washington and Jerusalem. While there are basic factors that provide for many of the common political interests, it would be unrealistic to accept continuous total agreement or understanding between both governments. It has, however, in the past eighteen years faced many crises and successfully withstood them.

16

The Test of a Winner

ONE way by which the success or failure of any political action may be assessed is by trying to determine whether it achieved what its initiators intended to achieve and how beneficial or detrimental were its unintentional consequences. In applying this test it will be well to resurvey several points.

Beyond the declared aims of Operation Peace for Galilee there were causes and motives more difficult to pin down and evaluate. Yet they have contributed no less significantly to the decisions that preceded the events. For example, to a large extent 1981 was a year of deadlock in Middle East peace efforts. The Palestine portion of the Camp David agreements remained a dead letter. As the months passed since the last year of President Jimmy Carter's term in office there was growing concern in Israel that the American government was increasingly opposed to the Israeli interpretation of autonomy.

The idea that the use of force can resolve political deadlock was always more at home in Herut philosophy than in that of the Labor movement. By early in 1982 it had gained ground in the government establishment and was given public voice by the chief of staff, the once taciturn but now increasingly vocal General Rafael Eitan.

Opponents and critics of Prime Minister Menachem Begin have insinuated that he wanted to have a dazzling victory of his own, to go down in history alongside the Six Day War of 1967. Lebanon of

1982 might have seemed to him the right place for the right purpose at the right time. For a brief period in the early summer, he believed this had happened. "We have overcome the trauma of the Yom Kippur War," he exclaimed proudly.

The declared aim of Operation Peace for Galilee was to eliminate the constant threat of attack on the towns, villages, and kibbutzim that were within range of the PLO guns in southern Lebanon. In July 1981 large numbers of Israelis fled their homes in northern Israel; they were mainly from Kiryat Shmona in the east but also from Nahariya in the west and some of the agricultural settlements in between. Those people were no longer willing to passively accept the repeated Katyusha and artillery attacks that had forced them to spend a considerable number of their nights in shelters. Jews were again becoming refugees—this time in their own country.

Toward the end of that month, following several Israeli acts of retaliation and American presidential envoy Philip Habib's peregrinations between Jerusalem and several Arab capitals, the PLO stopped their attacks, and an almost complete cease-fire prevailed in the following ten months. Thus, when Israel attacked in June 1982 in retaliation for the shooting of Ambassador Argov in London, it was after ten months of outward peace and tranquility, in which not a single Israeli in Galilee had been killed or wounded by the PLO. But, as Israeli spokesmen point out, the threat remained and, with it, the constant fear of sudden bomb or rocket attack in the middle of the night. To live in the shadow of another attack, to go to sleep seven nights a week knowing that the sound of siren alerts may soon wake you to rush to the shelters, is an experience few people get used to, even under the best of material and social conditions. Kibbutzim, being socially cohesive, are fairly well equipped to deal with problems of stress. Kiryat Shmona and other towns in close proximity to the border were definitely not in shape to take such pressure for long. For the residents of these towns and settlements—a majority of whom were immigrants and children of immigrants from Moslem countries—the strain and problems were becoming too heavy to bear.

The threat and the worry were strong enough to become a major political issue in northern Israel. Prime Minister Begin's statement that "there will be no more Katyushas in Kiryat Shmona" became in the eyes of his critics an example of his political irresponsibility, but in the eyes of his followers, both a symbol and test of his leadership.

PLO leader Yasser Arafat was pushing things too far. When he presented Israel a challenge no government could ignore, Begin's response was at least in part emotional. And the fact that it took the form of a clear and absolute promise to a public most of whom were his constituents made matters inevitably explosive. Begin turned himself and Israel into a hostage to Arafat's will and restraint. It was a challenge that neither side could stand up to, but it was Begin who made the first move.

When Israeli troops entered southern Lebanon, fairly large PLO arms caches were discovered in many places. Soon the reports of "unbelievable arsenals of modern arms," nourished by statements from government sources, became a retroactive justification of the invasion: the PLO was on the way to becoming a *military* threat, so the official case put it, and Israel had nipped it in the bud.

There were both domestic and foreign propaganda reasons for exaggerating the size and especially the potential effectiveness of the weapons stocks in PLO hands. But there is also the interesting question of why the PLO had amassed such a large, mixed quantity of the latest rockets and World War II armored vehicles, modern heavy artillery and forty year-old tanks, as well as similar small arms from a dozen different countries.

The PLO attempt to become a regular army was in the classic pattern of so-called liberation movements, which according to "the book" must reorganize in that way before the final push to seize the fatherland. Theoretically, this reshaping should take place in "liberated areas" of the country. The PLO realized that, for the time being, there was little chance of "liberating" parts of Palestine by force of arms. Instead, the process was to be reversed: political action on the international scene was to be used against Israel to get it out of the West Bank, which would then become the first of the so-called liberated areas of Palestine.

The fact that meanwhile the PLO was using its state within a state in southern Lebanon for this purpose was no contradiction of this doctrine. Liberated areas require a liberation army and such an army must have guns and tanks and rockets. If you don't have T-62s

or T-72s to roll down the streets of Nablus, Ramallah, and Bethlehem, T-34s will do almost as well. The ultimate aim, under both
strategies, was the takeover of the entire area of what had been
British Palestine, at least west of Jordan.

The wider strategic aims of both the PLO and Israel thus crossed
in Tyre and Sidon. For the PLO, southern Lebanon was a transit
station to the Palestinian state on the West Bank. To the Israel
government strategists, for this very reason, destroying the PLO
infrastructure and power in Lebanon seemed an essential move to
prevent the establishment of the Palestinian state. Unlike the public, at least part of which was skeptical, the Israeli government
professed to be convinced that if the PLO were destroyed in Lebanon
the Palestinians on the West Bank would be ready to negotiate on a
limited autonomy dictated by Israel. This appears to have been the
political aim of the war in Lebanon.

There was another reason, quite different and officially unstated,
and that was to reaffirm and cement the concept of "strategic
cooperation" between Israel and the United States. An outgrowth of
the thesis that Israel was a strategic asset for America, the idea of
strategic cooperation was fostered by Defense Minister Ariel
Sharon with the acquiescence of Secretary of State Alexander Haig,
but against the apparent inclinations of the U.S. Department of
Defense and its head, Caspar Weinberger. Since Defense Minister
Sharon described the 1981 "Memorandum of understanding" on
U.S./Israel Strategic Cooperation as a major breakthrough in the
country's security arrangements, destroying the center of Soviet
sponsored international terrorism and showing the vulnerability of
Soviet weapons should have proven the importance of Israel's contribution to this partnership.

The Israeli government operated in Lebanon under what were
for it favorable international conditions. The Arabs were once again
divided along their traditional lines of enmity and split by the
interminable Iran-Iraq war. The Soviet Union was busy with
Poland, Afghanistan, and the impending succession to Leonid
Brezhnev. The United States was approaching congressional elections. The world, Western Europe in particular, was gradually
becoming less dependent on Arab oil in a glutted international
market. But it faced major domestic difficulties as well as unfore-

seen complications. The war started at a time when, in Washington, there was a team of president and secretary of state who seemed closer to Israel than at any time in recent memory. They were promoting global ideologies and strategic concepts that coincided with the Likud's world view.

The Israeli government was also faced with an already hostile international public opinion and a large domestic Opposition, which challenged Begin's policies that many believed were mortgaging the future shape of life in Israel. While the Labor alignment unenthusiastically supported the government in the initial phase of the Lebanon invasion, their ways parted when the army was ordered to proceed beyond the initial 40- to 45-kilometer line. This was in contrast to past wars in which Herut and the entire hawkish Likud faction had unquestioningly supported whatever action against the Arabs Israel was engaged in. In pursuing the shifting and expanding aims of the war in Lebanon, the Israeli government was obliged simultaneously to counter strong domestic criticism. When the 48-hour campaign extended to months, and then to a year and more, it affected the government's determination and sense of self-confidence when pressing to obtain benefits from the war.

There were other unforeseen developments. Had the harmful nature of Western television coverage and its immediate political impact been anticipated, its cost might have been minimized; unfortunately it was not, and the damage proved severe. The assassination of Bashir Gemayel was unforeseeable and a serious blow to Israel. The tragic events in the Sabra and Shatilla camps were certainly not of Israel's making but they also gravely affected the attainment of the political aims of the operation.

Early in the campaign the tacit acceptance of the Israeli operation by the White House seemed to confirm the closeness of the American-Israeli alliance in pursuit of joint strategic interests in the Middle East. But things changed substantially with the departure of Alexander Haig from the State Department and his replacement by George Shultz. Israel's extension of the war beyond its original limits, the horrors of the fighting shown on TV, and the impact of Arab and especially Saudi pressure on the American administration ended the apparent cooperation between Washington and Jerusalem and replaced it for more than nine months with a conflict that strained relations between the two countries to a degree unprecedented for decades.

It is too early to pass definitive judgment on the success or failure of the strategic aims of the Lebanon war. The infrastructure of the PLO has been smashed; their state within a state has been destroyed; and the status of Yasser Arafat and his associates, despite their initial hero's welcome, has dropped considerably in the Arab world. There is some evidence that the PLO status among the Palestinians on the West Bank has also diminished.

But then, skillful PLO propaganda and distorted media reporting helped turn natural sympathies for the underdog into a big new pro-Palestinian international public opinion groundswell. It was more difficult to assess what tangible benefits this sympathy conveyed. The fighting focused world attention again on the plight of homeless Palestinians and seemed to confirm the basic PLO claim that there would be no peace in the Middle East as long as the Palestinians remain stateless. Thus, if Israel hoped that smashing the PLO in Lebanon would deal a fatal blow to prospects of Palestinian statehood and the Palestinian people, the war, if it did anything, increased international support for the idea.

Besides eliminating the direct threat to settlements in northern Israel and destroying the PLO infrastructure, Israel had two other openly declared political aims in moving into Lebanon: to restore Lebanese sovereignty over the country by ending PLO and Syrian occupation and to establish normal peaceful relations with a new, truly free Lebanese state. In the year following the start of the war neither of these aims was achieved, nor was it certain that they would be in the immediate future. There is no question, however, that the war has brought them closer to realization.

The extent and weight of the PLO presence and the predominant influence of Syria in Lebanese politics is much smaller than it was before the war. At the same time, it is significant that even such a close ally as Bashir Gemayel made it clear shortly before his murder that the idea of a formal peace treaty between Lebanon and Israel would have to be postponed for the time being. The Israeli government ultimately came to accept this fact in its talks with Bashir's brother and successor, Amin Gemayel.

The success or failure of a war initiated as part of a national policy cannot be judged solely by the achievements of its declared or hidden aims and by its human, political, and material costs. It must also be tested against the essential premises and postulates of the nation and its existence.

A fundamental premise of Israel has always been that the existence of a Jewish state should and would prevent the recurrence of the tragedy that befell the defenseless Jewish people during the Holocaust. Under the leadership of Menachem Begin, this historical motivation has provided the framework for both an active policy and a means of appealing to public opinion. That has led to what many consider to be the government's sometimes distorted perception of international events and developments. Neo-Nazi revival and the specter of another Holocaust were seen to be hiding behind every hostile act or intention against Israel, and the government's reactions were portrayed as responses to mortal threats to Israel's—and the Jewish people's—very existence.

Although the actual encounter between the Israeli army and the PLO and the practical military value of the stores of weapons discovered in southern Lebanon indicate that any talk of the PLO as a serious military threat to Israel was greatly exaggerated, the setting up of a *de facto* PLO state in southern Lebanon—as a prelude to the establishment of a Palestinian state on the West Bank—was seen by Begin and his associates in this light. Observers friendly to the Israeli government's approach therefore had reason to say that PLO policies based on such grounds were misguided.

The assumption that superiority in trained manpower and armaments can compensate Israel for the quantitative superiority of the Arabs has always been fundamental to Israel's strategic thinking. For thirty years a quantitative troop strength and weapons ratio of 3:1 in favor of the Arabs was accepted as tolerable as long as the qualitative advantage was on Israel's side. Technological advances claimed by arms manufacturers as capable of compensating for any lack of operator sophistication, enormous increases in quantities of weapons accumulated by the Arabs, and the limits of Israel's financial capability to purchase the increasingly more expensive weapons systems all have raised the question of how long Israel will be able to maintain a defense deterrent to counter Arab numerical superiority. When he was defense minister, Ariel Sharon announced publicly that Israel would no longer strain its economic resources to maintain the 3:1 ratio but would seek other means to defend itself. He did not specify what these other means might be and one must presume that they involve decisions to be taken on the political level. Attempting to destroy the PLO by a preemptive strike in the summer of 1982 could be construed as falling within the framework of such a policy.

The substantiation of the premise of qualitative advantage was tested only partially in this war. The PLO and its arsenals were greatly inferior to that of the invading Israeli army, not only qualitatively but also quantitatively. The PLO, moreover, though more highly motivated than most of the regular Arab armies, was not as well trained. Confronted with the Syrians, the Israeli armor and air force proved its qualitative edge—dramatically so in air battles and in attacks on SAM antiaircraft batteries. But not only did the Israelis have considerably better pilots and electronic equipment, the Syrians did not have the best and latest from the arsenal of their Soviet suppliers. No wonder that after the end of the war, it was hotly debated in Israel whether, under such circumstances, Israel should have disclosed some of the aspects of its own superior capabilities.

It is a time-honored belief that politically the Arabs are always one war behind in their readiness to talk with and recognize the existence of Israel. It took five wars and tens of thousands of casualties before Egypt was ready to negotiate a formal peace treaty. Lebanon, the only country that had no disputes with Israel, was always considered the second country that would make peace. Yet it refused to do so because its internal weaknesses and perceived economic interests exposed it to the *de facto* veto of the other Arab countries. Only after Israel had waged the first real war on Lebanese soil did Lebanon appear ready to replace its thirty-four-year-old armistice agreement with Israel, unilaterally canceled by them in June 1967, with a nonbelligerency agreement that would provide practical normalization of relations. Yet even then Beirut was not prepared to sign a full peace. It is significant in this context that Jordan, despite repeatedly flirting with the possibility of approaching the negotiating table, has found it difficult to summon the courage or faith in the potential benefit needed to take a seat.

The principle that Israel will never talk to the PLO was not laid down by Begin and the Likud but a decade earlier by a more moderate Labor government. The late Golda Meir denied the existence of a Palestinian nation, in the sense of their being a separate national branch of the family of Arab peoples. But the Likud government translated this position into a virtually total refusal to talk to anybody—West Bank mayors or Jordanians—who wanted to speak in the name of the Palestinians. Nor would the government discuss the matter with any Arab or other government who refused to accept Begin's interpretation of autonomy.

Still, Israel has for many years made a great effort to convince the world, and particularly Western public opinion, that it is opposed only to the PLO, which wished to destroy the Jewish state, and not to the Palestinians and their legitimate rights, the definition of which, the Israelis have suggested, should be discussed in the autonomy negotiations. This distinction never was—and probably never could be—clearly related by the Israelis to the population of the West Bank and the Gaza Strip. It was almost completely erased in the war in Lebanon. The PLO controlled, defended, and represented the Palestinians in Lebanon—and it located its military installations in their midst. In Israel's attempt to destroy the PLO, the IDF therefore inevitably hit the Palestinian population, so that when it came to be tested in Lebanon, Israel's principle of separating the PLO from the Palestinian population was necessarily violated by Israel's own military actions.

In the past, Israeli governments recognized the difference between PLO acts of terror and the Palestinian wish for self-determination, notwithstanding the PLO's claim that they were in the service of the latter. To combat terror and the PLO as a terrorist organization was a matter for the police, the security services, or the army; the PLO as such and Palestinian rights were political matters that had to be dealt with politically. Here, too, the revisionist Likud government's policies retrenched into more rigid, dogmatic positions. The PLO was seen only as a gang of terrorists who under no circumstances should benefit from any political treatment. This ideological concept was translated into an operational thesis by Chief of Staff Eitan, who declared that the PLO could be destroyed by military means. This dictum became the official credo of the Begin government and formed the theoretical motivation behind the invasion of Lebanon. Even by the Likud-Eitan definition, however, without completely smashing the PLO infrastructure everywhere —and not only in southern Lebanon—the PLO could not be destroyed. Since even General Eitan and his political chief, Defense Minister Sharon, did not expect to occupy all of Lebanon, let alone PLO bases in any other Arab countries, the theory of eliminating the PLO by military means alone was in fact impossible to apply.

The thesis of a friendly democratic Israel in the Middle East as a strategic asset to the West and to the United States in particular was born as a political concept. It was later promoted to support Israel's constantly growing requests for American political, economic, and military support. As such, it was generally appreciated in Washington by senators, congressmen, and opinion makers, though not necessarily in the Pentagon or the State Department. Israel's intelligence capabilities, the combat-testing of Western weapons systems against Soviet ones, and the capture of Soviet weapons systems for close inspection gave some practical content to the political concept. It was again the Likud government, and Defense Minister Sharon in particular, who translated this approach into delusions of equality in partnership and unrealistically high expectations of American support for Israeli aims. Attempts to sign an agreement on strategic cooperation between the United States and Israel fizzled out in an inoperative memorandum the original import of which was questionable. Yet not long afterward, Defense Secretary Weinberger signaled a shift by the United States, saying that "the revival or restitution of that memorandum could take place at virtually any time, depending on the wishes of the Israeli government."[1]

Ariel Sharon had apparently convinced Prime Minister Begin that destroying the PLO infrastructure, the Syrian influence, and thereby the Soviet prestige in Lebanon would exemplify for Washington the value of Israel as a partner in long-term strategic cooperation. For services rendered in Lebanon, so ran this thesis, a grateful Washington would ease pressures for autonomy for the Palestinians and give Israel a freer hand on the West Bank.

This thesis, perhaps more than any other formulated by the government, exploded in the face of its originators. The combat against the PLO, the plight of the refugees, and, most of all, the siege of Beirut had quite the opposite effect from that intended, especially after the resignation of Secretary of State Haig. Cooperation with Israel came to be seen by Washington as a liability; the PLO got fresh publicity and, in Western Europe, a boost of sympathy and political respectability. Most important, the idea of Palestinian self-determination for the first time acquired the support of the Reagan White House, which until then had shared in the perception of the PLO as purely an organization of terrorists. The concept of a war in Lebanon as a means to avoid concessions to the Palestinians in the West Bank had thus failed.

In addition to evaluating Israeli axioms and concepts in the light of the test of war in Lebanon, it is relevant to list some conclusions that appear pertinent for outside parties involved in events in the region.

For the Soviets, distance from the scene is a major handicap when American and Israeli determination to act requires their quick reaction. The loss of their position in Egypt aggravated this problem, while the continued absence of diplomatic relations with Israel drastically limits alternative political options. Being an interested party and very much involved, without fair chances to reap the benefits of its involvement, Moscow seems due for a reassessment of its Middle East policies—toward higher risks or lower involvement.

The first lesson for the United States to consider seems to be the continuous inadequacy of its intelligence (and, especially, interpretation of the data) from the Middle East. The trail of surprises, from the fall of the shah of Iran to Sadat's visit to Jerusalem, continued, though less spectacularly, in the war in Lebanon and in its diplomatic aftermath. Equally serious appears to be the failure to project clear, forceful messages of what U.S. interests are. Washington seems particularly unable to do so sufficiently far in advance so that the Israelis, the Arabs, the PLO, or Washington's European allies can take those interests into account when formulating their own policies. It is not clear that the American administration realizes that though it may gain less praise and immediate friendship, it receives more respect and influence in most Arab capitals when American and Israeli policies appear as parallel and mutually supportive, which the Arabs expect them to be in any case.

There is no evidence as yet that the Arab states' huge investments in armaments have brought about a major change in the military superiority of Israeli quality over Arab quantity. The Arabs could learn from the events of 1982 that mistakes of the Israeli government accelerate the change in Western public opinion and sympathies for the Palestinians in particular far more than do efforts fostered and financed by the Arabs themselves. This does not, however, portend more sympathy for the PLO, as distinct from the Palestinians, or a breakdown between the United States and Israel.

For Israel, the first lesson from the war was the old and general rule that a government's quest for domestic popularity is a risky guide in formulating foreign policy. The second is just as time honored and should be expanded in the light of the Lebanon experience: wars are too serious a matter for generals to be permitted to determine when they should start; nor should generals decide how wars should be waged. More abstract is the lesson that history, even so traumatic an experience as the Holocaust, must not become the yardstick for present dangers and responses.

The most important conclusion ultimately relates to the policy of the Israeli government toward the Palestine question. The efficacy of smashing the PLO state within a state in Lebanon can be argued at length one way or the other. Eliminating or minimizing the PLO influence on the West Bank may indeed be essential to a solution compatible with the safe existence of Israel.

The war in Lebanon was not a war of survival, not even a defensive war in the usual Israeli meaning of those words. Therefore, in assessing the achievements and failures of its aims and targets, one must, more than ever before, balance the successes against the more than 500 Israeli lives lost, the thousands wounded, and the enormous damage caused to Israel's international name and its own self-image. But as long as the Israeli government insists that *de facto* annexation, with no hope of some form of self-determination or human and civil rights, is the only acceptable solution, even the successful elimination of the PLO is unlikely to bring about the cooperation of the Palestinians or the disappearance of the problem.

17

Instead of an End

E ARLIER in 1983, before the Lebanese-Israel treaty was signed, the State Department argued that the longer Israel postponed its retreat from Lebanon, the more damage was done to its image and to the goodwill reserved for it in the U.S. Congress. However, as the attacks on Israeli forces in Lebanon, usually by PLO or other guerrillas, continued despite tighter security measures, and the strain of the longer reserve duty disrupted the economy, there was added urgency in the demand shared by the majority of the cabinet and the public—to go ahead with a partial withdrawal of Israeli forces in Lebanon, in order, it was hoped, to reduce the cost of the continued occupation of the rest of southern Lebanon.

Although the areas of south Lebanon, where most of the attacks on the Israeli forces occurred, would still remain under Israeli occupation, experts believed that with much less territory to control Israel would be in a far better position to block infiltration by terrorists and to prevent their moving around and hiding out. Also, supporters of the partial withdrawal, euphemistically called "redeployment," maintained that it would be a clear signal to the people of the region that Israel was ready to stay there for a long time. This, as experience in other places has shown, works positively with the attitude of the local population: instead of cooperating with the terrorists, it makes them cooperate with the police against the terrorists.

This implication of a protracted stay was one of the main reasons why Washington appeared so unenthusiastic about the idea of "redeployment." It could imply a *de facto* partition of Lebanon, for many years to come, into three sections: one held by Israel, one by the Syrians, and one—the smallest one—by the Lebanese government. But probably the more urgent reason for the American administration's opposition to the redeployment was the concern that it would oblige the United States to send more Marines to Lebanon and station them in those particularly dangerous areas of the Shouf Mountains evacuated by the Israeli forces, where the Christian militias and the Moslem Druse conduct their generations-old war-within-the-war. This attitude was buttressed by the growing opposition in Congress to any form of Marine presence in the Lebanon.

After the secretary of state failed to persuade Syrian President Assad to withdraw his forces from northern Lebanon and from the Al-Bika'a valley in the southeast, there was no doubt that the Israelis would nonetheless sooner or later implement the partial withdrawal. Israeli troops in the southeast still remain less than twenty miles from Damascus, obviously the most effective inducement to ultimately bring about the Syrian withdrawal from Lebanon.

Thus when, at the President's invitation, Foreign and Defense Ministers Shamir and Ahrens traveled to Washington late in July, reportedly carrying the plans for a unilateral unconditional IDF retreat from the outskirts of Beirut and the Shouf Mountains—even if the Syrians did not withdraw, the Reagan administration seemed unenthusiastic at best. Washington seemed to worry that the Syrians would fill the power vacuum.

The Israelis kept the Americans abreast of their plans in the ten weeks that preceded the redeployment of their troops, but when it actually took place in the first week of September, and the Moslem Druse unleashed ferocious attack and counterattack, the tenuous balance of forces around Beirut was upset, and both Americans and Israelis were caught unprepared.

After Professor Moshe Ahrens replaced Ariel Sharon as Minister of Defense, and General Moshe Levi replaced General Rafael

Eitan as Chief of Staff, unilateral partial withdrawal of the troops from the Beirut area and the Shouf Mountains became official Israeli policy. Despite the absurd spectacle of Washington, Beirut—and even Damascus—opposing the Israeli pullback, after several postponements at the request of the White House, Jerusalem finally ordered the troops back to the Awali River line. In the northeast, facing the Syrians, Israeli forces stayed and kept control of the strategic radar-crowned Mt. Baroukh. But from there to Beirut in the west, the evacuated areas became a bloody battleground between the Christian militias and the Druse, supported by Palestinian terrorists and backed by Syrian artillery.

President Amin Gemayel's government, which spent the intervening weeks trying to distance itself from Israel to curry Arab favor but refusing to make compromises with the Druse, discovered that it had miscalculated on both counts. Arab governments could not prevent the Syrian-backed Druse advance, and a disillusioned Israel was unwilling to lose more soldiers fighting Gemayel's and the Christians' war.

The retreat, and the renewed civil war and massacres that followed, underscored also the failure of Israel's political aims and ambitions in Lebanon. Two of Israel's three war aims have clearly not been achieved, and the third was in danger: the establishment of a free, strong central Lebanese government, master of the country's fate and able to reach a peace settlement with Israel, seemed more than ever to be mere wishful thinking. Gemayel's troops were fighting in the outskirts of Beirut, and the country appeared to be destined for a long division among foreign armies and warring religious and ethnic militias. The removal from Lebanon of Syrian physical presence and political influence seemed as distant, if not more so, than it was before the Israeli tanks rolled across the border in June 1982. Damascus, in alliance with the Druse, had set out to prove that not only could it prevent the implementation of any Lebanese settlement contrary to its wishes; it had come close to being able to force solutions to its liking.

The power of the PLO has, indeed, been broken and the West now appeared to pay, more reluctantly than before, only lip service to the "Palestinian cause." But in their new-found, possibly only temporary alliance with the Druse, the Palestinian terrorists may have

247

found a path back to Beirut and to the western-central parts of Lebanon. Israeli Chief-of-Staff General Moshe Levi conceded in an interview in September that "it is possible that the terrorists will establish a new infrastructure in Lebanon."

To Israelis, it was clear that such a development would set events back to where they had been in May 1982, before more than 500 Israelis lost their lives and thousands were injured in pursuit of Begin's and Sharon's "Peace for Galilee" and new order in Lebanon.

At the end of the summer of 1983, the Grand Design that had led Menachem Begin into Lebanon fifteen months earlier appeared to be in deep disarray. It may still be too soon to judge whether there was or is a chance for a stable Lebanese nation to reemerge. Lebanon's vacillations, those of the Israelis and, no less, the Americans' in the winter and spring of 1982–3, had enabled the Syrians to seize the initiative in the region and thwart moves toward molding a new, peaceful Lebanon. As often in the past, the Lebanese clans, perhaps unwittingly, seem determined to hasten the collapse of the central government.

Although the cautious breeze of optimism had not completely dissipated, the future of the Middle East appeared less decipherable than ever.

A physically exhausted Menachem Begin unexpectedly tendered his resignation as prime minister in September 1983. Ariel Sharon, although still a minister, had lost his power base, and the government, now to be headed by Itzhak Shamir, was set, in tune with the national mood, to avoid if possible any new political or military adventures.

In Israel, the departure of Menachem Begin confirmed the feeling of many that an epoch had ended.

When the Lebanese-Israeli troop withdrawal agreement was signed on May 16, 1983, and ratified by the Lebanese parliament on June 14, the state of war between the two countries was terminated and Lebanon became the second Arab country within five years to give recognition to Israel and to enter into nearly normal relations with the Jewish state.

Compared with the fanfare surrounding the change in Israel's relations with Egypt, the initial meetings between the Lebanese and the Israelis received modest coverage. Perhaps rightly so: it is invariably the first breakthrough that gets the full glare of publicity.

Possibly, the discussions between Lebanon and Israel were accorded little importance or scorned by people who felt that not much good could come out of talks. The negotiations were, after all, forced upon Lebanon by the more powerful Israelis, who insisted on the normalization of relations before they would withdraw their troops. Yet both ancient history and recent events in Europe have shown, time and again, that countries successful in armed conflict have expected to secure their borders in order not to feel compelled to repeat their invasions. Only in the Middle East wars from 1948 to 1973 was the victorious Israeli army forced by international pressure to accept a cease-fire or, at best, an armistice agreement.

From a historical viewpoint, there may today be hope that Israel is on the way to peace with its neighbors, which had seemed impossible until the thirtieth year of the existence of the state. Until Sadat's visit to Jerusalem in November 1977, most Israelis pessimistically doubted they would have peace in their lifetime—today many are worried about the dangers threatening that tenuous process. Unlike a familiar highway, the road to peace is neither well mapped nor clearly marked; this particular road has not been traveled at all until recently and is full of obstacles, if not landmines.

The younger generation of Israelis, if they can extricate themselves from the political morass and find their way out of the maze of Middle East pressures, finally may look forward to some form of peace in the future.

As 1984 approaches, it appears that bloodletting in the Middle East will go on. Soon after completing this writing, hundreds of American young men and many Frenchmen lost their lives in Beirut. The tragedy is closely connected and yet quite similar to the events described in this book. There has been terror throughout history. Its escalation in recent years was at first spearheaded against Israelies. But we should always remember that terror can and often is armed against any open society and every free people.

249

Notes

CHAPTER 2. THE PLO

1. "The Palestinians and the PLO," *Commentary*, January 1975.
2. Leila S. Kadi, ed., *Basic Political Documents of the Armed Palestinian Resistance Movement*, PLO Research Center, Beirut.
3. Khaled al-Hassan, political adviser to Yasser Arafat, in an interview with "Sada al-Usbu, Bahrain," as quoted by the United Arab Emirates News Agency, January 12, 1982.
4. Hani al-Hassan, a political adviser to Yasser Arafat and member of the Fath Central Committee, at a student rally at the American University of Beirut marking the seventeenth anniversary of Fath activity, as quoted in *An-Nahar*, January 9, 1982.
5. *Foreign Affairs*, July 1978.
6. "The PLO's War Chest," *New York Post*, January 21, 1982.
7. *Al Watan*, Kuwait, June 1979.
8. *Wall Street Journal*, January 14, 1982.

CHAPTER 3. THE LEBANON—A HOUSE DIVIDED

1. Lebanese ambassador Nagib al-Dahdah, in a report to the Democratic European Union meeting in Lisbon, Portugal, June 24,

1980, page 2, *Lebanon since April 13, 1975.* Issued by the Lebanese Forces Command in April 1982.
2. Reported by Loren Jenkins, *The Guardian,* London, October 24, 1982.

CHAPTER 4. A CHANGE OF MIXED BLESSINGS

1. *Financial Times,* London, December 3, 1982.

CHAPTER 5. ONE WAR, THREE BATTLES

1. "Sayings of the Year," *The Observer,* London, January 2, 1983.
2. *Air Force Magazine,* Washington, November 30, 1981, quoting Assistant Secretary of Defense Richard Perle.
3. Commander in Chief Rafael Eitan, testifying before the Foreign Affairs and Defense Committee of the Knesset, December 29, 1982.
4. "Play It Again, SAM-8," *The Economist,* August 28, 1982.
5. Ibid.
6. Robert Fisk, "Sidon," June 19, 1982.
7. Ibid.
8. Dr. Joyce R. Starr, "A Report from Lebanon," Center for Strategic and International Studies, Washington, D.C.
9. Kelly H. Burke, "Electronic Combat, Warfare of the Future," *Armed Forces Journal International,* December 1982, pp. 53–54.

CHAPTER 7. MOSCOW KEEPS A LOW PROFILE

1. *Time,* International Edition, June 28, 1982.

CHAPTER 8. AN ARAB MAZE

1. Thomas I. Friedman, "Pique in Washington over Those 'Moderate' Saudis," *The New York Times,* January 23, 1983.

2. *The Guardian,* London, January 30, 1983.
3. Ahmed Iskandar, Syrian Minister of Information, in an interview to *Monday Morning,* June 20-26, 1983.

CHAPTER 9. THE TARNISHED IMAGE

1. Robert MacNeil, *The Right Place at the Right Time* (Boston: Little, Brown, 1982).
2. *The Economist,* January 8, 1983.
3. "How the PLO Terrified Journalists in Beirut," *Commentary,* January 1983.
4. Ibid.

CHAPTER 10. THE LONGEST NIGHT

1. London, December 25, 1982.
2. *Final Report of the [Kahan] Commission of Inquiry into the Events at the Refugee Camps in Beirut,* Jerusalem, February 8, 1983.
3. Ibid.
4. Ibid.
5. Ibid.
6. Ibid.
7. Ibid.

CHAPTER 12. THE PLO AND THE PALESTINIANS

1. Yasser Arafat, speaking in San'a, October 5, 1982, as reported by Sana'a radio.
2. Bassam Abu-Sharif, spokesman of George Habash's Popular Front, at a news conference in Kuwait, quoted by the Middle East News Agency, October 22, 1982.
3. *Al Talak,* official organ of the PLO's Al-Saika faction, cited by Radio Damascus, November 1, 1982.
4. Connor Cruise O'Brien in *The Observer,* February 23, 1983.
5. *The Third Way—A Journal of Life in the West Bank* (New York: Quartet Books, 1982), p.

CHAPTER 13. THE NEW LEBANON

1. Fadi Frem speech to the Kataeb in memory of Bashir Gemayel, October 24, 1982.
2. Joseph Abu Halil, in *Al Amal,* Beirut, October 30, 1982.
3. "Monday Morning," Beirut, January 17, 1983.
4. Thomas I. Friedman, "Survivors and Thrivers: Coping with 8 years of violence in Beirut," *International Herald Tribune,* July 27, 1983.
5. Ibid.

CHAPTER 14. ISRAEL'S ECONOMIC NEEDS
AND INDEPENDENCE.

1. GAO Report on U.S. assistance to the State of Israel by the Comptroller General of the United States. June 24, 1983, pp. 27-28.
2. GAO Report, p. 1.
3. GAO Report, p. 1.
4. Ibid., p. 7.
5. Wolf Blitzer, "Weighing the Cost of Alliance," *The Jerusalem Post,* December 7, 1982.

CHAPTER 16. THE TEST OF A WINNER

1. Quoted in *The New York Times,* June 14, 1983.

Index